THE MEMOIRS OF
FRÉDÉRIC
MISTRAL

Mistral in his old age. (*Roger-Viollet*)

THE MEMOIRS OF
FRÉDÉRIC
MISTRAL

TRANSLATED BY
GEORGE WICKES

A NEW DIRECTIONS BOOK

The translations of chapters III and VIII, "The Magi" and "How I Passed My Baccalaureate Exam," were first published in *Translation* magazine, Fall 1985.

Manufactured in the United States of America
First published clothbound and as New Directions Paperbook 632 in 1986
Published simultaneously in Canada by Penguin Books Canada Limited

Library of Congress Cataloging-in-Publication Data

Mistral, Frédéric, 1830–1914.
   The memoirs of Frédéric Mistral.
   (A New Directions Book)
   Translation of: Moun espelido.
   Includes index.
   1. Mistral, Frédéric, 1830–1914—Biography—Youth.
2. Poets, Langue d'oc—19th century—Biography.
3. Lexicographers—France—Biography.   4. Félibrige.
5. Provence (France)—Social life and customs.   I. Title.
PC3402.M5Z47513   1986   849'.14 [B]   86-8768
ISBN 0-8112-0992-X
ISBN 0-8112-1009-X (pbk.)

New Directions Books are published for James Laughlin
by New Directions Publishing Corporation,
80 Eighth Avenue, New York 10011

CONTENTS

LIST OF ILLUSTRATIONS

Frontispiece: Mistral in his old age.

Pages xvi–xvii: Map. The heart of Mistral's Provence.

Following page 162:
   The Judge's Farm.
   Five of the original Félibres, and friends, 1854.
   Title page of the first *Provençal Almanac.*
   Bilingual edition of *Mirèio.*
   Mistral in 1863, studio portrait by Nadar.
   Mistral reading from his poem *Calendau* to a group of Félibres in
     1866.
   Daudet and Mistral.
   Mistral in 1913.

INTRODUCTION

In his old age Frédéric Mistral looked like Buffalo Bill and was
almost as famous. A big, handsome man with a flowing white
mane and goatee, he sported a broad-brimmed felt hat like
those worn by the cowboys of the Rhone delta. In fact, the
story is told that Buffalo Bill came to call on him with Sitting
Bull and several other Indians from the Wild West Show when
they were touring Europe. Whether or not the story is true, it
suggests the legendary character of Mistral's reputation. His
very name was legendary, the name of the great wind that
whistles down the Rhone, rattling houses and setting nerves on
edge. The poet's presence was equally pervasive, but his influ-
ence was benign. In the words of one American visitor, he was
"the greatest man in the south of France, universally beloved
and revered."

He was without a doubt the greatest modern Provençal poet
and the greatest champion of his native Provence. His fame
dated from the appearance of his pastoral epic in twelve cantos,
Mirèio (1859), which Gounod translated into a rather dull opera,
Mireille, a few years later. More important to Mistral was the
Provençal renaissance in which he played a leading role. He was
the guiding spirit of a group of latter-day troubadours who
revived and refined their native language as a literary medium,
and he was their lexicographer. For this achievement and for
his poetry Mistral was awarded the Nobel prize in 1904. Char-

acteristically, he gave the prize money to a folklore museum he had founded at Arles to preserve the customs and traditions of his region.

Two years later, in his seventy-sixth year, he published his charming book of Memoirs, which is not so much an autobiography as a recollection of the life of ordinary country people during his early years. The Memoirs provide a unique record of a traditional way of life that had existed for centuries but was rapidly disappearing during Mistral's lifetime. Like the folklore museum, they attempt to preserve that vanishing way of life, recording for posterity the traditional ways, legends, rituals, and beliefs that had shaped the lives of country folk from time immemorial.

The Memoirs describe the circumstances in which Mistral spent his childhood and youth, the landscapes, the seasonal life of the farm, the religious observances and festivals associated with the various times of the year, many of them of obviously pagan origin. Although well educated in Avignon and Aix, he feels out of place among the bourgeois, never loses touch with simple farming people, and devotes his life to writing for them in their language. He begins writing a long poem with a heroine modeled on the young women who work on his father's farm, drawing his materials and inspiration from the peasants of his region. At the same time he and six other young men band together to form the Félibrige, a society dedicated to restoring the Provençal language and preserving local traditions. The Memoirs culminate with the death of Mistral's beloved father and the publication of Mirèio, so quietly understated that one would hardly suspect the author had been hailed as a major poet while still in his twenties.

Mistral's long life (1830–1914) spanned a whole era, and from his father, who had been a soldier in the French Revolution of 1789, he heard about life in the previous century. Mistral himself was caught up in the lesser revolution of 1848, but after that outburst of youthful fervor, he no longer engaged in politics, although frequently urged to do so. Instead he devoted his life to the patriotic cause of Provence and its culture. He was a patriot of his region, a Provençal first and last.

Provence, the old Roman province, was a different world from the north of France, with a different language, a different landscape and climate, a different outlook and temperament. The Provençaux considered themselves heirs of ancient Rome, whose monuments were conspicuous reminders of their past. They resented the standardization and centralization of all French institutions from Paris. Mistral's father exemplified the old Roman virtues, and Mistral based his writings on classical models. He was not a French writer, and he refused to be considered for the Académie Française.

As a boy growing up in the country he regarded French-speaking city-dwellers as foreigners, and he was miserable when sent to school in the city. As a matter of fact, his education distanced him somewhat from the people he had grown up with, who now treated him as a "Monsieur," but to the end he remained loyal to his peasant origins, distrustful of the citified bourgeois, and when forced by his father's death to leave the farm where he was born, he moved scarcely more than a mile away to the village of Maillane, where he remained for the rest of his life.

The Memoirs provide a guided tour of Mistral's world. Maillane is situated in the middle of the stony plain of Crau, its southern horizon bounded by the mountain range of the Alpilles, with a smaller range of hills, the Montagnette, to the west. Historically and culturally, the farmers and shepherds of this plain belong to the land of Arles rather than to Avignon, the city of the medieval Popes. Some distance farther to the southeast is Aix, the old capital of Provence, where Mistral spent three years not too zealously studying law. Across the Rhone to the west are the desolate marshlands of the Camargue, home of the white horses, fighting bulls, and cowboys. The Memoirs record a jaunt through the Camargue and another up around Mount Ventoux, the most prominent feature of the Provençal landscape, dominating its northern reaches. Mistral seldom strayed beyond these boundaries.

The Memoirs are entitled *Moun Espelido: Memòri e Raconte*, which can be translated as *My Beginnings: Memories and Tales*, that is, reminiscences of his early years and stories he heard others tell, such as the old folks of his village. Mistral assembled these memories and tales in his old age, but he had been collecting them all his life and had published quite a few of them in the annual *Provençal Almanac* he and his fellow Félibres founded in 1855 and in other publications. The earliest to be published was his obviously fictionalized account of playing hooky, which he elaborates in Chapter IV of the Memoirs; and a representative sampling of his tales, ranging from folktales to realistic narrative, appears in Chapter XIII. All of these writings, whether based on fact or fiction, are written in a rambling, conversational manner, with a style and syntax close to the language of everyday speech. The effect is to put one in the presence of an elderly man reminiscing about the old days.

Mistral wrote his Memoirs in Provençal and translated them into French. The only previous translation into English, published in 1907, was done by an English noblewoman who worked only from the French and took many liberties with the text, freely adding, dropping, or altering passages on almost every page and even eliminating a whole chapter. Her translation is rendered in a stilted English that has none of the flavor of the original and totally misrepresents Mistral's style and spirit, making his peasants speak like Shakespeare's clowns.

Provençal is not a dialect of French, as many suppose, but of another language derived from Latin, the *langue d'oc* then spoken by nearly twelve million people, according to Mistral, throughout the southern third of France. It has many affinities with other Romance languages but is closest to French in vocabulary, usage, and syntax. It is unique among Romance languages in having feminine endings in -*o* and hence, rather surprisingly, feminine names like Lauro, Jano, and Marìo for Laura, Joanna, and Mary. Provençal is pronounced like French for the most part, except that *e* and *ai* are pronounced as in Italian, *n* is pronounced *ng* after all vowels but *u*, and *un* is pronounced like French *une*. Accent marks on the vowels indicate that they are open (*è, ò*) or closed (*é, ó*). Tonic stress falls on one of the last two syllables, and the cadence resembles that of Spanish or Italian more than French.

My translation is based on the definitive bilingual edition of the Memoirs published by Pierre Rollet in 1969, with the original Provençal and Mistral's French translation on facing pages. The French follows the Provençal quite closely but tends to be more abstract, less pungent and earthy. In translating I have followed the Provençal but have frequently found that Mistral elaborates or clarifies his meaning in French. And I have been aided enormously by his monumental Provençal-French dictionary, *Lou Tresor dóu Felibrige*, in which he documented and explained his language.

The dictionary is also an encyclopedia, a treasury of information about Provençal life and an invaluable resource for interpreting all manner of things in the Memoirs, explaining, for instance, the songs and proverbial sayings that Provençal children learned, the lore about the creatures of the field, superstitions, old wives' tales, in short, folk wisdom as well as the language used to express it. To call Mistral the Samuel Johnson of Provençal would be an understatement; he spent twenty years of his life compiling linguistic and ethnographic data from people of the seacoast, the mountains, and the plains, not only of Provence but of the entire area that spoke *langue d'oc*. His Provençal is based on the speech of his immediate neighborhood, but his dictionary takes other regional variations into account.

Mistral's prose is close to the homely speech of the peasants he knew, full of expressions and images that spring from the soil and everyday life. I have tried to keep as many as possible, but some simply cannot be rendered intelligibly into English, such as *la man de Diéu* ("the hand of God") for a sovereign remedy, *au nis de la serp* ("in the snake's nest") for dire extremity, or *touca li cinq sardino* ("to touch the five sardines"), meaning to shake hands. Peasant speech is deeply rooted in tradition and full of proverbial expressions that come readily as the occasion requires, not all of them familiar to us by any means. For instance, in Chapter IV, when young Mistral is forced to take shelter for the night in an abandoned hut, he uses a traditional saying to express his resignation to the inevitable: "There's no resisting a hanging in Aix." Or in Chapter XVII, when the old dowser says, "Then Bertha spun; now Martha unwinds," his listeners understand him, but we need an interpretation: "Those were the good old days; now my life is running down."

Provençal speech is also rich in exclamations and interjections that Mistral sprinkles liberally throughout his narrative as well as his dialogue. My Provençal grammar lists some forty exclamations to express joy, pain, sympathy, surprise, etc., all of which English can only render as "oh," "ah," or "alas." Similarly, the many expletives still current in Provençal have long since vanished from English speech. The Memoirs are full of watered down oaths invoking thunder, for instance, that would be meaningless in modern English. Despite these obvious differences, I have endeavored to keep my translation as close as English permits to Mistral's idiom.

This translation is dedicated to all those who have aided and encouraged me in a variety of ways and above all to my wife, Louise Westling, who by now feels as if she has lived the life of Mistral. I owe much to friends in Avignon, Louisa Jones, Bernard Dupont, and Clément Serguier, for guidance and assistance, and to Madame Mireille Bosqui for pleasant hours in the Archives Iconographiques of the Palais du Roure. Three French scholars answered many questions and offered much enlightenment on Mistral and the Provençal language: Claude Mauron and Henri Moucadel of the Université de Provence and Charles Rostaing, professor emeritus of the Sorbonne. Madame Marcel Mistral, the present owner of the Judge's Farm, hospitably invited us to visit the setting that figures so prominently in the Memoirs.

American colleagues generously shared their expertise in matters botanical, historical, linguistic, poetic, and miscellaneous: Thomas Hart, Richard Heinzkill, Roy Rosenstein, George Sheridan, Annette Smith, Sanford Tepfer, and Steven White. It was my rare good fortune to have Peter Glassgold, translator and poet, as my editor at New Directions. The office staff of the English Department at the University of Oregon, and particularly Germaine Beveridge, Donna Holleran, Marilyn Reid, and Michael Stamm, have been helpful and forbearing beyond the call of duty.

I am grateful to the Office of Research of University of Oregon and the Oregon Committee for the Humanities for summer research fellowships and to The Translation Center of Columbia University for permission to reprint two selections from the Memoirs that first appeared in *Translation*.

George Wickes

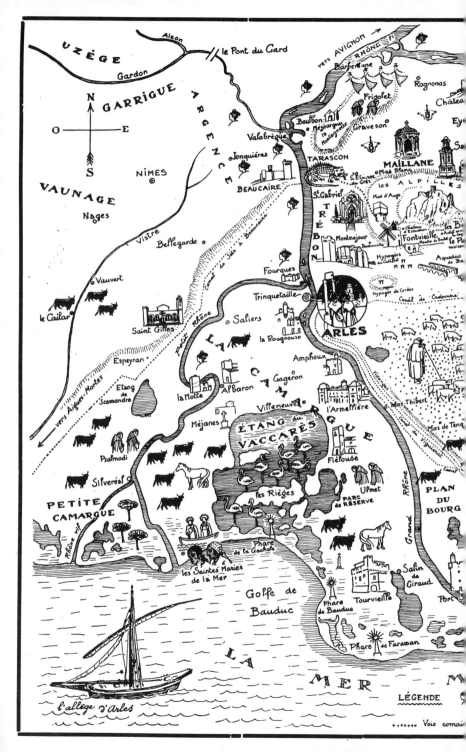

The heart of Mistral's Provence. Avignon is just off the top of the map.

I

AT THE
JUDGE'S
FARM

For as long as I can remember, I can see before me off there to the south a wall of mountains, whose hills, slopes, cliffs, and hollows cast great blue shadows, sometimes light, sometimes dark, from morning to evening. This is the chain of the Alpilles, girdled by olive trees like a range of rocky Greek crags, looking down on a land of glorious deeds and legends. At the foot of this rampart the savior of Rome, Caius Marius ("Càius Màius," as our peasants call him, for he is still popular throughout the region) awaited the barbarians behind the walls of his camp. And for two thousand years since, the monuments to his victory have been gilded by the sun at Saint-Rémy-les-Antiques. On the slope of those hills you come across the remains of the great Roman acqueduct that brought the waters from Vaucluse, they say, to the amphitheater of Arles, a conduit the people call "the Saracens' Channel," because the Moors took Arles through that passage. On the rocky escarpments of those hills the princes of Les Baux had their stronghold. In those aromatic vales, at Les Baux, Romanin, and Roque-Martine, beautiful chatelaines held their courts of love in the days of the troubadours. At Montmajour our kings of Arles sleep under the flagstones of the cloister. In the caves of the Valley of Hell at Cordes our fairies still wander, and under those Roman or medieval ruins the Golden Goat lies buried.

My village of Maillane stands facing the Alpilles in the middle of a wide plain which perhaps in memory of the Consul Caius Marius is still called *"Lou Caïéu."* An old wrestler of the town called "the little Maillanais" once said to me, "In the days when I used to wrestle, I traveled far and wide in Languedoc as well as Provence. But never," he said, "did I see land as level as this plain. If you were to plough a furrow as straight as a candle from the Durance down there to the sea, a furrow of twenty leagues, the water would run by itself, simply flowing down the slope."

Although our neighbors scorn us as "frog-eaters," the people of Maillane have always believed that there is no prettier village under the cope of heaven. And once when they asked me for some verses for the village choir, here is what I wrote:

> Maiano es bèu, Maiano agrado,
> E se fai bèu toujour que mai;
> Maiano s'óublido jamai,
> Car es l'ounour de l'encountrado
> E tèn soun noum dóu mes de Mai.

> Fugue à Paris e fugue à Roumo,
> Pàuri couscri, rèn vous fai gau;
> Trouvas Maiano sènso egau:
> I' amarias mai manja 'no poumo
> Que dins Paris un perdigau.

> Nosto patrìo n'a pèr bàrri
> Que li grand lèio de ciprès
> Que Diéu pèr elo a facho esprès;
> E quand s'enauro un vènt countràri,
> Tant soulamen brando lou brès.

> Tout lou dimenche se caligno;
> Pièi au travai, sènso cala,
> Se l'endeman se fau gibla,
> Bevèn lou vin de nòsti vigno,
> Manjan lou pan de nòsti blad.

> Maillane is fair and pleasing,
> Grows prettier day by day;

Maillane is so appealing,
It's the pride of the countryside
And takes its name from the month of May.

When in Paris or in Rome,
Nothing charms you there;
You find Maillane without compare:
And you'd rather eat an apple at home
Than a partridge in Paris.

Our village has no walls,
Only great hedges of cypress
Which God created for us;
And when the mistral blows,
It only rocks the cradle.

All day Sunday we go courting,
Then down to work without respite,
Though on Monday we must bend,
We drink wine from our own grapes,
We eat bread from our own grain.

The old farm on which I was born, facing the Alpilles and adjoining the Clos-Créma, was called the Judge's Farm. It was quite an estate, with four pairs of draft animals, a head carter, several plowmen, a handyman, a shepherd, a servant (whom we called the "aunt"), and a varying number of workers hired by the day or by the month to help with the silkworms, the hoeing, the haying, the wheat harvest, the threshing, the grape harvest, the sowing, or the olive picking.

My parents were landed farmers from families that live on their own land, tilling the soil from one generation to the next. These yeoman farmers form a class apart in the region of Arles, a sort of aristocracy who make the link between peasant and bourgeois and who, like all others, are proud of their caste. For while the peasant lives in a village and labors over his little patches of land with spade and hoe, the landowner who farms on a large scale, whether on the farms of the Camargue, the Crau, or elsewhere, works with his hand on his plow, standing erect and singing a song. That is what I said in these verses on the occasion of my nephew's wedding:

Avèn tengu l'araire	We have held the plow
Proun ounourablamen	With self-respect
E counquist lou terraire	And subdued the soil
Em' aquel estrumen.	With this implement.
Avèn fa de seisseto	We have made our wheat
Pèr lou pan calendau	For the Christmas bread
E de telo rousseto	And fine linen cloth
Pèr prouvesi l'oustau.	To furnish the house.
Tout camin vai à Roumo:	All roads lead to Rome,
Leissés dounc pas lou mas,	So don't ever leave the farm,
E manjarés de poumo,	And you'll have apples to eat,
D'abord que lis amas.	Since you like them so much.

But if indeed we wanted to blow our horn, as so many others do, we could claim without too much presumption that the family of Mistral is descended from the Mistrals of Dauphiné, who became by marriage lords of Montdragon and then of Romanin. The famous *"Pendentif"* they show you at Valence is the tomb of those Mistrals. And at Saint-Rémy, where my family had its roots (for my father came from there), you can still see the house of the Mistrals of Romanin, now known as the "Palace of Queen Jano."

The coat of arms of the noble Mistrals bears three clover leaves with the boldly inflated motto, "All or Nothing." For those like ourselves who read a person's future in family names or in the mystery of chance encounters, it is intriguing to find the courts of love of Romanin united in times past with the domain of the Mistrals, and the name of Mistral designating the great wind of the land of Provence, and those three clover-leaves indicating the destiny of our landed family.

"The four-leaved clover," Sâr Péladan once explained to us, "is a talisman, expressing symbolically the idea of the indigenous word, of development and slow growth, always in the same location. In divination the number three signifies the home: father, mother, son. Three clover leaves thus signify three harmonious generations in succession, or the number nine, which is that of the wise hermit of the Tarot. The motto 'All or Nothing' would readily correspond to those flowers which cannot be transplanted, a good emblem for a settled landowner."

Besides, the clover can also be found in the coat of arms of Ireland, and the Irish call it "Saint Patrick's flower," which represents for them the Holy Trinity.

But enough of these trifles. My father, left a widower by his first wife (by whom he had two children), was fifty-five years old when he remarried, and I am the product of that second marriage. Here is how he met my mother.

One year on the feast of Saint John, Master Francés Mistral was standing in the midst of his wheat as a band of reapers was cutting it down with sickles. A swarm of gleaners followed the harvesters, picking up the ears of grain that eluded the rakes. And my honored father noticed a handsome girl who lingered behind, as if ashamed of gleaning like the others. He went up to her and said, "Sweetheart, whose daughter are you? What's your name?"

The girl answered, "I am the daughter of Estève Poulinet, the mayor of Maillane. My name is Delaïdo."

"What!" said my father, "the daughter of Poulinet, the mayor of Maillane, goes gleaning?"

"Master," she replied, "we are a big family, with two boys and six girls, and although it's true that our father has enough property, when we ask him for money to make ourselves pretty, he replies, 'My little ones, if you want finery, go earn it.' And that is why I have come gleaning."

Six months after that meeting, so reminiscent of the Biblical story of Ruth and Boaz, the worthy landowner asked Master Poulinet for the hand of Delaïdo, and I was born of that marriage on the 8th of September in 1830.

My birth occurred about three o'clock in the afternoon, and my mother sent word from childbed to my father, who was in the middle of his fields as usual at that hour. The messenger cried out as he ran, from as far away as he could be heard, "Master, come! The mistress has just given birth."

"How many did she have?" asked my father.

"She's had a fine boy."

"A son? May the Lord make him grow big and good!"

And without further ado, acting as if nothing had happened, the good man finished his work and slowly returned home. Not that he was any less sensitive for all that, but brought up in the Roman tradition like the Provençaux of antiquity, he had the austere manners of the ancient *pater familias*.

They christened me Frederi in memory of a poor little fellow who, when my father and mother were courting, had sweetly run their errands of love, and who shortly after had died of sunstroke. But my mother always told me that she wanted to call me Nostradamus, first to thank the Mother of God, since I was born on the feast of Notre Dame of September, then in memory of the famous astrologer born in Saint-Rémy who was the author of *Centuries*. But neither the town hall nor the parish would allow that marvelous, mystical name, so felicitously chosen by maternal instinct.

Vaguely, as in a distant mist, I seem to recall my first outing in my mother's arms as she nursed me on her way to be churched, my dear mother in the full bloom of her youth and beauty proudly presenting her "king" to her friends, the friends and relatives welcoming our visit as good people do here by offering me a couple of eggs, a chunk of bread, a grain of salt, and a matchstick, saying, "Sweetheart, may you be full as an egg, wholesome as bread, wise as salt, straight as a matchstick."

Some may find it a bit childish to tell of these childish things. But after all, everyone does as he pleases, and it pleases me to go daydreaming back to my swaddling clothes, my cradle of mulberry, and my baby carriage, for I can thus relive the sweetest moments of my mother's joy.

When I was six months old, I was released from my swaddling band—for my grandmother Nanounet had recommended that I be kept well swaddled, because that way children would be neither knock-kneed nor bandy-legged. When I was six months old, they "gave me my feet" on the feast of Saint Joseph, according the custom of Provence. My mother brought me to the church in triumph, and holding me by my leading-strings, made me take my first steps on the saint's altar, while my godmother sang to me, "Come, come."

Every Sunday we went to Mass in Maillane, a walk of at least half a league, and my mother cuddled me in her arms all the way. What a soft and cozy nest was that mother's breast! I wanted to go on being carried that way forever and forever. But one day when I was five, my poor mother set me down halfway to the village, saying, "You're too heavy now. I can't carry you any more."

After Mass we used to go with my mother to visit my grandparents in their handsome kitchen with its white stone vaulting. There the local bourgeois, Monsieur Deville, Monsieur Dumas, Monsieur Ravoux, and the younger Rivière, usually came to talk politics while pacing back and forth on the flagstones from the fireplace to the sink. Monsieur Dumas, who had been a judge but had resigned in 1830, liked to give advice on all matters, like the following, which he repeated every Sunday in his loud voice to the young mothers dandling their little ones: "Never give children a knife, a key, or a book, for a child can cut himself with a knife, can lose a key, and can tear a book."

Monsieur Dumas did not come alone. With his ample wife and their eleven or twelve offspring, they filled the drawing room—that beautiful room of my ancestors, its walls covered with painted cloth from Marseille depicting little birds and baskets of flowers. And there to show off the learning of his progeny, he proudly had them declaim, one after another, each one a little, word by word and line by line, the "Speech of Théramène":

A peine nous sortions des portes de Trézène . . .
De Trégène . . . Il était sur son char . . . sur chon sar . . .
Ses gardes affligés . . . afflizès . . .
Imitaient son silence autour de lui rangés . . .
Lui ronzés.

Scarce had we left the gates of Trézène . . .
of Trégène . . . He rode on his chariot . . . on chis hariot . . .
His guards grieving . . . greasing . . .
Gathered in silence around him . . .
surround him . . .

Then he would say to my mother, "And your boy, Delaïdo, aren't you teaching him to recite?"

"Yes," my mother would reply naively, "he knows the jingle of 'Jan O'Pig.'"

"Go on, sweetheart," everyone would cry out, "'recite 'Jan O'Pig.'"

Then, lowering my head, I would mumble shyly:

—Quau es mort?	Who is dead?
—Jan dóu porc.	Jan O'Pig.
—Quau lou plouro?	Who mourns him?
—Lou rèi Mouro.	The Moorish king.
—Quau lou ris?	Who laughs at him?
—La perdris.	The partridge trim.
—Quau lou canto?	Who sings of him?
—La calandro.	The clothes wringer.
—Quau ié viro à brand?	Who tolls the bell?
—Lou quiéu de la sartan.	The skillet's bottom.
—Quau n'en porto dòu?	Who wears mourning?
—Lou quiéu dóu peiròu.	The cauldron's backside.

With such stories, nursery songs, and fairy tales our parents taught us in those days to speak the good Provençal tongue, while nowadays with vanity prevailing in most families, they teach children by the method of the worthy Monsieur Dumas and turn them into little simpletons who are like foundlings without ties or roots in their region, for it is the fashion now to repudiate absolutely all traditions.

I must now say a little about good old Estève, my maternal grandfather. Like my father, he was a landed farmer from a good family and of good stock, but with the difference that on the Mistral side they had no equals in all the region for being hard-working, thrifty, and acquisitive, while on my mother's side they were utterly carefree and always slow to work, they let the water run and ate up their property. To tell the truth, my grandfather Estève (may he be with God!) was a regular good-time Charley.

Although he had eight children, including six girls (who at mealtimes, when they had been served, took their plates and went out on the doorstep to eat), whenever there was a festival, off he went! He would be gone with his cronies for three days, playing and carousing while his money lasted. Then on the fourth day, when his pockets were empty, he would come home, gentle as a lamb. And then my grandmother Nanoun, who was a good soul, would cry out, "Aren't you ashamed to be such a squanderer, eating up your daughters' property?"

"Come now, old lady," he would reply, "what are you worrying about? Our little girls are pretty, they'll get married without dowries, and you'll see, my dear Nanoun, there won't be any left for the latecomers."

And mollifying and cajoling the good woman, he got her to take mortgages on the property in her dowry with usurers who lent him money at fifty or a hundred percent. Which did not prevent him, when his companions came around the next day, from spending the evening dancing in front of the fireplace and singing all together:

> Oh! la poulido vido que fan lis acabaire!
> Acò's de bràvi gènt,
> Quand n' an plus ges d'argènt,

> Oh, the lovely life that wastrels lead!
> They are such good fellows
> When they run out of money.

Or else this lively tune, which made them die laughing:

> Sian tres que n' avèn pa 'n sòu,
> Que n' avèn pa 'n sòu,
> Que n' avèn pa 'n sòu,
> E lou coumpaire qu'es darnié,
> Éu n' a pa 'n denié,
> Éu n' a pa 'n denié.

> We are three lads who haven't a sou,
> Haven't a sou,
> Haven't a sou.
> And the fellow who follows
> Has even less,
> Has even less.

And when my poor grandmother grieved to see the choice and fertile fields of her fine inheritance disappearing one after another, my grandfather would say to her, "Oh, you silly goose, why are you crying over a few plots of land? It rains there same as everywhere." Or else: "That barren soil? What it yielded, my dear, didn't even pay the taxes." Or else: "That wasteland? The neighbor's trees dried it out like a heath."

And he always had a good-humored answer ready like that. In speaking of those who practice usury, he even said, "By gad, we're very lucky there are such people. Otherwise what would we spenders and wasters do to find cash at a time when you know money is a commodity?"

That was the time when Beaucaire with its fair was the wonder of the Rhone. Multitudes came by water or by land from all nations, even Turks and Negroes. Everything made by the hand of man, all kinds of things man needs to feed, clothe, lodge, amuse, and cheat him, from millstones to pieces of linen or bolts of cloth, even to glass rings with rats carved on them, could be found there in profusion, in heaps or in bundles, in the big vaulted warehouses, under the arches of the market, on the ships in the harbor, or in the countless booths of the fairground. This was, so to speak, the universal exposition of the industries of the South, held every year under the July sun, but it also had its more popular side, teeming with life.

As you can well imagine, my grandfather Estève did not pass up such an occasion to go on a spree at Beaucaire for four or five days. So on the pretext of going to buy pepper or cloves or ginger for the household, he left for the fair with a handkerchief in every pocket—for he took snuff—and three other handkerchiefs in single, uncut pieces, which he wrapped around his middle as a sash. Then he strolled around all God's livelong day among the jugglers, the mountebanks, the actors, and especially the gypsies, as they wrangled and bargained, haggling over some skinny donkey.

For him Punch and Judy was a delicious treat. It was always new to him, and he was always enraptured, gaping and laughing like a pauper at the clowning and at the blows that rained incessantly on the Landlord and the Constable. As a result he never turned around as the pickpockets—and you can imagine how many there were at Beaucaire!—ever so gently lifted all his handkerchiefs, one after another, every year. And when he had no more—as he knew in advance would happen—he untied his sash without the least regret and used it to wipe his nose.

But when he came back to Maillane with his nose all blue from the dye that had run from the uncut handkerchiefs, my grandmother would say to him, "So they've stolen your handkerchiefs again?"

"Who told you that?" my grandfather would reply.

"Good Lord, your nose is all blue. You've blown your nose in your sash."

"Oh, I have no regrets," replied the good fellow, "that Punch made me laugh so much!"

In short, when his daughters (including my mother) came of marrying age, since they were attractive and not spoiled, suitors came around in spite of everything. But when their fathers said to my grandfather, "Seriously, how much are you giving your daughters?" Master Estève would turn red and reply, "How much am I giving them? Why you son of an ass, it's your loss! I would give your boy a fine girl all brought up and outfitted, and you expect me to throw in land and money besides? Anyone who doesn't want my daughters, let him leave them. Thank God there's bread in Master Estève's bin."

And indeed it's true that all six of my grandfather's daughters were taken for their pretty faces, and they all made good matches. As the saying goes, "A pretty girl has her face for a dowry."

But I don't want to leave the first flower of my childhood without picking another little bouquet for you.

Behind the house at the Judge's Farm where I was born, there was a ditch alongside the road that brought water to our old well with its pulley-wheel. The water was not deep but clear and sparkling, and when I was little, I could not resist going to play along its banks, especially on summer days.

That ditch of the pulley-well! It was the first book in which I learned a little natural history while playing.

There were little fish in it, sticklebacks and tiny carp, swimming by in schools, that I tried to net in a canvas nailbag hung at the end of a reed. There were green, blue, and black dragonflies that I would gently, oh so gently, catch in my little fingers when they alighted on the cattails—unless they escaped, lightly and silently fluttering their lacy wings. There were "cobblers," brown bugs with white bellies that skip on the water and wiggle their legs like a cobbler sewing. Then there were frogs, whose green backs flecked with gold emerged from the moss, frogs that quickly dove away when they saw me; tritons, a kind of water-salamander that rummaged in the ooze; and big beetles they call "eel-eaters" prowling in the depths.

Add to that a border of marshy plants, like those long woolly "cattails" that are the flowers of the reed mace; the water lily that makes a magnificent display on the surface of the water with its large round leaves and white calyx; the flowering rush with its cluster of pink blossoms; the poets' narcissus that admires its reflection in the water; duckweed with its tiny leaves; the "ox-tongue," with blossoms like a chandelier; and the "eyes of Baby Jesus" or forget-me-not.

But what pleased me most of all was the flower of the water iris. This is a big plant that grows in large clusters at the water's edge, with long sword-shaped leaves and beautiful yellow flowers rising up like golden halberds. It is quite likely that the golden fleur-de-lis, the emblem of France and of Provence, shining on an azure ground, were simply iris flowers, for "fleur-de-lis" comes from "fleur-d'iris," and the azure of the coat of arms could well represent the water in which the iris grows.

One summer day some time after the harvest, our sheaves were being threshed, and all the people of the farm were working on the threshing floor. Around the horses and mules that trod the grain vigorously about their masters were some twenty men in shirtsleeves, keeping pace, two by two and four by four, turning over the ears of wheat or removing the straw with wooden forks. This fine task they did cheerfully, dancing barefoot in the sun on the beaten grain.

The big winnowing sieve hung above the the threshing floor,

supported by the three legs of a crane made of three poles. Two or three girls or women with baskets threw the grain mixed with chaff into the hoop of the sieve, while the tall and vigorous master (my father) shook the sieve in the wind, thus bringing the bad grain together in the middle.

And when the wind died down, or at times when it stopped blowing for a spell, my father, holding the sieve motionless in his hands, would turn toward the wind and, looking into space as though speaking to a friendly god, would say quite seriously, "Come on, blow, blow, blow, sweetheart!" At that the mistral, obeying the patriarch, would suddenly breathe again, taking away the chaff, and God's beautiful grain would fall in yellow showers on the cone-shaped pile that rose before our eyes between the winnower's legs.

Then in the evening, when the grain had been shoveled up in a heap, when the threshing floor had been swept with a broom of dogberry, when the men all covered with dust went to the well to wash or to draw water for the animals, my father would measure the pile of grain with big strides and draw a cross on it with the handle of the shovel, saying, "May God make you increase!"

One fine afternoon of that threshing season—I was about four or five and still wearing little dresses—when I had had a good roll in the new straw, as children do, I made my way by myself toward the ditch of the pulley-well.

The beautiful iris flowers had begun to bloom several days before, and my hands were itching to pick some of those golden bouquets.

I came to the ditch, went slowly down to the water's edge, and reached out my hand to catch hold of the flowers. But since they were too far away, I bent over, I stretched out, and down I went, into the water up to my neck.

I cried out. My mother came running, pulled me out of the water, spanked me several times, made me run to the house ahead of her, wet as a duckling, saying, "Just let me catch you by the ditch again, you bad boy!"

"I was just going to pick iris flowers."

"Yes, go on back there and pick your iris and more of your iris. Don't you know there's a snake hiding in the weeds, good-for-nothing, a big snake that swallows birds and children?"

And she undressed me, took off my little shoes, my socks, my shirt, and to dry out my wet dress and my little shoes, she put on my wooden shoes and my Sunday dress, saying, "Now be careful not to get dirty."

I went right back to the threshing floor, made several somersaults on the fresh straw, saw a white butterfly fluttering about in a field of stubble, ran and ran after it, with my blond hair streaming in the breeze outside my bonnet, and suddenly there I was again, going toward the ditch of the pulley-well.

Oh, my beautiful yellow flowers! They were still there, standing proudly in the middle of the water, making me want them so much that I could not resist. I went down the bank very, very carefully; I placed my little feet on the very, very edge of the water; I reached out my hand, I stretched out, I stretched as far as I could . . . and down I went! into the mud right up to my bottom.

Ow, ow, ow! As I looked at the bubbles gurgling around me and thought I saw the big snake through the weeds, I heard someone on the threshing floor crying out, "Mistress, run quickly, I think the boy has fallen in again."

My mother came running, grabbed me, pulled me out of the stinking mud, all dirty, and the first thing she did was to tuck up my little dress and smack! smack! give me a good spanking.

"Now will you go back to your iris flowers, you stubborn child? Will you go back there and drown yourself? Here's a brand-new dress ruined, you little monster, you've spoiled your clothes, and you'll make me die of fright!"

And crying and covered with mud, I came back to the house, hanging my head. And again they undressed me and this time put on my little holiday dress. Oh, that elegant dress! I can still see its black velvet stripes flecked with gold on a blue background. Then when I had on my beautiful velvet dress, I said to my mother, "Now what shall I do?"

"Go watch the chickens," she said, "see that they don't go on the threshing floor, and stay in the shade."

"All right."

And full of good intentions, I ran toward the chickens that were wandering in the stubble pecking up the grain the rake had left behind.

But isn't it strange how things turn out? As I was watching, it so happened that a tufted pullet began chasing one of those grasshoppers with red and blue wings—you know? And both of them went hopping cross-country with me after them, because I wanted to see the grasshopper, with the result that we ended up at the ditch of the pulley-well.

There again were the golden flowers reflected in the stream and arousing my desire—such a passionate, delirious, excessive desire as to make me forget my two baths in the ditch.

"Oh, but this time," I said to myself, "don't worry, you won't fall in."

And going down the bank, I twisted a rush that grew there around my hand, and leaning very cautiously out over the water, I tried again to reach the iris flowers with my other hand.

But curse the luck! The rush broke, and I dove into the middle of the ditch headfirst.

I stood up as well as I could, bellowing like a lost soul, and all the people came running from the threshing floor.

"It's that little devil who's fallen into the ditch again. This time, you rascal of rascals, your mother's going to give you a sound whipping!"

But no. I saw her coming down the road, poor soul, all in tears, saying, "Dear God, I don't want to strike him because he might have an 'accident.' But Holy Mother, that boy is not like the others. He does nothing but run and pick flowers. He loses all his toys when he goes into the wheatfield to gather bouquets. Not satisfied with that, now he goes and throws himself into the ditch of the pulley-well three times in the last hour. Oh, patience, poor mother, resign yourself to cleaning him up. Who else would give him dresses? And yet it's a blessing—dear God, I thank you—that he didn't drown himself."

Thus we both went crying along the ditch.

Then once in the house, after taking off my clothing, the

saintly woman dried me, all naked, with her apron. And afterward for fear that I might take fright, she made me drink a spoonful of worming medicine and put me down in my bed, where I soon fell asleep, exhausted from crying.

And guess what I dreamed of!

My iris flowers, of course. In a beautiful, clear, limpid stream that snaked around the farm, azured like the waters of the Fountain of Vaucluse, I saw handsome clusters of big green iris plants crowned with a fairy treasure of golden flowers.

Dragonflies with blue silk wings alighted on them. And I swam naked in the sparkling water and picked the yellow fleur-de-lis by the handful, by the double handful, by the armful. And the more I picked, the more sprang up.

All of a sudden I heard a voice calling me, "Frederi!"

I woke up, and dear Lord, what did I see? A handful, a big handful of golden iris flowers glowing on my bed.

The patriarch, the Master, my honored father himself had gone to pick the flowers that made me happy. And the Mistress, my beautiful mother, had put them on my bed.

I I

MY FATHER

hus my earliest childhood was spent on the farm in the company of plowmen, harvesters, and shepherds. And sometimes, when some bourgeois happened by the farm, one of those who affected to speak only French, I was abashed and even humiliated to see that my parents suddenly became respectful toward him, as if he was superior to them.

"How come," I would ask, "that man doesn't speak like us?"

"Because he's a 'Monsieur'," they would reply.

"Well, then," I would say with a fierce little expression," I don't want to be a 'Monsieur'."

I had also noticed that when we had visitors such as the Marquis de Barbentane, whose adjoining land made us neighbors, my father, who ordinarily called my mother "the mistress" in the presence of the servants, then designated her formally as "my wife." The handsome marquis and the marquise, who was the sister of General de Galliffet, brought me pralines and other sweets whenever they came. But wild creature that I was, as soon as I saw them getting down from their carriage, I immediately ran away and hid in the hayloft, and poor Delaïdo called in vain, "Frederi!" Hiding in the hay, not breathing a word, I would wait to hear the wheels of the carriage taking the marquis away, and then listen to my mother down below in front of the house saying, "That impossible child! Monsieur de Barbentane and Madame de Barbentane, they came to see him, and he goes and hides."

And afterward, when I came fearfully out of my hiding place, instead of sugared almonds, whack! I got a spanking.

I much preferred to go with our foreman, Papoty, when with his hands on the handle of the plow drawn by his two mules he would call me invitingly, "Come quickly, little fellow, come, let me teach you to plow."

And at once I was in the furrow, barefoot, bareheaded, all excited, trotting and rummaging along the trench to pick up the "cuckoo-flowers" or the "blue penitents" torn up by the plowshare.

"Pick up some snails," Papoty would tell me.

And when I had a handful of snails in each hand, he would say, "Now with the snails grab the handles of the plow."

And when I gullibly took hold of the handles with my little fingers, he with his tough fingers pressed my two hands full of snails, squashing them against my flesh. Then the plowman would burst out laughing, "Now, little one, you can say that you have held the plow!"

They played all kinds of tricks on me. That's how they teach children on farms not to be stupid. Sometimes our shepherd Rouquet would call me as he came from milking, "Come, little fellow, drink straight from the *piau*." (The *piau* is a vessel of pottery or wood into which they milk.) Oh, when I saw the milkman coming out of the sheepfold, sweating, with his sleeves rolled up, carrying in his hand the foaming pail full to the brim with milk, I would come running, eager to swallow it all warm. But as soon as I knelt down to drink from the pail, bam! with his big hand Rouquet would push my head under up to the neck. Floundering and blinded, my hair tangled and my face streaming white with milk, I would run and roll on the grass like a puppy to dry myself, swearing to myself that I would not be tricked again . . . until I was tricked again.

Next it was a harvester who would say to me, "Little fellow, I've found a 'heel-striker's' nest. If you give me a boost, I'll keep the mother and you can have the babies."

Oh, the rascal! I would go off down the windrow, all excited.

"Look, you see that hollow on top of that big willow?" the fellow would say. "That's where the nest is. Come on, bend over."

And I would bend over with my head against the tree. And pretending to climb on my back, the joker would beat the back of my heel.

Thus amid the practical jokes of our farm workers—for which I have no regrets—my childhood education began.

How cheerful, how wholesome was that scene of farm work! Each season brought a new sequence of tasks. Plowing, sowing, shearing, mowing, the silkworms, the wheat harvest, the threshing, the wine harvest, the picking of olives—all displayed before my eyes the majesty of farm life, forever hard but forever independent and serene.

A whole world of workers, of men hired by the month or by the day, with a goad, a rake, or a fork on their shoulders, of women who weeded or made hay, came and went on the fields of the farm, working always with noble gestures as in the paintings of Léopold Robert.

When the men came into the farmhouse one after another for dinner or supper and sat down around the big table, each according to his rank, with my honored father at its head, he would solemnly ask them questions or make comments on the flocks, on the weather, on the work of the day, whether it was more or less easy, whether the soil was hard or soft or in good condition. Then when the meal was over, the head carter would close the blade of his knife, and immediately everyone would get up.

Among all these country people my father dominated by his height, by his judgment, and by his noble character as well. He was a big, handsome old man, dignified in his speech, firm in his authority, charitable to the poor, hard only on himself.

In the evening he took pleasure in telling stories about his old wars when he signed up as a volunteer to defend France during the Revolution. At the height of the Terror he was asked to transport wheat to Paris where famine reigned. This was during the period when the king had been killed. France was in a state of panic and dismay. One winter day, he told us, coming back through Burgundy with a cold rain beating his face, with mud on the roads up to the wheel hubs, he met a carter from his village. The two compatriots shook hands, and my father spoke, "Say, neighbor, where are you going in this devilish weather?"

"Citizen," the other replied," I am taking the saints and the bells to Paris."

My father went pale, tears came to his eyes, and removing his hat before the saints of his village and the bells of his church, which they had put up for auction and which he met thus on a road in Burgundy, he said to him, "You villain, do you think they'll make you a representative of the people for that when you return?"

The iconoclast bent his head in shame and with a curse against his God set his team going.

My father, I must say, had a profound faith. In the evening, in summer and winter alike, he prayed for all, kneeling at his chair, with his head bare, his hands crossed on his forehead, and his pigtail tied with a ribbon hanging down his back. Then in autumn, when the evenings grew longer, he read the gospels to his children and servants.

My father had read but three books in his life: the New Testament, *The Imitation of Christ,* and *Don Quixote* (which reminded him of his campaign in Spain and diverted him when it rained). "Since schools were rare in our day," he used to tell us, "a poor man who came by the farms once a week taught me my ABC." On Sunday, after vespers, following the practice and custom of the ancient *pater familias,* he recorded his business transactions, his accounts and expenditures, together with his reflections, in a big diary called the "Record Book."

Whatever the weather, he was always happy. And sometimes when he heard people complaining about windstorms or heavy rains, he would say to them, "Good people, He who is up there knows quite well what it's doing and what we need. What if those big winds which invigorate Provence never blew, who would disperse the marsh vapors and fogs? Likewise, if we never had heavy rains, who would fill the wells and the springs, the fountains and the rivers? We need everything, friends."

Although he would pick up a piece of wood by the wayside to bring it to the hearth, although he was satisfied with a humble diet of boiled vegetables and dark bread, although he was frugal amid abundance and watered his wine, his table, his hand, and his purse were always open for any poor person who came along. And when someone was being discussed, he would first ask if he was a good worker, and if they said yes, he would say, "Then he's a good man, and I am his friend."

Oh, he was faithful to the old ways, and for him Christmas Eve was the greatest holy day. On that day, the plowmen unhitched early. My mother gave each of them a fine oil cake, a slice of nougat, a double handful of dried figs, a fresh cheese, a bunch of celery, and a bottle of spiced wine, all wrapped in a napkin. And they all went off hither and thither to "put the log on the fire" in their homes and villages. Only the poor devils who had no family remained at the farm, and sometimes relatives, such as some old bachelor, would arrive at nightfall, saying, "Happy holidays! Cousins, we have come to put the log on the fire with you."

All together, we would go joyfully to get the Yule log, which always had to be from a fruit tree. We would bring it into the house, all in a row, the oldest at one end and I, the youngest member of the family, at the other. Three times we would make it go on a tour of the kitchen. Then arriving in front of the hearthstone, my father would solemnly pour a glass of spiced wine on the log, saying:

Alègre! alègre!
Mi bèus enfant, Diéu nous alègre!
Emé Calèndo tout bèn vèn . . .
Diéu nous fague la gràci de vèire l'an que vèn,
E se noun sian pas mai, que noun fuguen pas mens!

Good cheer! good cheer!
My dear ones, God give us good cheer!
At Christmas, all good comes.
God grant us grace to see the coming year,
And if there are not more of us, may there not be fewer!

And we would all cry out, "Good cheer, good cheer, good cheer!" as the tree was put on the andirons, and as soon as the bright flames burst forth, my father would cross himself, saying:

Cacho-fiò,	To the log,
Bouto fiò!	Let it burn!

Then we would all sit down to the table.

Oh, that holy gathering, truly holy, with the entire family all around the table, peaceful and happy! On that day three candles shone on the table, instead of the oil lamp hanging from a reed that gave us dim light during the year. And if the wick happened to turn toward someone, that was a bad omen. In a little plate at each end was a bunch of green wheat sprouts that had been placed in water to germinate on the feast of Saint Barbara. On the triple white tablecloth the traditional dishes appeared one after another: snails that everyone pulled from their shells with a long thorn, fried cod, mullet with olives, artichokes, cardoons, celery in a peppery sauce, followed by a lot of special delicacies, such as oil cakes, dried raisins, nougat, paradise apples, and on top of everything the big Christmas bread, which was never cut until a quarter had been given reverently to the first poor person who came by.

The evening, spent waiting for midnight Mass, was long that day, and around the fire they spoke at length of ancestors and praised their deeds. But gradually and willingly, that good man my father got around to Spain and his memories of the siege of Figueras.

"If I told you," he would say then, "that when I was in the army over there in Catalonia at the height of the Revolution I found a way to come from Spain in spite of the war and in spite of everything to celebrate Christmas with my family! Here is how it happened, I swear to God.

"At the foot of the Canigou, which is a big mountain between Perpignan and Figueras, we had been going and coming for quite a while, attacking and retreating, while fighting the Spanish troops. Oh, what a lot of dead and wounded, what suffering and misery! You would have to have seen it to know what it was like. Besides, there was a shortage of everything in camp. It was December, and for lack of fodder, the mules and horses gnawed on the wheels of the baggage wagons and gun carriages.

"Now what should happen to me but one day while prowling in the bottom of a ravine near the seacoast I discovered a tree full of oranges bright as gold!

"'Ah,' said I to the owner, 'you must sell them to me, no matter what the cost or price!' And when I had bought them, I came hurrying back to camp and went straight to the tent of Captain Perrin (who was from here, from Cabannes) with my basket and said to him, 'Captain, I have brought you some oranges.'

"'Where on earth did you get them?'

"'Where I could, Captain.'

"'Oh, what a rascal! Look, that's the greatest pleasure you could give me. So ask me what you wish, and you'll have it if it's in my power.'

"So then I said, 'I would like to go one more time, before a cannonball cuts me in two, like so many others, to bring in the Yule log at home with my family in Provence.'

"'That's easily done,' said he. 'Here, give me the writing-desk.'

"And Captain Perrin (may God have locked him up in heaven, that fine man!) scribbled the following on a piece of paper that I still have:

'The Army of the Eastern Pyrenees.
'We, Perrin, Captain in the Military Transport, give leave to Citizen François Mistral, a brave soldier of the Republic, twenty-two years of age, height five feet, six inches, hair and eyebrows brown, eyes russet, nose regular, eyes ditto, chin round, forehead average, face oval, to go to his region, via all the Republic, and to the devil, if it suits him.'

"And so, my friends, I arrived in Maillane on the beautiful eve of Christmas, and you can imagine the amazement of everyone and the embraces and celebrations. But the following day the mayor (I won't mention the name of that noisy braggart, for his children are still alive) summoned me to the town hall and said, 'In the name of the law, Citizen, how come you have left the army?'

"'It so happens,' I replied, 'that a fancy took me to come to Maillane this year to bring in the Yule log.'

"'Is that so? In that case, Citizen, you'll go explain your conduct to the district court at Tarascon.'

"And, just as I tell you, I let myself be conducted by two national guardsmen before the district judges. Those three grim faces with red caps and beards down to here said to me with eyes like fists, 'Citizen, how come you have deserted?'

"Thereupon I took my passport from my pocket and said, 'Here, read this.'

"Oh, my dear friends, as soon as they had read it, they stood up and shook my hand, exclaiming, 'Good Citizen, Good Citizen! Go, go, go! With papers like that you can send the mayor of Maillane to bed.'

"And after New Year's Day—I certainly could have stayed longer, but one must do one's duty—I went back and joined up again."

Here, reader, is what I wanted to show you, just as it was, the portrait of my family and the patriarchal home in all its noble simplicity.

On New Year's Day—to end with this other memory—a crowd of children, old people, women, and girls would come early in the morning to greet us:

> Bon-jour! vous souvetan en tóuti bono annado,
> Mestresso, mèstre, acoumpagnado
> De tant que lou bon Diéu voudra!

> Good morning, we wish you all a good year,
> Mistress and master, blessed with
> As much as the good Lord wills.

"And we wish you a good one," my father and mother would reply, giving each of them a couple of long loaves and round loaves of bread as a New Year's gift.

It was the tradition in our house, as in several others, to

distribute two ovenloads of bread thus at the New Year to the poor people of the village.

Cènt an viéurai,	If I live a hundred years,
Cènt an couirai,	A hundred years will I bake,
Cènt an i paure dounarai.	A hundred years will I give to the poor.

My father repeated these words in the prayer he said every night before going to bed. And so at his funeral the poor had reason to say in mourning him, "May as many angels accompany him in heaven as loaves of bread he gave us! Amen!"

III

THE MAGI

omorrow is the Feast of Kings. If you want to see them arriving, hurry, little ones, go meet them and bring them some offerings."

That's what our mothers used to tell us in our day on the eve of the Epiphany.

And off we would go, all the children of the village, leaving eagerly to meet the Magi Kings, who were coming to Maillane with their pages, their camels, and all their retinue to adore the Infant Jesus.

"Where are you going, little ones?"

"We are going to meet the Kings."

And all together, tousled urchins and fair young maidens, in our hoods and little wooden shoes, we would set out on the road to Arles, our hearts throbbing with joy, our eyes full of visions. And we carried in our hands, as we had been told, cakes for the Kings, dried figs for their pages, and hay for the camels.

Jour creissènt,	Days growing longer,
Jour cousènt.	Days of stinging cold.

The north wind whistled—in other words, it was cold. A pallid sun was going down toward the Rhone. The little streams were frozen. The grass on their banks was brown. The leafless willow branches were turning red. The redbreast and the wren hopped from branch to branch, lively and friendly.

And there was no one to be seen in the fields except some poor widow who filled her apron with firewood and loaded more on her head or some ragged old man looking for snails at the foot of a withered hedge.

"Where are you going so late, little ones?"

"We are going to meet the Kings."

And with our heads in the air, proud as young roosters, laughing, singing, running on one foot, or sliding, we would go straight down the white road swept by the wind.

Then daylight faded. The steeple of Maillane disappeared behind the trees, behind the big, black, pointed cypress trees. And the countryside stretched off in the distance, vast and naked. We looked as far as we could, as far as the eye could see, but in vain. Nothing appeared but some bunches of thistles carried off in the stubble by the wind. Like the winter nights of January, all was sad, silent, and bleak.

Sometimes, however, we would meet a shepherd wrapped in his cape who had just been watching his sheep.

"Where on earth are you going so late, children?"

"We are going to meet the Kings. Could you tell us if they are still far away?"

"Ah yes, the Kings. That's right. They're back there coming along. You'll soon see them."

And we would run and run to meet the Kings, with our cakes, our little flat cakes, and handfuls of hay for the camels.

Then daylight faded. The sun, covered by an enormous cloud, disappeared little by little. Our playful chatter died down. The north wind grew colder. And the bravest walked with restraint.

Suddenly all our voices gave a wild cry of joy, "There they are!"

And our eyes were dazzled by a magnificent display of royal grandeur. An outburst, a triumph of splendid, sumptuous colors flamed out and set the west ablaze. Great flashes of purple flared, and a half-crown of gold and ruby shot a circle of long rays in the heavens, lighting up the horizon.

"The Kings! The Kings! Look at their crown! Look at their coats! Look at their flags! Look at their horses and camels!"

And we stood amazed. But soon that splendor, soon that glory, the last glow of the setting sun, dissolved and died out little by little in the clouds. And we found ourselves all alone in the dark countryside, gaping sheepishly.

"Where did the Kings go?"

"Behind the mountain."

An owl hooted, fear seized us, and we turned back in the dusk, crestfallen, nibbling the cakes, the little flat cakes, and the figs we had brought for the Kings.

And when we reached home, our mothers said to us, "Well, did you see them?"

"No, they went farther away, on the other side of the mountain."

"Why, which road did you take?"

"The road to Arles."

"Oh, my poor lambs! The Kings don't come from there. They come from the East. Good Lord, you should have taken the road to Rome. Oh, how beautiful it was, if you could have seen, if you could have seen, when they entered Maillane! The drums, the trumpets, the pages, the camels, Lord, what a racket! Now they are in the church, worshiping. After supper you'll go see them."

We would eat supper quickly—I at my grandmother Nanoun's—then run to the church. And as soon as we entered the church full of people, the organ would begin slowly, then swell powerfully, accompanying the whole congregation singing the superb carol:

> De matin
> Ai rescountra lou trin
> De tres grand Rèi qu'anavon en vouiage;
> De matin
> Ai rescountra lou trin
> De tres grand Rèi dessus lou grand camin.

> This morning
> I met the retinue
> Of three great Kings going on a journey;
> This morning

> I met the retinue
> Of three great Kings on the great highway.

Overwhelmed, we would worm our way between the women's skirts to the chapel of the Nativity. And there above the altar we saw the Beautiful Star and the three Magi Kings in red, yellow, and blue cloaks hailing the Infant Jesus, King Gaspard with his golden casket, King Melchior with his censer, and King Balthazar with his jar of myrrh. We gazed in wonder at the charming pages holding the train of their long cloaks; the humped camels raising their heads above the Ass and the Ox; the Blessed Virgin and Saint Joseph; and all around them on a little mountain of darkened paper the Shepherds and Shepherdesses bringing cakes, baskets of eggs, and swaddling clothes; the Miller carrying a bag of flour; the old Spinning Woman; the Awestruck Man staring; the Knife-grinder grinding; the Innkeeper opening his window with amazement; and all the traditional figures that appear in the Crèche. The one we stared at the most was the Moorish King.

Many a time since then I have happened to go for a walk on the road to Arles at nightfall when the Kings are coming. The redbreast and the wren continue to flutter there along the hawthorn hedges, there is always some old man still looking for snails in the grass, as in the past, and the owl still hoots. But in the sunset clouds I no longer see the visionary gleam, I no longer see the glory or the crown of the old Kings.

"Where have the Kings gone?"

"Behind the mountain."

Alas, alas, the melancholy, the sadness of things seen in times past, in youth! However big and beautiful the familiar landscape, when we want to see it again, when we want to return there, someone or something is always, always missing.

> Oh! vers li plano de tousello
> Leissas me perdre pensatiéu,
> Dins li grand blad plen de rousello
> Ounte drouloun iéu me perdiéu!
>   Quaucun me bousco
>   De tousco en tousco

En recitant soun angelus;
E, cantarello,
Li calandrello
Iéu vau seguènt dins lou trelus . . .
Ah! pauro maire,
Bèu cor amaire,
Cridant moun noum t'ausirai plus!
(Isclo d'Or)

Toward the fields of grain
Let me lose myself in thought,
In the tall wheat full of poppies
Where I'd lose my way as a boy.
Someone is looking for me
Going from sheaf to sheaf
While reciting the angelus;
And the skylarks
Are singing above;
I follow them in the sunshine.
Ah, poor mother,
Dear loving heart,
I shall never hear you calling my name again!
(Golden Isles)

Who will give me back the delight, the heavenly bliss of
ignorance, when my soul opened like a flower, fresh and new to
the songs, the jingles, the laments, the fabliaux that my mother
told me and sang me in the sweet language of Provence while
she was spinning and I snuggled at her knees: "The Pater
Noster of Christmas," "Mary Magdalen, the Poor Sinner,"
"The Ship's Boy from Marseille," "The Swine-Maiden," "The
Wicked Rich Man," and so many other stories, legends, and
beliefs of our Provençal people that rocked my childhood in a
cradle of dreams and moving poetry. After nursing me with her
milk that good woman nourished me thus with the honey of
tradition and of the Lord.

Nowadays, with the harsh and narrow system that no longer
takes into consideration the wings of childhood, the angelic
instincts of the budding imagination, or its need for the marvel-
ous—which is what makes saints and heroes, poets and art-
ists—nowadays, as soon as the child is born, its heart and soul

are dried up with raw, naked learning. Alas, poor dreamers, with age and school, especially the school of life, only too soon do they learn the shabby truth and become disillusioned by scientific analysis of everything that enchanted us.

If some tiresome anatomist came to us at the age of twenty or thirty, when we are in the grip of love for a beautiful girl bursting with youth, and said, "Do you want to know the truth about this creature who charms you so? If her flesh fell off, you would see a skeleton"—don't you think we would send him packing immediately?

Good Lord, if we always had to get to the bottom of the well of truth, we might as well return to the Middle Ages, which came from the opposite direction from modern science and arrived at the same result in depicting life as a *danse macabre*.

But enough. To give some idea of the fancies and phantoms, ghosts and goblins that I had seen frisking around my childhood, I put on stage somewhere a superstitious old woman I knew in those days, Dame Renaudo. And I believe that piece will be appropriate here.

Old Renaudo sits in the sun on a block of wood in front of her cottage. She is withered, wizened, and wrinkled, poor woman, like an overripe fig. Shooing away the flies from time to time that settle on her nose, she drinks in the sun, drowses, and dozes.

"So, Aunt Renaudo, you're having a little nap there in the good warm sunshine?"

"Well, what would you have me do? To tell the truth, I am neither sleeping nor waking. I am daydreaming and praying. But then in praying to God, you end up falling asleep. How time drags when you can no longer work! You're bored as a dog."

"You'll catch a cold in the glare of this bright sunshine."

"Me catch cold? Nonsense! Can't you see that I am dry as tinder, alas. If they boiled me, I probably wouldn't yield a spot of oil."

"If I were you, I'd go and visit old ladies of your age. You'd have a good time."

"What do you mean, old ladies of my age? Soon there won't

be any more. Let's see, who's left? Poor Genevivo, who's deaf as a plow; old Patantano, whose wits are wandering; Catarino of the Oven, who does nothing but complain. I have plenty of troubles of my own. I'd just as soon be alone."

"Why don't you go to the washhouse? You could chat a while with the washerwomen."

"Go on with your washerwomen! They're silly gossips who spend the whole day knocking this one and that one. They say only unpleasant things. They make fun of everyone, then laugh like fools. Some day the good Lord will teach them a lesson. No, no, it's no longer the way it was in our day."

"And what did you talk about in your day?"

"In our day? Oh, we told stories, tales, bits of nonsense that you'd love to hear: 'The Beast with Seven Heads,' 'John Who Seeks Fear,' 'The Big Body without a Soul.' Just one of those stories would sometimes last three or four evenings.

"In those days we used to spin wool and flax. In the winter after supper we would take our distaffs and gather in some big sheepfold. Outside we could hear the mistral blowing and the dogs barking at the wolf. But we were nice and warm sitting there on the sheep's bedding. And while the men were feeding or milking the sheep, and the pretty lambs were on their knees bumping their mothers' udders and waggling their tails, we women, as I say, listened and told stories as we turned our spindles.

"I don't know how it is, but in those days they spoke of many things that no one speaks of any more, of things that plenty of trustworthy people we knew nevertheless assured us of having seen.

"Look, my Aunt Mïan, the Chairmaker's wife, whose grandsons live at the Clos de Pain-Perdu, one day went out to gather firewood and met a White Hen, a fine hen that seemed tame. My aunt bent over and reached out her hand. But suddenly the hen moved away and went a little farther off to peck around in the grass. Stealthily Mïan again approached the hen—which seemed to crouch down to let itself be caught—calling, 'Here, chick, chick, chick!' But just as she thought she had her, suddenly the hen jumped, and my aunt followed her more and more eagerly. She followed and followed her, for perhaps an hour. Then as the sun had already set, Mïan got frightened and went back home. It seems she did well, for if she had followed that White Hen at night, Holy Virgin Mary, who knows where she would have led her!

"They used to speak also of a Horse or a Mule—others said a Big Sow—that sometimes appeared to dissipaters as they came out of the tavern. One night in Avignon a group of worthless characters who had been carousing saw a black horse coming out of the drain of Cambaud.

"'Oh, what a fine horse!' said one of them. 'Wait till I jump on him.'

"And the horse let him mount.

"'Say, there's room for one more,' said another, 'I'm going to get on him too.'

"And immediately he got on too.

"'Look, there's still room,' said another youth.

"And he too climbed on. And as they mounted, the Black Horse grew longer and longer and longer, so long indeed that twelve of those fools were already on horseback when the thirteenth cried, 'Jesus, Mary, holy Saint Joseph! I believe there's room for one more!' But at these words the creature disappeared, and our twelve carousers all came to their senses sheepishly and found themselves standing on their feet—fortunately, fortunately for them! For if the very last fellow had not cried out, 'Jesus, Mary, holy Saint Joseph!' that evil beast would surely have carried them all to the devil.

"Do you know what else they spoke of? Of the kind of people who went dancing on the moors at midnight, then took turns drinking from the Silver Cup. They called them Sorcerers or Warlocks, and in those days there were a few of them in every village. I even knew several—whom I don't want to name out of consideration for their children. Anyway, it seems they were a bad lot, for once my grandfather, who was a shepherd over there at Grès, in passing behind the Priests' Farm looked through the gate, and my Lord! what did he see? In the kitchen of that old abandoned house he saw men playing ball with children, little naked children they had taken from their cradles and were throwing from hand to hand, from one to another. It made me shudder!

"What else? Weren't there Sorcerer Cats? Yes, there were black cats they called Matagots that brought money to the houses where they stayed. You knew old Tartavello, didn't you, who left so many crowns when she died? Well, she had a black cat to which she always threw the first mouthful under the table at every meal. She never failed to do so.

"I always heard it said that one night in going to bed my Uncle Cadet saw a kind of black cat crossing the road in the moonlight.

"Without thinking he threw a stone at it. But the cat turned around and said to our uncle with an evil look, 'You have hit Robert!'

"How strange, though! Today all that seems a dream, no one speaks of it any more, and yet there must have been something, since everyone was afraid of it.

"Well," said Renaudo, "there were plenty of other goblins that have since disappeared. There was the Chaucho-Vièio, who crouched on your chest at night and took away your breath. There was the Garamaudo, there was the Fouletoun, there was the Loup-Garou, there was the Tiro-Graisso, there was . . . I don't know what-all.

"But look at what I was forgetting—the Fantastic Spirit! That one, it can't be said that he wasn't real. I heard him and saw him. He haunted our stable. My poor father (may he be with God) was sleeping once in the hayloft. Suddenly he heard the door opening down below. He looked through the crack, the crack in the window, and what did he see? He saw our animals, the jack-mule, the jenny, the donkey, the mare, and the little colt, neatly yoked together, going off in the moonlight to drink at the trough. My father soon saw—for he was not new to such charms—that it was the Fantastic who led them to drink. He lay down again in the straw and said nothing. But the following morning he found the stable door wide open!

"What attracts the Fantastic in the stables, they say, is the sleigh bells. The sound of sleigh bells makes him laugh, laugh, laugh, like a one-year-old child when a rattle is shaken. Other-

wise he's not harmful, far from it. But he's capricious and a
trickster. If he's in a good humor, he will curry your animals,
plait their manes, give them white straw, clean their manger.
It's noteworthy that one animal is always healthier than the
others when the Fantastic is around because the Spirit has
chosen to favor it on a whim, and then at night he comes and
goes in the manger and takes hay from the others.

"But if by mistake or by chance you disturb something in the
stable against his will, my, oh my, oh my! he will give you a
witches' sabbath the following night. He will snarl the animals'
tails, he will tangle their feet in their halter and straps, he will
upset the rack of horsecollars with a crash, he will rattle the
frying pan and the pothanger in the kitchen, in short, he will
make a nuisance of himself in every way—to such a point that
my father, annoyed by all that racket, once said, 'This must
stop!'

"He took a peck of vetch seed, climbed up to the hayloft,
scattered the tiny grain in the hay and in the straw, and called
out to the Fantastic, 'Fantastic, my friend, sort out these grains
of vetch for me, one by one.'

"The Fantastic Spirit, who takes pleasure in minute detail and
who likes everything to be tidy, set to work, it appears, sorting
out the vetch seed. He was very painstaking, for we found little
piles all around the hayloft. But as my father knew, that metic-
ulous work finally bored him, and he left the hayloft, never to
be seen again.

"Ah yes, but to finish, I saw him one more time. Just imagine
that one day—I might have been eleven—I was coming back
from catechism. In passing by a poplar I heard laughter in the
top of the tree. I looked up and saw the Fantastic Spirit laugh-
ing in the foliage on top of the poplar, beckoning me to climb
up. Ah, I ask you now! Not for a hundred onions would I have
climbed! I ran off like a madwoman, and that's been the end of it
ever since.

"All the same, I assure you that when night came and they
told stories about those things around the lamp, we didn't
venture to go out. Oh, how frightened we poor little girls were!
But then we grew up, the time of courtship arrived, as you

know, and in the evening the boys would call us, 'Come on, girls, let's go dance the farandole in the moonlight.'

"'We're not that foolish!' we would reply. 'What if we met the Fantastic Spirit or the White Hen?'"

"'Oh, how silly,' they would say, 'can't you see those are blind grandmothers' tales? Come on, don't be afraid, we'll keep you company.'

"And so we went out, and indeed, little by little, in talking with the boys—boys of that age, you know, have no sense, they only talk nonsense and make you laugh—little by little, little by little, we were no longer afraid. And since then, I tell you, I have no longer heard tell of those nocturnal spirits.

"It's true that since then we've had plenty of work to keep us from being bored. Look at me, I have had eleven children, all of whom I brought up, and I have nursed fourteen, without counting my own!

"Ah, when you're not rich and you have such a brood to swaddle, rock, nurse, and clean, that's a pretty bagpipe tune!"

"Well, now, Aunt Renaudo, may the good Lord keep you."

"Oh my, now we are ripe. He'll come pick us, when He wishes."

And with her handkerchief the old lady chased away the flies. And lowering her head, she settled down again peacefully, drinking in the sunshine.

I V

PLAYING
HOOKY

t about the age of eight and no sooner, with my blue bookbag, my notebook, and my lunch, I was sent to school. No sooner, thank God, for as far as the development of my nature and emotions was concerned, the training and growth of my young poetic soul, I certainly learned more in the somersaults of my childhood among common people than in the regurgitation of all the rudiments of learning.

In our time the dream of all of us little rascals who went to school was to play hooky. The one who had done so was regarded by the others as a rogue, a scoundrel, a thoroughly accomplished fellow.

"Ditching"—not that you don't know—is a child's escapade far from his father's house without warning his parents and without knowing where he is going. Little Provençal boys run away like that if they have done something wrong, some serious misdeed, some act of disobedience that makes them expect a good hiding when they get home. Therefore, as soon as they suspect what is hanging over their ears, these little wretches "ditch" school and father and mother. Come what may, they go wandering off with the wind, and long live liberty!

At that age there's nothing so delightful as to feel oneself absolute master, without a bridle, free to go wherever you wish. Off into the brush! Off to the marsh! Over by the mountain!

Only then comes hunger. If it's a summertime ditch, you're in the land of Cockaigne. There are gardens of beans, orchards with apples, pears, and peaches, cherry trees that catch your eye, fig trees that offer you their ripe figs, round-bellied melons that beg to be eaten, and beautiful vines with bunches of golden grapes—ah, I can almost see them!

But if it's a wintertime ditch, you need to use your wits. Good Lord, there are little vagrants who go to farms where they aren't known and ask for hospitality. Then if they can, the little beggars steal eggs from the henhouses, even the nest-eggs, and swallow them raw, gulp!

But the proudest, the most sensitive, those who have quit school and family not so much out of idleness as from a desire for independence or on account of some injustice that has wounded their hearts—they flee humanity and its habitation. They spend their days lying in the wheat, in ditches, in millet fields, under bridges, or in huts. The night they spend in piles of straw or in haystacks. When hunger comes, they eat wild blackberries, wild plums, almonds left on the tree, or bunches of wild grapes. They eat the fruit of the elm—which they call "white bread"—onions that have sprouted again, wild pears, beechnuts, and acorns, if necessary.

The whole day is but a game, every leap a caper. What need is there for companions? There you have all the animals and little creatures for company. You understand what they do, what they say, what they think, and they seem to understand everything you say to them.

If you catch a cicada, you look at its little singing "mirrors," you rub it in your hand to make it sing, and then you let it go with a straw in its tail.

Or when you're lying on a bank along comes a ladybug and climbs your finger. Whereupon you sing to her:

Parpaiolo, volo!	Ladybug, fly away!
Vai-t'en à l'escolo!	Go away to school!
Prene ti matino,	Take your prayer book,
Vai à la dóutrino . . .	Go to Sunday School.

Then spreading her wings, the ladybug says to you as she flies away, "Go to school yourself. I already know enough."

If a praying mantis kneels and looks at you, ask it:

> Prègo-Diéu, ié venès, prègo-Diéu, tu que sabes tout,
> > Ounte es lou loup?

> Praying mantis, come, praying mantis, you who know everything,
> > Where is the wolf?

And the praying mantis, stretching out its leg, points toward the mountain.

If you discover a lizard sunning himself, say:

> Lesert, ié venès, lesert,
> > Aparo-me di serp:
> Quand passaras vers moun oustau,
> Te baiarai un gran de sau.

> Lizard, come, lizard,
> > Protect me from snakes;
> When you come near my house,
> I'll give you a grain of salt.

"To your house?" the sly lizard seems to say, "to which you're not returning?" and whish! he vanishes into his hole.

Or if you see a snail, you say to her:

Cacalaus mourgueto,	Snaily snail,
Sorte ti baneto,	Stick out your horns,
O vau souna lou manescau	Or I'll call the blacksmith
Pèr que te roumpe toun oustau.	To break down your house.

And again and again the house keeps obsessing you, so finally when you have spoiled enough nests, and pants too, when you have trimmed enough barley straws, peeled enough willow shoots to make whistles, and set your teeth well on edge with green apples and other unripe fruit (ow!), then homesickness overwhelms you, and you come home, hanging your head.

Being of Provençal stock like my companions, I too played hooky—don't let this surprise you—after I had been hardly three months at school. And here's why:

Three or four of those urchins who on the pretext of going to cut grass or gather manure wandered about all day long were waiting for me when I was leaving for Maillane and said to me, "Hey, you fool, what do you want to go to school for? to stay the whole day behind four walls? to be put in the corner? to have your fingers struck with a ruler? Come and play."

Ah me, the clear water sparkled in the streams; the larks were singing on high; in the sunshine the bluets, the iris, the poppies, the corncockles blossomed in the green wheatfields. And I said, "School, oh well, you'll go tomorrow."

And then with our pants rolled up we jumped into the stream and went wading. We splashed, we paddled, we fished for tadpoles, we made mud pies, flip! flop! then we smeared ourselves with black mud up to the calves (to make ourselves boots), and set off at full tilt down a sunken road in the dust:

Ra-pa-ta-plan!	Ratatatat!
Li sóudard s'envan,	The soldiers are going,
A la guerro van!	To war they are going!
Garas-vous davans!	Make way up ahead!

Lord, what fun! The King's children had nothing on us—not to mention that with the bread and the snack in my bag we had a nice little lunch on the grass. But all things must end.

It happened that one day my father—the schoolmaster must have told him—said to me, "Frederi, if you miss any more school to go wading in the ditches, remember this: I'll break a willow switch on your back."

Three days later I recklessly skipped school again and went wading again. I don't know if my father had kept an eye on me, or if it was chance that brought him, but just as I was frisking about in the water without my pants in the company of the other rascals, suddenly I saw him appear thirty paces away. My heart did a somersault.

My father stood there and shouted to me, "All right. You know what I promised you. Go on, I'll be waiting for you tonight."

He said no more than that. Then he went away.

My honored father, good as the holy bread, had never given

me a flick of the finger. But he had a loud voice and spoke roughly, and I feared him like fire.

"Ah," I said to myself, "this time, this time, your father will kill you. He must surely have gone to prepare the switch."

On top of that my rascally companions clapped their hands and sang to me, "Ow! ow! ow! what a tanning! Ow! ow! ow! of your hide!"

"Well, then," I said, "since all is lost, I must clear out and ditch."

So I left. I remember that I took a road that led over there toward Crau d'Eyragues. But at that time, poor little wretch, did I have any idea where I was going? And then, to tell the truth, when I had traveled about an hour or an hour and a half, it seemed to me that I must be in America.

The sun began to go down in earnest, I was tired, I was scared. "It's getting late," I thought to myself, "now where am I going to find supper? I must go ask for hospitality at some farm."

And leaving the road, I slowly made my way toward a little white farm that looked as hospitable as could be, with its pig shed, its manure ditch, its well, and its grape arbor, all nicely sheltered by a row of cypress trees.

Timidly I went up to the doorstep and saw an old woman pouring soup, a kind of dirty woman, all disheveled, so that you would have to be really hungry to eat what she touched.

The old woman had taken the pot down from the pothook, had put it on the floor in the middle of the kitchen, and while twisting her tongue and scratching herself, poured the broth with a big ladle and spread it slowly on thin slices of moldy bread.

"Well, grandmother, so you're preparing soup?"

"Yes," she replied, "and where do you come from, little one?"

"I am from Maillane," I told her, "I have ditched, and I come to ask you for hospitality."

"In that case," replied the ugly old woman in a peevish tone, "sit down on the stairs so that you won't wear out my chairs."

And I crouched down on the first step.

"Grandmother, what do they call this place."

"Pamparigousto."

"Pamparigousto!"

You know that when speaking to children of a place far away people will sometimes call it Pamparigousto in jest. You can imagine that at that age I fervently believed in Pamparigousto, in Zibo-Zoubo, in Never-Never Land, and other fanciful places. So when the old woman mentioned that name, I felt a cold sweat run down my back, to find myself so far from home.

"Now then," the old woman said to me when she had finished her work, "that's not all, little one. In this country lazy people get nothing to eat. If you want your share of soup, do you hear, you'll have to earn it."

"Gladly. And what must I do?"

"Look, we are both going to stand at the bottom of the stairs and play at jumping. The one who jumps farthest, sweetheart, will have his share of good soup, and the other, if he wishes, will eat with his eyes."

"I'm willing." Not only that, but I was proud of earning my soup, especially while enjoying myself.

"It will be too bad," I thought, "if that old crab jumps farther than you."

No sooner said than done. With feet together we both took our places at the foot of the stairs—which in farmhouses, you know, are to the right of the door and very near the doorsill.

"And I say 'one!'" cried the old lady, swinging her arms to give herself momentum.

"And I say 'two!'"

"And I say 'three!'"

I sprang with all my might and cleared the doorstep. But the old crook, who had only pretended, immediately closed the door, quickly shot the bolt, and cried out to me, "Go, you rascal, go back to your parents, they must be worrying."

Poor me, I felt as foolish as a basket with a hole in its bottom. And now where should I go? Home? I wouldn't have gone back there for a hundred onions, for it seemed to me that I could see the switch flexing in my father's hand. And then it was almost night, and I no longer remembered the road I should take.

"God help me!"

Behind the farm there was a path that went uphill between two high banks. I took it on a chance, and off went little Frederi. After I had gone up and down a long time I was exhausted. You can well imagine—at that age with nothing in my stomach since noon. Finally I discovered a dilapidated hut in an abandoned vineyard. It must have been burned, for the cracked walls were blackened by smoke. There was neither door nor window, and the beams, which only held at one end, bit the dirt at the other. It looked like the den where the Nightmare nested.

But there's no resisting a hanging in Aix. Weary, collapsing, and dead tired, I climbed up on the biggest beam and stretched out. And in the blink of an eye I fell asleep.

I couldn't say how long I remained thus, but in the middle of my heavy sleep I suddenly thought I saw a flaming brazier with three men seated around the fire, chatting and laughing.

"Are you dreaming?" I said to myself in my sleep, "are you dreaming, or is this true?"

But that strong sense of well-being that slumber gives you removed all my fear, and I kept on sleeping quietly.

However, it must have been the smoke that finally made me uneasy. I awoke with a sudden start and gave a cry of terror. Oh, since I did not die of fright then and there, I shall never die!

Just imagine three faces of gypsies, all three turning their eyes toward me at once, terrible eyes.

"Don't kill me! don't kill me!" I cried out to them, "don't kill me!"

Then the three gypsies, who had surely had as great a fright as I, began to laugh, and one of them said to me, "Never mind, you can brag, you little brat, of having given us quite a scare."

But when I saw that they were laughing and that they talked like me, I took heart a little. And then I smelled a very, very pleasant odor of roasting meat rising in my nostrils.

They made me get down from my perch, they asked me where I came from, who I belonged to, how I came to be there, what-have-you.

Completely reassured at last, one of the robbers (for they were really three robbers) said to me, "Since you have ditched, you must be hungry. Here, take a bite of that!"

And he threw me, as he would to a dog, a bloody, half-cooked shoulder of lamb. Only then did I notice that they had just roasted a young sheep on the brazier—which they must have stolen, probably from some shepherd.

As soon as we had eaten well in that fashion, the three got up, picked up their clothes, and whispered among themselves. Then one of them said, "Look, little one, since you say you're a good fellow, we don't want to hurt you. However, we're going to put you in a barrel, that barrel over there, so that you won't see where we go. When it's daylight, you can shout, and the first passerby will get you out, if he wants."

"All right, put me in the barrel," I answered submissively.

I was still quite satisfied, you see, to get off so lightly. And indeed in a corner of the hut there was a battered barrel in which the winemakers must have made wine at harvest-time.

They grabbed me by the butt and stuck me in the barrel. And there I was, all alone in the middle of the night in a barrel on the floor of a dilapidated hut.

I curled my poor self up into a ball and waited for dawn, praying quietly to keep away the evil spirits.

Would you believe that all at once I heard something prowling and sniffing around my barrel in the dark?

I held my breath as if I were dead and commended myself to God and the holy Blessed Virgin. I heard something turning and returning, snuffling and worrying, then going away, then coming back. What the devil could it be? My heartbeat sounded loud as a clock.

To end my story, when the day began to grow light and the trampling that frightened me went away a little, I peeked cautiously, cautiously, through the bunghole of the barrel, and what did I see? A wolf, my dear friends, the size of a small donkey, an enormous wolf with two eyes that glowed like two candles.

Apparently he had come at the scent of the lamb, and when he found only bones, my tender young Christian flesh took his fancy.

Then, strange enough but true, once I saw what it was, my

blood ran a bit slower. I had been so afraid of having to do with some ghost that the sight of the wolf restored my spirits.

"Oh, my, that's not all," I said, "if that beast should notice that the barrel is smashed, he will surely jump inside and strangle you with one bite. If you could find some way. . . ."

As I made a move, the wolf heard it and returned to the barrel in one bound. And there he was circling around and whipping the staves with his long tail. I reached my little hand through the bunghole very carefully, grabbed the tail, pulled it inside, and hung on with both hands.

The wolf took off as if he had five hundred devils on his tail, with the barrel after him, through fields, through vineyards, across the stony plain. We must have rolled over all the hills and valleys of Eyragues, Lagoy, and Bourbourel.

"Oh, my God, Jesus, Mary! Jesus, Mary, Joseph!" I cried, "who knows where he'll take you? And if the barrel breaks, he'll slash your throat and eat you."

Crash! smash! the barrel burst, the tail got away from me. I saw my wolf fleeing far off in the distance, and lo and behold! I found myself at the New Bridge on the road from Maillane to Saint-Rémy, fifteen minutes from our house. The barrel must have struck the parapet broadside and broken to pieces there.

No need to tell you that after such a shock the aforementioned switch hardly frightened me. I came running home as if I still had the wolf behind me. Along the path behind the house my father was breaking up clods. Smiling over the handle of his mattock, he straightened up and said, "Ah, you rascal, run quickly to your mother. She didn't sleep a wink all night."

I ran to my mother. I gave my parents a fresh, blow-by-blow account of what had just happened to me. But when I came to the part about the robbers, the barrel, and the enormous wolf, they said to me, "Come, silly, can't you see that it's fear that made you dream all that?"

In vain did I say, swear, and insist that it was nothing but the truth. In vain. No one would believe me.

V

AT SAINT-MICHEL-
DE-FRIGOLET

hen my parents saw that my love of playing led me astray and that I continually skipped school to go waste time in the fields with the peasant children every day, they said to themselves, we must lock him up. So one morning the servants loaded the farm cart with a little folding bed, a pine box to store my papers, and a shaggy pigskin trunk to hold my dress clothes and everyday wear. And accompanied by my mother, who comforted me, and our big dog Jusiòu, I left with a heavy heart for a place called Saint-Michel-de-Frigolet.

It was an old monastery located two hours away from our farm in the Montagnette between Graveson, Barbentane, and Tarascon. At the Revolution the lands of Saint-Michel had been sold piecemeal for paper currency, and the abandoned abbey remained like a widow up there on those hills, stripped of its goods, deserted and solitary in the middle of a wasteland open to the four winds and the wild beasts.

Smugglers sometimes made powder there, and when it rained, shepherds stabled their ewes in the church. To give the gendarmes the slip gamblers from neighboring villages—the Lout from Graveson, the Cape from Maillane, the Chill from Barbentane, the Menace from Château-Renard—came there on the sly at midnight in winter to play cards, and there by the dim light of several candles, while gold changed hands with the cards, the swearing and blaspheming reverberated under the arches, instead of the psalms that were once heard there. Then when the card game was over, the revelers ate, boozed, and caroused until dawn.

About 1832 several mendicant friars had settled there. They had put a bell back in the old Romanesque belfry, and they rang it on Sundays. But they rang in vain, no one came up to their services, for the people had no faith in them. And because the Duchess of Berry had landed in Provence at that time to stir up the Carlists against King Louis-Philippe, it was rumored, I remember, that under their black robes those unlicensed friars were partisans who must be involved in some suspicious plot.

After those friars had gone, a worthy citizen of Cavaillon named Monsieur Donnat came and founded a boarding school for boys at the monastery of Saint-Michel, which he had purchased on credit. He was an old bachelor, of a sallow, swarthy complexion, with lank hair, a flattened nose, a large mouth, and big teeth, who wore a long black frock coat and brown shoes. Very pious and poor as a church rat, he had found a way of setting up his school and recruiting boarders without a sou in his purse.

For example, he would go to Graveson, to Tarascon, to Barbentane, or Saint-Pierre and find a prosperous landed farmer who had sons, to whom he would say, "I wish to inform you that I have opened a boarding school at Saint-Michel-de-Frigolet. You have there within easy reach an excellent institution to educate your children and make them progress in their studies."

"Come now, sir," the father would answer, "that's all right for rich folks. People like us don't need to give that much reading to our boys. They'll always know enough to till the soil."

"Look here," Monsieur Donnat would say, "there's nothing finer than education. Don't worry about paying. You will give me so many bushels of grain per year, so many kegs of wine, or so many pipes of oil. Then at the end of the year we will settle our accounts."

And the good farmer would send his little boys to Saint-Michel-de-Frigolet.

Then Monsieur Donnat would go and find a shopkeeper, I suppose, and make this proposal to him: "What a handsome boy you have there! How alert he looks! You don't want to make a pepper grinder of him, do you?"

"Ah, sir, if we could," the father would reply, "we would indeed give him a bit of education, but private academies are expensive, and when you're not too rich. . . ."

"Who needs academies?" Monsieur Donnat would say. "Send him to me at my boarding school up there at Saint-Michel, and we will teach him Latin and make a man of him. Then for payment we'll take credit. You will have me as one more customer, a good customer, I assure you."

And immediately the shopkeeper would entrust his son to him.

Another day he would pass in front of a carpenter's house and see, I daresay, an anemic-looking child playing near his mother in the drain of the sink.

"What's the matter with that sweet child?" Monsieur Donnat would say to the mother, "he's quite pale. Is he subject to fevers, or has he been eating ashes?"

"Oh, no," the woman would reply, "it's the love of playing that ails him. Playing, sir, takes away his appetite and thirst."

"Well, then," Monsieur Donnat would rejoin, "why not place him in my institution at Saint-Michel-de-Frigolet? There the fresh air alone will restore his color in a couple of weeks. Then too, the child will be supervised and will do his lessons. And when he has finished his studies, he will soon have a job and will never have to work as hard as he would pushing a plane."

"Ah, sir, when you are poor!"

"Don't worry about that. We have many windows and doors to be repaired up there. Your husband is a carpenter. I promise him more work than he'll be able to do, my good woman, and we will cut down the room and board."

And so the little darling also went to Saint-Michel, as did that of the butcher, the tailor, and others. By this method Monsieur Donnat had gathered some forty children from the neighborhood in his boarding school, and I was one of that number. There were several in the bunch like me who paid cash, but the majority and then some paid in kind, in supplies or foodstuffs or in the work of their parents. In a word, before the democratic and social Republic, Monsieur Donnat had quite simply and without so much fanfare solved the problem of the Exchange Bank which the celebrated Proudhon attempted in vain to establish in Paris in 1848.

Of these schoolboys I remember one in particular. He was gentle, with a pretty face, the look of a young girl, and something sad in his countenance. They called him Agnel, and I believe he was from Nîmes. Our parents often came to see the rest of us and brought us goodies for our afternoon tea. But Agnel, you would have said he had no relatives, for he never spoke of them, and no one came to see him or brought him anything. Only once, a fat man came, a mysterious, haughty man, who spoke to him privately for perhaps half an hour. Then he went away and never came back. That led us to believe that Agnel was a child of superior birth, born under a bar sinister, and that he was being brought up in hiding at Saint-Michel. I never saw him again.

Our teaching staff consisted of, first, the master, good old Monsieur Donnat, who taught the lower classes when he was at home, but half the time he was away recruiting pupils; then two or three poor devils, unfrocked seminarians who were quite satisfied to earn room, board, and several crowns; then a chaplain of sorts called Monsieur Talon to say Mass for us; and a little hunchback called Monsieur Lavagne as music teacher. In addition, there was a Negro who cooked for us and a woman of about thirty from Tarascon to wait on tables and do the laundry. Finally, Monsieur Donnat's parents: his father, a poor old man in a red cap who went with his donkey to the neighboring village to get provisions, and his mother, a poor old lady in a white coif who sometimes cut our hair when we needed it.

At that time Saint-Michel was much smaller than it is today. There was only the cloister of the old Augustinian monks with its little courtyard in the middle of the square; the refectory to the south with the chapter hall; the little church of Saint-Michel, quite dilapidated, with frescoes on the walls representing hell with its red flames, its damned souls, and its devils armed with pitchforks, and the battle of the Devil against the great Archangel; and finally, the kitchen and the stables.

But outside that main group of buildings there was a chapel to the south dedicated to Our Lady of Remedies with buttresses and with a porch on its façade. Great masses of ivy covered the walls, and the interior was paneled with gilded woodwork all around, which framed paintings depicting the life of the Virgin Mary. Queen Anne of Austria, the mother of Louis XIV, had had it furnished with that decoration in fulfillment of a vow she had made to the Blessed Virgin in order to give birth to a son.

The little chapel, a veritable jewel lost in the mountains, had been saved during the Revolution by good people who heaped a pile of faggots on the porch to hide the door. There we were taken to Mass every morning of the year, at five o'clock in the summer, six o'clock in the winter. There on Sunday we sang Mass and vespers, holding our missals and our vesperals in our hands. And there on holy days the country folk admired the voice of little Frederi, for at that age I had a pretty voice, clear as a girl's, and it was I who did the solo part when we sang motets at the Elevation. I remember one where I apparently distinguished myself particularly, which goes like this:

> O mystère incompréhensible!
> Grand Dieu, vous n'êtes pas aimé!
>
> Oh, incomprehensible mystery!
> Great God, you are not loved!

In front of the little chapel and around the monastery there were several African lotus trees on which we tore our pants climbing in autumn to pick the sweetish little fruit that hung there in clusters. There was a well dug and carved in the rock that drained its water through an underground pipe into a tank down below and from there watered a vegetable garden. And below the garden, farther down the little valley, a clump of white poplars brightened the wasteland.

For it was a real wasteland, that little plateau of Saint-Michel where our parents had caged us, and the Latin inscription on the monastery gate expressed it well:

Behold, I have withdrawn in flight and remained in solitude because I saw injustice and discord in the city. Here I shall have my repose for ever, for here have I chosen to live.

The old monastery was built on the narrow plateau of a mountain pass which must have had a bad reputation in the past, for it is noteworthy that chapels dedicated to the Archangel Michael are always in lonely and fearsome places.

The surrounding hills were covered with thyme, rosemary, asphodel, boxwood, and lavender. There were several small vineyards, which as a matter of fact produced a renowned vintage, the wine of Frigolet; several patches of olive trees planted in the bottom of the valleys; several rows of crooked, blackened almond trees, stunted by the rocky soil; several wild fig trees growing in the clefts of the rock. That was all the cultivated land scattered about that mass of hills. The rest was nothing but wasteland and rubble, but how good it smelled! As soon as the sun shone, we were intoxicated by the fragrance of the mountains.

In school students are usually cooped up between four walls in big cold courtyards. But we had the run of the whole Montagnette. On Thursdays or even during the hours of recreation we were turned loose like a flock of goats, and off we would go over the mountain until the bell sounded the recall.

So in a little while we grew as wild as a litter of scrub rabbits. You may be sure we were in no danger of being bored. Once away from our studies we went off like partridges across hills and valleys.

Far off, in the bright, limpid, dazzling heat the ortolans sang: *chi-chi begu, chi-chi begu.*

And we rolled around in clumps of thyme; we gleaned almonds or green grapes that had been left unpicked; we gathered mushrooms underneath the thistles; we set snares for birds; we searched the ravines for the fossils they call "Saint Stephen's stones" in the region; we poked around in caves to ferret out the Golden Goat; we slid, we climbed, we tumbled down so much that our parents could not keep us in shoes or clothes.

We were as ragged as a band of gypsies.

And how we marveled at all those hills, those gorges, those ravines with their wonderful Provençal names—expressive, resounding names on which the people of Provence have stamped their genius in grand lapidary style. *Lou Mourre de la Mar*, "the Hill of the Sea," from which the seacoast could be seen glowing white in the distance; on the feast of Saint John we went to its top at sundown to light the bonfire; *la Baumo de l'Argènt*, "the Silver Cave," where counterfeiters used to forge their money; *la Roco-pèd-de-biòu*, "Bull's Foot Rock," where we could see the imprint of a bovine hoof engraved as if some wild bull had kicked against it; *la Roco d'Arciè*, "the Rock of Steel," which had a commanding view of the Rhone, with boats and rafts passing at its foot—eternal monuments of our land and of our speech, all perfumed with rosemary and lavender, all illuminated with azure and gold. What fragrance, what brightness, what pleasure, what vision, what peace of sweet nature, what a dream of paradise you revealed to my childhood!

In winter or when it rained, we remained in the cloister, playing hopscotch, leapfrog, or high-cockalorum. Inside the monastery church, which as I said was abandoned to the winds, we played hide-and-seek and hid in the open vaults full of the old monks' skulls and bones.

One winter evening before supper, when the wind was bellowing down the long corridors, the master, Monsieur Donnat, was supervising our studies as we all huddled against our desks. Nothing could be heard but our pens scratching the paper and the wind whistling through the doors. All of a sudden we heard a voice outside, a hollow, sepulchral voice crying, "Donnat! Donnat! Donnat! give me back my bell!"

Frightened out of our wits, we all looked at the master. And Monsieur Donnat, pale as death, slowly got down from his dais, signaled to the biggest boys to accompany him outside, and the rest of us little boys all went out after them, crowding behind.

By the light of the moon, which shone up above on a rock facing the monastery, we then saw a shadow or perhaps a giant in a long black robe, who spoke in the wind, saying, "Donnat! Donnat! Donnat! give me back my bell!"

We all stood there, trembling at the sight and sound of such an apparition. Monsieur Donnat only said in a low voice, "It's Brother Philip," and without answering, he went back into the monastery with us after him, looking backward as we walked. We were quite disturbed as we resumed our studies, but we knew no more that evening.

This Brother Philip, we later learned, apparently was one of those hermits who had occupied Saint-Michel some years before us and who had put a bell in the empty belfry. Then when they left, since it could not be carried away like a hand bell, the steeple bell had remained up there on the church, and naturally Monsieur Donnat had kept it.

Brother Philip was a good man who had undertaken the task of restoring the ruined hermitages that are scattered hither and yon through the mountains of Provence. Long afterward I met him several times: tall, thin, a bit stooped, taciturn, with his broad-brimmed black hat and his cassock in patches, begging from door to door and carrying a long sack of blue linen on his shoulder, half in front, half in back.

When he decided to restore some abandoned hermitage, he would buy it from the owner with the alms he had collected, repair its walls, hang a bell there, and having searched and found some good fellow who wanted to become a hermit, he would grant him the cell with its little gardens. Then he would begin again, patiently begging and fasting to rebuild another hermitage.

The last time I saw him he told me he had restored almost thirty of them. It was at the train station in Avignon, where like him I had gone to take the one-thirty train. It was very hot, and poor Brother Philip, who was then not much under eighty years old, walked in the sun in his black habit, bent under his bag, which was nearly full of wheat.

"Oh, Brother Philip, Brother Philip!" a big boy wearing a red sash and scarf called out to him, "isn't that bag heavy? Let me carry it a while."

And the good boy took up the friar's bag and carried it to the room where tickets are sold. Now that boy, whom I knew slightly, was a "Red" from Barbentane, and since our democrats are hardly on good terms with the black robes, I was reminded of the parable of the good Samaritan, and I realized how popular that man of God was.

At the end Brother Philip retired with some monks who had taken him in. But since the government had the monasteries closed about that time, the poor old holy man went, I believe, to the hospital of Avignon to die.

To return to Saint-Michel, I said we had a chaplain who was called Monsieur Talon, a squat, pot-bellied little priest from Avignon with a face as florid as a beggar's gourd. Because he lifted his elbow too much, the archbishop of Avignon had deprived him of the power to confess and had sent him to us to get rid of him.

It so happened that one Thursday, on the feast of Corpus Christi, we were taken to Boulbon, a nearby village, to walk in the procession, the bigger boys as incense-bearers, the little ones as flower-boys. And they had very unwisely given the place of honor to Monsieur Talon.

At the moment when the men, women, and girls paraded down the streets, which were draped with white sheets, at the moment when the brotherhoods waved their banners in the sun, when the choir girls all in white sang their hymns with virginal voices, when we boys piously and solemnly perfumed the air with incense and scattered our flowers before the Blessed Sacrament, suddenly a clamor arose and, good Lord! what did we see but poor Monsieur Talon taking up the whole street, staggering like a cowbell, with the monstrance in his hands and the golden cope on his back.

It appears that in dining at the rectory he had drunk or perhaps they had made him drink a little more than necessary of that charming Frigolet wine that goes to the head so quickly, and the poor man, as red with shame as with wine, could no longer stand up straight. Two priests in dalmatics, acting as his deacon and subdeacon, quickly took him by the arms, the procession entered the church, and once in front of the altar, Monsieur Talon began to sing, *"Oremus, oremus, oremus,"* and could say no more. Between them the two led him off to the sacristy.

But think of the scandal!

Fortunately, however, that happened in a parish where the blessed wine has preserved its rites as in the time of Bacchus. On the mountain near Boulbon there is an old chapel called Saint-Marcellin, where on the first of June the men of Boulbon go in procession, each one carrying a bottle of wine in his hand. Women are not admitted because in times past our wives drank only water, in keeping with Roman tradition, and to get our girls used to that custom, we always told them and still tell them that "water makes you pretty."

Father Talon never failed to take us to the Procession of the Bottles every year. Once in the chapel, the parish priest of Boulbon would turn toward the people and say, "My brothers, uncork your flasks and may every beard be silent. I am going to invoke the blessing." And in a red cope he solemnly chanted the prescribed words to bless the wine. Then saying *"Amen,"* all of us made the sign of the cross and took a big swallow. And the priest and the mayor, clinking glasses together on the steps of the altar, solemnly drank. On the following day, which was a holiday, they carried the statue of Saint Marcellin in procession across the land when there was a drought, for the people of Boulbon have a saying:

| Sant Marcelin, | Saint Marcellin, |
| Bon pèr l'aigo, bon pèr lou vin. | Good for water, good for wine. |

Another pilgrimage, also quite jolly, that we saw on the Montagnette and that has now gone out of style, was that of Saint Anthime, observed by the people of Graveson.

When the rain was too slow in coming, the penitents of Graveson, drawling their litanies and followed by a crowd of people with sacks over their heads, took Saint Anthime—a bug-eyed, mitred, bearded, high-colored statue—to the church of Saint-Michel. There in the woods with a picnic spread out on the fragrant herbs to await the rain all God's livelong day they devoutly swigged good Frigolet from the bottle—and would you believe it?—more than once a downpour bathed their return. Well, why not? Singing makes it rain, as the old folks used to say.

But beware! If in spite of the litanies and pious libations, Saint Anthime did not make clouds appear, on returning to Graveson the jolly penitents dunked him three times in the Ditch of Lones—splash!—to punish him for not having heeded them. This curious custom of soaking the saint's statue in the water to force him to make rain could be found in different places—in Toulouse, for example, and as far as Portugal.

When as little boys we went with our mothers to Graveson, they never failed to take us to the church to show us Saint Anthime, and afterward Beluguet, a wooden Jack who struck the hours on the clock above.

Now to finish what I have left to tell about my sojourn at Saint-Michel, it comes back to me like a dream that at the end of the first year, before letting us go on vacation, they made us perform *The Children of Edward* by Casimir Delavigne. They gave me the role of a young princess, and for my costume my mother brought me a muslin dress she had borrowed from young ladies in our neighborhood. This white dress was later the cause of a little love story, which I shall tell in its place.

The second year of my studies, as they had started me on Latin, I wrote to my parents to go buy me some books. And several days later we saw from the valley of Bull Foot's Rock my honored father climbing toward the monastery mounted on Babacho, an old familiar mule who was perhaps thirty years old and who was known in all the markets of the surrounding region where my father rode him when he went traveling. He so loved that good creature that in the springtime when he went riding in his wheatfields he always took Babacho, and mounted astride, armed with a long-handled hoe, he cut the thistles and the wild mustard.

When he had arrived, my father unloaded a big full bag which he had attached to the packsaddle with a rope, and while untying the knot cried out to me, "Frederi, I have brought you some books and a little paper."

Thereupon he took from the bag one by one four or five dictionaries bound in parchment, a load of books bound in boards (*Epitome, De Viribus Illustribus, Selectae Historiae, Conciones,* etc.), a big pot of ink, a bundle of goose quills, and such a bale of reams of paper that I had enough for seven years, right to the end of my studies. Eager to provide his son with those supplies of learning, the good patriarch had gone to Monsieur Aubanel, printer in Avignon and father of the dear "Félibre of the Cleft Pomegranate." (At that time we were still far from being acquainted.)

But I did not have time to use much paper at the pleasant monastery of Saint-Michel-de-Frigolet. For one reason or another, our master, Monsieur Donnat, did not spend enough time at his institution. And when the cat's away, as he said, the rats dance. He was constantly on the move, either in search of students or to raise money. The professors, who were badly paid, always had some pretext for shortening classes. When parents came, they often found no one. "Where are the children?"

Sometimes we were busy repairing some dry stone wall along an inclined way. Sometimes we were among the vines joyfully gleaning bunches of grapes or hunting for morel mushrooms. And all that did not increase confidence in our master. Besides, to enlarge his boarding school, Monsieur Donnat unfortunately took children who paid little or nothing, and it was not those who ate the least. But a funny incident precipitated its downfall.

We had a Negro as cook, as I have told you, and a woman from Tarascon as servant, who was the only woman in the house (not counting the old mother of our principal, who was at least seventy years old). Since the Devil, as you know, never wastes his time, one day our maid found herself "embarrassed," as they say, and there was a terrible scandal in the boarding school. Some said the slut was pregnant by Monsieur Donnat, some asserted that it was the professor of humanities, some Father Talon, some the master of studies. In the end the burden was put on the back of the Negro. He, who probably felt guilty, packed his bag and left, either from fear or from anger; and the woman from Tarascon, who had kept her secret, also took off to go and set down her burden.

It was the signal for retreat. No more cook, no more bad food. One after another the professors left us in the lurch.

Monsieur Donnat disappeared. His mother, the poor old woman, boiled us some potatoes for several more days. Then one morning his father told us with tears in his eyes, "My children, there is nothing more to eat. You must go back to your homes."

And suddenly, like a flock of weanling kids released from the fold, we went running to tear up bunches of thyme on the hill before separating—to carry away a souvenir of our beautiful Frigolet. Then with our little bundles, four by four and six by six, some above, some below, we scattered down the valleys and the pathways, but not without regret and not without looking back on the way down.

Poor Monsieur Donnat! After having gone round and round in every way from one place to another to re-establish his institution—for we all have our touch of madness—he ended his days like Brother Philip, poor man, at the hospital.

But before leaving Saint-Michel-de-Frigolet, I must say a word about what became of the ancient abbey after us. After it had fallen into neglect for a dozen years, a White Monk, Father Edmond, bought it (1854) and re-established there, under the rule of Saint Norbert, the Premonstratensian Order, which no longer existed in France. Thanks to the energy, the preaching, and the collections of that ardent zealot, the little monastery assumed grandiose proportions. A good many buildings clustered around it, with a crown of crenelated walls. A new church, magnificently decorated, raised its three naves and two steeples; about one hundred monks or lay brothers occupied the cells; and every Sunday the neighboring population went up there by the cartload to behold the pomp and majesty of their services.

So popular did the abbey of the White Fathers then become that when the Republic closed the monasteries (1880), a thousand peasants or inhabitants of the plain came and shut themselves in to protest in person against the execution of the radical decrees. And then we saw a whole army on the march, cavalry and infantry, with generals and captains, with supply wagons and war equipment, come and camp around the monastery of Saint-Michel-de-Frigolet and seriously undertake the siege of that comic-opera citadel, which three or four gendarmes could have brought to terms if they had wished.

I remember that while the siege lasted—and it lasted a whole week—people left in the morning with their lunches and posted themselves on the slopes and hills that dominate the abbey to spy out the day's maneuvers from a distance. The prettiest sight was the girls, from Barbentane, from Boulbon, from Saint-Rémy, or from Maillane, who waved their handkerchiefs in encouragement:

Prouvençau e Catouli,	Provencaux and Catholics,
Nosto fe, nosto fe n'a pas fali.	Our faith, our faith has not faltered.
Canten, tóuti trefouli,	Let us sing, thrilling with joy,
Prouvençau e Catouli!	Provencaux and Catholics!

—all that mixed with invective, raillery, and hoots against the officials who rode fiercely past in their carriages down below.

Apart from the indignation that the injustice of those events aroused in every heart, the "Siege of Caderousse" by the Vice-Legate Sinibaldi Doria—which gave Father Favre the material for a farce so full of laughs—was surely not as ridiculous as that of Frigolet, and perhaps another priest will turn it into a poem that will sell thousands of copies in France. Daudet at any rate, who had already set his story called "The Elixir of Brother Gaucher" in the White Fathers' monastery, shows us Tartarin barricading himself bravely in the abbey of Saint-Michel in his last novel about Tarascon.

V I

AT MONSIEUR MILLET'S BOARDING SCHOOL

hen it was necessary to find me another school not too far from Maillane and not too grand, for we country folk were not proud. And they placed me in Avignon with Monsieur Millet, who kept a boarding school in rue Petramale.

This time it was my Uncle Benòni who drove the carriage. Although Maillane was but three leagues from Avignon, in those days when there was no railroad, when the roads were damaged by heavy wagons, and when it was necessary to cross the wide bed of the Durance on a ferry, the trip to Avignon was still an undertaking.

We embarked on our journey a little after sunrise, three of my aunts, my mother, my Uncle Benòni, and I, all comfortably seated on a long sack of oat straw that padded the cart.

I said three of my aunts. Hardly anyone ever saw as many aunts at one time as I did. I had a whole dozen of them. There was Great-aunt Mistral, Aunt Janetoun, Aunt Madeloun, Aunt Verounico, Aunt Poulineto, Aunt Bourdeto, Aunt Franceso, Aunt Marìo, Aunt Rioun, Aunt Terèso, Aunt Melan, and Aunt Lisa. They are all dead and buried now, but I like to recite the names of those good women I saw fluttering around my cradle like so many good fairies, each with her own charm. Add to my aunts the same number of uncles, together with the swarm of cousins they produced, and you have some idea of our family.

Uncle Benòni was my mother's brother and the youngest of that generation. Thin, dark, slender, he had a turned-up nose and two jet-black eyes. A surveyor by trade, he was considered lazy and even boasted of it. But he had three passions, dancing, music, and joking.

There was no dancer more charming in Maillane, none more spirited. When he danced outdoors in the "green room" on the feast of Saint Eloi or Saint Agatha, doing the country dance with Jesèto the wrestler, people crowded around to see him "beat the pigeon wings." He played all sorts of instruments more or less well: the violin, the bassoon, the horn, the clarinet. But it was the Provençal flute to which he finally devoted himself the most. In his youth he had no equal for playing aubades to the pretty girls or for singing midnight serenades in the month of May. And whenever there was to be a pilgrimage to Our Lady of the Lights, to Saint-Gent, to Vaucluse, or to the Saintes-Maries, who was the life of the party and who drove the cart? Benòni, always ready and always delighted to leave his job, his surveying square, and his house to go running about the countryside.

You would see cartloads of fifteen or twenty girls going off singing:

| A l'ounour de sant Gènt, | In honor of Saint Gent, |

or

Alis ma bono amigo,	Alis, my sweetheart dear,
Sarié tèms de quita	It's time to leave
Lou mounde e sis entrigo	The world and its intrigues
Emé si vanita,	With all its vanity,

or

Li tres Marìo	The three Marys
Parton davans jour,	Left before daybreak,
S'envan adoura lou Segnour,	Going to worship the Lord,

with my uncle on the shaft of the cart accompanying them on his flute. And off they went, tickle-you, tickle-me, hugging and laughing and shrieking all the way.

Now he had taken quite an extraordinary notion into his head: that if he married, he would pick a noblewoman.

"But noble girls want noble men," people told him, "and you will never find one."

"What!" Benòni replied, "aren't we noble ourselves? Perhaps you think we are peasants like you. Our grandfather was an émigré. He wore a coat with a red velvet lining, buckles on his shoes, and silk stockings."

He ran around so much that one day over by Carpentras he heard there was a practically ruined family of authentic nobility that had seven daughters, all marriageable. The father, a spend-thrift, sold a piece of land every year to his tenant farmer, who finally even got his chateau. My good Uncle Benòni got all dressed up and introduced himself to the eldest of the seven, the daughter of a Marquis and a Commander of the Knights of Malta, who, seeing that she was about to become an old maid, decided to marry him. It's about the fall of that noble family of Vaucluse to the level of commoners that Enri de la Madeleine of Carpentras wrote his charming novel, *The End of the Marquisat d'Aurel*.

I said that my uncle was lazy. In the middle of the day, when he went to his garden to dig or cultivate, he always took his flute. After a little while he would throw down his hoe, sit down in the shade, and try out a rigadoon. The girls working in the nearby fields would promptly come running to the music, and he soon had them dancing the saltarello.

In winter he seldom got up before noon.

"Well," said he, "where can you be better off than snuggled up nice and warm in your bed?"

"But aren't you bored there, Uncle?" we would say to him.

"Oh never! When I'm sleepy, I sleep. When I'm no longer sleepy, I recite the psalms for the dead."

And what is remarkable is that this jolly man never missed a funeral, and after the ceremony he was always the very last to remain in the cemetery. Then he would come back alone, praying for his relatives and for others—which did not keep him from repeating this quip every time: "Ah me, there's always someone to be carted off to Eternal Rest."

His turn came when he had to go there too. He was eighty-three years old, and the doctor let it be known that there was no hope. "Bah!" said Benòni, "what's the use of getting frightened? Why, only the most seriously ill die of it."

He had his flute on his night table, so I said to him one day when I went to see him, "What are you doing with that fife, Uncle?"

"Those idiots," he said, "have given me a little bell to ring when I need tea. How much better is my fife! Instead of calling or ringing a bell I take my fife and play a tune whenever I want something to drink."

So he died with his flute in his hand, and they put it in his coffin with him. Which gave rise the morning after his death to the following story. On the day after my uncle was put in the ground, a girl arrived at the silk-spinning mill, where the girls of Maillane went to work, all agitated and with a frightened look, and said to the others, "Didn't you girls hear anything last night?"

"No, only the mistral and the cry of the owl."

"Oh, how can you say that, girls? We who live not far from the cemetery didn't sleep a wink. Just imagine that on the stroke of midnight old Benòni took his flute, which they had put in his coffin with him, got out of his grave, and began playing a demonic farandole. All the dead arose, carried their coffins to the middle of the cemetery, and lit them with Saint Elmo's fire to warm themselves. Then to the rigadoon that Benòni played they danced a wild dance around the fire until dawn."

So with Uncle Benòni, whom you now know, with my mother, and my three aunts, we had got under way for the city of Avignon. You know how village folk behave when they go somewhere in a group. All along the way they exclaimed or made remarks about the farms, the alfalfa, the wheat, the fennel, the seedlings that we passed as the cart went jogging along.

When we went through Graveson, where there is a beautiful steeple decorated all around with stone artichokes, my uncle exclaimed, "Look, little one, the navels of the people of Graveson, do you see them up there, nailed to the steeple?"

Whereupon he laughed and laughed at that gibe that has amused the people of Maillane for seven or eight centuries—to which the people of Graveson respond with a song that goes:

> A Gravesoun—avèn un clouchié:
> Quau que lou vegue,—dison qu'es bèn dre.
> A Maiano,—lou siéu es redoun:
> Sèmblo uno gàbi—pèr li passeroun.

> At Graveson we have a steeple;
> Everyone says it's good and straight.
> In Maillane their steeple is round;
> It looks like a cage—for sparrows.

Thus they reeled off for me the usual stories of the road to Avignon, one after another: the Bridge of Folly where the warlocks danced their brawl, the Crossroads of the Highwaymen, the Milestone Cross, and the Needle Rock. Finally we arrived at the sandy shores of Durance. The floodwaters had carried away the bridge the previous year, and the river had to be crossed by a ferry. There we found more than a hundred carts awaiting their turn. We waited like the others for a couple of hours at the landing. And then we embarked, after shouting "Go home!" and chasing our big dog Jusiòu, who had followed us.

It was after noon when we reached Avignon. Like the people of our village, we stabled our horse at the Hôtel de Provence, which was a little inn on the Place des Corps-Saints, and spent the rest of the day gawking around the city.

"Would you like me to treat you to a play?" my uncle said. "This evening they are playing *Maniclo, or the Sophisticated Cobbler* with *Castro Abbey*."

"Oh!" we all replied, "we must go see *Maniclo*."

It was the first time I ever went to the theater, and fate decreed that they put on a Provençal comedy that night. We did not understand much of *Castro Abbey*, which was a gloomy drama. But my aunts found that *Maniclo* was performed much better in Maillane. For at that time comedies and tragedies were staged in our village in winter. There I have seen *The Death of Caesar, Zaïre,* and *Little Jóusè* played by our peasants. They made Roman, Turkish, or Hebrew costumes with their wives' skirts and with bedspreads. The common people, who love tragedy, listened with great pleasure to the melancholy declamation of those plays in five acts. But they also performed *Lawyer Pathelin,* translated into Provençal, and various comedies of the Marseille repertory, such as *Monsieur Just, Fresquiero or the Ass's Tail, The Sophisticated Cobbler,* and *Mademoiselle Galineto.* Benòni was always the director, and he accompanied the songs on his violin, nodding his head. I remember that I played a part in *Mademoiselle Galineto* and in *The Ass's Tail* when I was about seventeen and even received a good round of applause from my compatriots.

But enough of that. The following day, after kissing my mother goodbye with a heart swollen like a pea that's been soaking for nine days, I had to shut myself up at Monsieur Millet's boarding school in rue Petramale. He was a big man, big and tall, badly shaved and dirty, with shaggy eyebrows and a red face. Add to that pig's eyes, elephant's feet, and ugly square fingers constantly stuffing his nose with snuff. His chambermaid Catarino, a fat, sallow woman from the mountains, did the cooking for us and ran the household. I have never eaten as many carrots as I ate there, boiled carrots in a flour sauce. Poor me, in three months I wasted away to nothing.

Avignon, the city where the art of the troubadours was destined to be reborn one day, did not have its present liveliness, far from it. The Place de l'Horloge had not been widened nor Place Pie expanded nor had the main street been cut through. Up above the city, the Rocher des Doms, which is now laid out like a royal garden, was bare then, and there was a cemetery on top. The city walls, half in ruins, were encircled by moats full of refuse, with pools of slimy water. The rough stevedores, organized in a guild, laid down the law on the banks of the Rhone and even in the city when they wished. With their leader, a kind of Hercules they called "Four-Arms," they were the ones who cleared out the city hall of Avignon in 1848.

As in the cities of Italy, there was a Black Penitent with a hood over his face and two holes for his eyes who came by all the houses once a week, rattling his money box and saying in a deep voice, "For the poor prisoners!" In the streets you frequently ran into local characters like Sister Cooking-Pot with her covered basket on her arm, her silver crucifix dangling over her ample bosom, or like the plasterer Barret, who when he lost his hat in a brawl with the liberals, swore never again to wear a hat until Henry V ascended the throne and went bareheaded all his life. But what you encountered most with their big tall hats and their long blue coats were the veterans living in Avignon (where there was a branch of the Invalides of Paris), the venerable debris of our old wars, minus an eye or an arm or limping on their wooden legs, slowly tapping the sharp cobbles of the streets.

The city was going through a confused and difficult kind of molting period between the two regimes, the old and the new, which were still battling it out in secret. Frightful memories of past strife, insults, and recriminations were still alive and still bitter among people of a certain age. The Carlists spoke of nothing but the Tribunal of Orange, of Jourdan the Headsman, of the massacre of La Glacière. The liberals hadn't swallowed the events of 1815, constantly remembering the assassination of Marshal Brune, his corpse thrown into the Rhone, his baggage plundered, his murderers unpunished, among others "The Spike," who had left a fearful name. And if some ever so slightly insolent upstart succeeded in his business, the people would say, "There, now you can see Marshal Brune's *louis d'or* turning up."

However, the people of Avignon, like those of Aix and of practically all the cities of Provence, generally yearned for the white flag with the fleur-de-lis. (That has changed since.) Our ancestors' enthusiasm for the royal cause was not so much a political opinion, it seems to me, as an unconscious protest of the people against the increasingly excessive centralization that Jacobinism and the First Empire had made hateful. The fleur-de-lis of yore was for the Provençaux (who had always seen it on the coat of arms of Provence) the symbol of an age when governments had more respect for our customs, traditions, and freedoms. But to believe that our fathers wanted to return to the abuses of the regime before the Revolution would be a complete mistake, for it was Provence that sent Mirabeau to the States-General and Provence where the Revolution was most fervent.

In that connection I remember a time when the people of Marseille had just elected Berryer as deputy. When that illustrious orator was to come through Avignon, the prefect barred the gates of the city to keep out the legitimists who were coming in throngs from elsewhere to receive him in triumph, and on that occasion a crowd of Whites was locked up in the prison of the Papal Palace.

Some time after that my lord the Duc d'Aumale came through on his return from Africa. They took us to see him at Saint Lazare's Gate. Accompanied by his soldiers, who were tanned like him by the sun of Algeria, he was all white with dust, and with his blond hair and blue eyes, radiant with youth and glory. The women of the suburbs kept crying out, "Long live our beautiful prince!"

In 1889 when I was in Paris and had the honor of being invited to Chantilly, I reminded His Grace of that tiny detail of his visit to Provence, and after forty-five years my lord Aumale readily remembered the good women who cried out as they saw him go by, "How pretty he is! How gallant he is!"

Old Avignon is so steeped in glorious events that you cannot take a step without treading on some memory. It turned out that the convent of Saint Clare used to be in the block of houses where our boarding school was located, and it was in the chapel of that convent that Petrarch first saw Laura on the morning of April 6, 1327.

We were also very near the rue des Etudes, which still had an ominous reputation among the common people at that time. We could never persuade the chimney sweeps or shoeshine boys to come clean the chimneys in our boarding school or shine our shoes. Because the University of Avignon and the School of Medicine were formerly located in the rue des Etudes, rumor had it that the students caught little street urchins when they could in order to bleed them, flay them, and study their cadavers.

Most of us were village children, who found it interesting to prowl around in our neighborhood when we went out into that labyrinth of the alleys of Avignon, like Little Paradise Street, which had been a red-light district and which still showed signs of being one, the Street of Firewater, the Street of the Cat, the Street of the Rooster, the Street of the Devil. But how different it was from our beautiful vales all flowering with asphodel, from our good fresh air, from our peace and liberty at Saint-Michel-de-Frigolet!

There were days when my heart ached with homesickness. Yet Monsieur Millet, who was after all a good fellow, had something about him that finally won me over.

As he was from Caderousse, the son of a yeoman farmer like myself, and had always spoken Provençal at home, he professed an incredible admiration for the poem of *The Siege of Caderousse*. He knew it all by heart. And sometimes in class in the midst of explaining some fine battle of Greeks and Trojans, he would suddenly shift his gray forelock with a movement of his forehead that was peculiar to him and say, "Well now, look, that's one of the finest passages in Virgil, isn't it? And yet listen, my children, to the piece I am going to recite, and you will see that the bard of *The Siege of Caderousse* often crowds the heels of Virgil himself:

> Un noumat Pergòri Latrousso,
> Lou pus ventrut de Cadarousso,
> S'acoussavo contro un talhur . . .
> L'aurié crebat! Mai, pèr malur,
> Anèt brounca contro uno mouto
> E barrulèt coumo uno bouto.

> A certain Pergòri Latrousse,
> The fattest man in Caderousse,
> Had flung himself against a tailor.
> He would have killed him, but by chance,
> He went and stumbled over a clod
> And went rolling away like a barrel.

How it pleased us, that quotation from our delicious language! Big fat Millet would burst out laughing, and I would relish that tasty tidbit, for I had kept the bittersweet taste of honey from my childhood and had the language in my blood like nobody else.

Every day about five o'clock Monsieur Millet went to the café to read the gazette, the Café Baretta, which he called "the Café of the Talking Animals," and which, unless I'm mistaken, was kept by the uncle or perhaps the grandfather of Mademoiselle Baretta of the Théâtre-Français. Then on the following day, when he was in a good mood, he would mimic for us the eternal grumbling of the old politicians of that establishment, who at that time spoke only of the "Little One," as they called Henry V.

That year I made my first communion at the church of Saint-Didier, which was our parish church. And it was Fanot, the bell-ringer later celebrated by Roumanille in his *Bell-Raising*, who summoned us to catechism. For two months before the ceremony Monsieur Millet took us to the church every day to recite our catechism. And there, mixed in with the other children who were to make their communion together, girls as well as boys, we were lined up and seated on benches in the nave of the church. And it happened that I, being the very last of the row of boys, found myself placed next to a charming girl who was the first of the row of girls. She was called Presseto, and she had two delicate blushes on her cheeks that looked like two fresh blooming roses.

Just see what children are like! As we met every day, sitting next to each other, as we touched elbows without giving it a thought, and as we whispered our little jokes, breathing in each other's ears—God help me!—didn't we end up falling in love?

But that was a love so innocent and so steeped in mystic aspirations that it must surely be like that if the angels on high experience love among themselves. We were both twelve years old, the age of Beatrice when Dante saw her, and that vision of the blossoming young maiden is what made the great Florentine poet's *Paradiso*. There is a very expressive word in our language for the delight of the soul that intoxicates couples in their early youth: we suit each other. We were happy when we saw each other. It's true we only saw each other in church, but merely to see each other filled our hearts. I smiled at her, and she smiled at me. We united our voices in the same hymns of love and thanksgiving, exalting our simple, eager faith toward the same mysteries. Oh dawn of love when innocence blooms joyfully like a daisy in a cool brook, oh daybreak of love, pure dawn that has fled!

She has remained in my memory, Mademoiselle Presseto, as she was the last time I saw her. Dressed all in white, with a crown of hawthorn blossoms, ravishingly pretty under her transparent veil, she went up to the altar right near me, like a bride, a beautiful little bride of the Lamb.

Once we had made our communion, it was all over. For a long time when we went down her street (she lived in rue des Lices) I cast yearning glances under the green blinds of Presseto's house—in vain. I was never able to see her again. Alas, they had placed her in a convent.

To think that my charming friend with the smile on her rosy-cheeked face was taken from me forever! Partly for that, partly for other reasons, I fell into a decline, lost all appetite, and almost pined away.

When I went home for vacation, my mother, seeing that I was so pale and had attacks of fever from time to time, decided on an act of faith to take me to Saint Gent, the patron of the feverish, as much to divert me as to cure me.

Saint Gent, who also has the power of making rain, is a sort of demigod for the peasants on the banks of the Durance. My father used to say, "I went to Saint Gent before the Revolution. And we walked barefoot with my dear mother when I was no more than ten years old. But in those days people had more faith."

So we left in a covered cart about midnight by the light of a bright September moon, with my Uncle Benòni, whom you already know, driving. And after joining other pilgrims going to the feast of Saint Gent all along the way—at Château-Renard, at Noves, at Le Thor, or at Pernes—we saw many other carts behind us, covered like ours with cloth stretched over wooden hoops, coming to join the caravan.

Singing more or less together the hymn of Saint Gent—which is magnificent, by the way, and which Gounod used in the opera of *Mireille*—we went through sleeping villages at night to the sound of cracking whips and arrived about four o'clock the following afternoon at the gorge of Le Bausset in a throng crying, "Long live Saint Gent!"

There on the very spot where the saintly hermit had lived in self-denial, the old people gave the young a lively account of what they had been told. "Gent," they said, "was the son of peasants like ourselves, a good lad from Monteux, who at the age of fifteen withdrew to the wilderness to dedicate himself to God. He tilled the soil with two cows. One day when a wolf killed one of them, Gent caught the wolf, harnessed it to his plow, and made it work, yoked to the other cow. But in Monteux, after Gent left, it did not rain for several years. The people of Monteux said to Gent's mother, 'Imberto, you must bring back your son, for not a drop of rain has fallen since he left.' And Gent's mother, after much searching and calling, finally found her son, right here where we are now, in the gorge of Le Bausset. And since his mother was thirsty, Gent stuck two of his fingers in the rock of the cliff to give her a drink, and two fountains gushed forth, one of wine and one of water. The fountain of wine has dried up, but the fountain of water still flows, and it's a sovereign remedy for bad fevers."

People go to the hermitage of Saint Gent twice a year. First in the month of May, when his compatriots of Monteux carry his statue from Monteux to Le Bausset, a pilgrimage of three leagues which they make on the run, symbolizing and commemorating the flight of the saint. Here is the ecstatic letter that Aubanel wrote me one year when he had gone there (1866):

> My dear friend, I have just come from Saint-Gent with Grivolas. The festival is astonishing, wonderful, sublime. The race by night of those who carry the saint is unbelievably poetic and has enchanted my soul. The Mayor of Monteux had given us a carriage, and we followed the pilgrims through the fields, the woods, and the rocks

by moonlight to the singing of nightingales from eight o'clock in the evening to half past midnight. The mystery grips you, so strange and beautiful that it brings tears to your eyes. Those four youths in nankeen breeches and gaiters, running like hares, flying like birds, with a man on horseback galloping ahead of them letting off pistol shots; the people from the farms who come as the saint passes, men, women, children, and old people, stopping the youths to kiss the statue, calling, weeping, gesticulating; then as they leave again more quickly than ever, the women who cry out to them, "Have a good trip, boys!" and the men who add, "May the great Saint Gent keep up your strength!" And off they go running again, running until they pant for breath. Oh, that journey by night, that little band in the keeping of God and of Saint Gent, plunging into the darkness and the wilderness to go who knows where, all that, I say to you again, is so grand and so profoundly poetic that it leaves you with an indelible memory.

The second pilgrimage takes place in the month of September, and that is when we went. Seldom have I seen such fervor. Since Saint Gent has only been canonized by popular acclaim, priests seldom go there, much less the bourgeois. But the people who till the earth believe in that unpretentious saint who was of their soil, who spoke like them, who farmed like them, who sent them rain and cured their fevers without requiring too many alleluias. The people believe in his deification and honor him with a devotion so fervent that up to twenty thousand pilgrims have sometimes been seen in that narrow gorge where the legend lives.

Tradition has it that Saint Gent slept in a stone bed with his head down and his legs up, and all the pilgrims devoutly and merrily do a headstand on "the bed of Saint Gent," which is a standing stone trough—even the women, who hold each other's skirts wrapped tight.

We did a headstand there like the others. With my mother we went to see "the Fountain of the Wolf" and "the Fountain of the Cow" and then the chapel of Saint Gent, surrounded by several old walnut trees, where his tomb is located, and "the hideous rock," as the hymn calls it, from which the miraculous water flows for the feverish.

Marveling at all those tales, at all those beliefs, at all those visions, with my soul intoxicated by the look of the place, by the scent of plants still perfumed by the saint's footprints, with my fine twelve-year-old's faith, I plunged my face into the spring and drank, and—say what you will—from that day I had no more fever. Don't be surprised then if the daughter of the Félibre, poor Mirèio, lost in the plain of Crau and dying of thirst, commends her soul to good Saint Gent:

O bèu e jouine labouraire	Oh, fine young plowman
Qu'atalerias à voste araire	Who harnessed to your plow
Lou loup de la montagno, etc.	The wolf of the mountain, etc.
(*Mirèio*, cant VIII)	(*Mirèio*, Canto VIII)

It still delights me to recall that memory of my youth.

Back in Avignon, we continued our studies under a new arrangement. While we remained boarders with fat Monsieur Millet, we were brought to the Royal College twice a day to take the university courses as non-resident students. And thus in that lycée I finished my studies in the course of five years (from 1843 to 1847).

At the college our teachers were not, as nowadays, stylish young graduates of a normal school. The grim old graybeards of the former university still occupied their chairs: in fourth year, for instance, good old Monsieur Blanc, a former sergeant-major of the Napoleonic era, who hurled books at our heads when we did not answer well; in third year, Monsieur Monbet, who spoke through his nose and kept a fetus his wife had produced in a jar on his mantel; in second year, Monsieur Lamy, a peevish classicist who couldn't stand the innovations of Victor Hugo; finally, in rhetoric, a rough patriot named Monsieur Chanlaire, who hated the English and who gave us emotional declamations of the warlike songs of Béranger while banging on his desk.

I can still see myself at the prize awards one year with all Avignon society filling the college church. That year I had won all the prizes—I don't know how—even the prize for "excellence." Every time they called my name I went up shyly to collect the beautiful prize book and the crown of laurels from the hands of the principal. Then passing through the applauding crowd, I went and placed my honors in my mother's apron. And with a look of curiosity and astonishment, everyone eyed that beautiful Provençal woman who piled her son's laurels in her basket with calm dignity and happiness. Then back at home we put them behind the cooking pots above the fireplace to preserve them. *Sic transit gloria mundi.*

But whatever was done to divert me from my natural inclination (as is done only too often to children of the South, nowadays more than ever), I could not wean myself of the memory of my language, and everything brought it back to me. Once I read in some journal or other these lines from Jasmin to Loïsa Puget:

Quaṇd dins l'aire,	When you make
Pèr nous plaire,	The air resound
Sones l'aire	To please us
De tas noubellos cansous,	With your new songs,
Sus la terro tout s'amaiso,	All the earth grows
Tout se taiso,	calm and silent
Al refrin que fas souna,	To the sound of your refrain,
Mai d'un cop se derebelho	But at a stroke awakens
E fremis coumo la felho	And quivers like a leaf
Qu'un bent fres fai frissouna.	Shivering in a cool wind.

In a fine transport of enthusiasm at seeing that poets still brought glory to my language, I promptly wrote a little tribute to the famous hairdresser which began thus:

Pouèto, ounour de ta maire Gascougno!

Poet, honor to your Gascon mother!

But little shrimp that I was, I received no reply. I know my poor apprentice verses hardly deserved it. Still—why deny it?—that snub hurt me, and later when I in turn received letters from all comers, I always made a point of welcoming them, remembering my verses that had remained without thanks.

Homesickness for my countryside and my language had never left me and finally gave me the worst heartache ever when I was about fourteen. "How much happier are the hired hands and shepherds of our farm down there, who eat the good bread my mother provides them," I said to myself, like the Prodigal Son, "and my childhood friends, my companions in Maillane, who live freely in the country and plow and harvest and gather grapes and olives under God's blessed sun, while I wither away between four walls over compositions and translations."

And my sadness was mixed with a great distaste for that artificial world in which I was walled up and an attraction toward a vague ideal that I saw as a blue haze on the distant horizon. Then it happened one day while reading *The Family Magazine*, I believe, I fell upon a passage that described the Charterhouse of Valbonne and the silent contemplative life of the Carthusians.

And do you know what? I got carried away, and escaping from school one fine afternoon, I left all alone, taking the road along the Rhone to Saint-Esprit, which I knew was not far from the Charterhouse of Valbonne.

"You will go," I said to myself, "knock on the door of the monastery. You will pray, you will cry, until they are willing to accept you. Then once accepted, you will go like one of the blessed, walking all day long under the trees of the forest, and sinking deeper into the love of the good Lord, you will become holy like Saint Gent."

That memory of Saint Gent, whose legend haunted me, arrested me on the spot. "And your mother," I said to myself, "you haven't said goodbye to her! And when she knows that you have disappeared, she will be in a state and will search for you everywhere, over hill and dale, poor woman, crying disconsolately like the mother of Saint Gent!"

Hesitating then and deeply moved, I turned back in the direction of Maillane, supposedly to embrace my parents one last time before withdrawing from the world. But the closer I came to my father's house, behold, my monastic plans and my proud resolutions melted in the warmth of a poor little boy's filial love, like a snowball in a bright fire. And when I came to the door of the house late in the day, my mother was astonished to see me standing there and said, "But how come you have left school before vacation?"

"I was homesick," I said, crying with shame, "and I don't want to stay any more with that fat Monsieur Millet, who makes us eat nothing but carrots."

And the following morning they had me driven back by our shepherd Rouquet, back to my hateful prison, promising however to take me away from there quite soon, after vacation.

VII

AT MONSIEUR DUPUY'S SCHOOL

ike mother cats who move their young, my mother took me at the beginning of the school year to Monsieur Dupuy, a bespectacled man from Carpentras who kept another boarding school in Avignon, near the Pont-Troué. But here with my budding taste for the Provençal language, I had my muzzle in the nosebag, as they say.

Monsieur Dupuy was the brother of the late deputy of Drôme, Charle Dupuy, the author of "Little Butterfly," one of the choice selections in our modern Provençal anthology. The younger Dupuy also wrote Provençal verse, but he did not boast of it—with reason.

Some time afterward it happened that a young professor with a fine black beard came to us from Nyons. He was from Saint-Rémy, and his name was Jóusè Roumanille. Since we were neighbors—Maillane and Saint-Rémy are in the same district—and our parents, all people of the soil, knew each other from way back, we were soon friends. Still, I did not yet know that the native of Saint-Rémy also took an interest in Provençal poetry.

On Sundays they took us to Mass and vespers at the Carmelites' church. There they placed us in the choir stalls behind the high altar, and with our young voices we accompanied the singers at the lectern, among them Danis Cassan, another Provençal poet, who was in great demand at neighborhood festivities, and whom we saw in a surplice, with his droll look, his bald head, and his imperturbable manner, intoning hymns and antiphons. Since then his name has been given to the street where he lived.

Now one Sunday when we were all singing at vespers, the idea occurred to me to render the penitential psalms into Provençal verse. So surreptitiously I wrote with a pencil stub on a sheet of paper in my open book the quatrains of my translation one by one:

Que l'isop bagne ma caro,	When hyssop bathes my face
Sarai pur; lavas-me lèu,	I will be pure; wash me
E vendrai pu blanc encaro	And I shall be whiter
Que la tafo de la nèu!	Than the whiteness of snow!

But Monsieur Roumanille, who was the proctor, came up from behind, took away the paper I was writing, read it, had Monsieur Dupuy read it—who, it appears, wisely decided not to trouble me. And after vespers, when we went on a walk around the walls of Avignon, he said to me, "So, young Mistral, you entertain yourself in that fashion by writing Provençal verse?"

"Sometimes I do," I answered.

"Do you want me to recite some to you? . . . Listen."

And in a soft and sonorous voice Roumanille recited "The Two Lambs":

Entendès pas l'agnèu que bèlo?
Ve-lou que cour après l'enfant . . .
Coume fan bèn tout ço que fan!
E l'innoucènci, coume es bello!

Do you hear the lamb bleating?
See it run after the child.
How well they do all that they do!
And how beautiful is innocence!

And then "Jejè":

Lou paire es ana rebrounda	The father has gone to trim
E, pèr vèndre lou jardinage,	And sell the garden tillage,
La maire es anadó au vilage,	The mother has gone to the village,
E Jejè rèsto pèr garda.	And Jejè watches the house.

And then "Pauloun" and then "The Poor Man" and "Madaleno" and "Louviseto," a veritable blossoming of April flowers, of meadow flowers, of flowers heralding the Félibrean spring. Overwhelmed with delight, I exclaimed, "This is the dawn that my soul was awaiting to awaken!"

Until then I had read a little Provençal from time to time. But I was annoyed to see our language generally used with derision by modern writers, with the exception of Jasmin and the Marquis de Lafare, whom I did not know. And Roumanille, the handsome lead, sang with dignity in a fresh and simple style, expressing all the feelings of the heart in the current speech of the people of Provence.

Then in spite of a dozen years' difference in age (Roumanille was born in 1818), we shook hands as children of the same god, he happy to find a confidant ready to understand his poetry, I thrilled to enter the sanctuary I was looking for, and we became friends under such a happy star that we labored together in the same patriotic endeavor for half a century without any slackening of enthusiasm or friendship.

Roumanille had contributed his first poems to *Bouillabaisse*, a Provençal weekly published by Jóusè Désanat in Marseille, which was like a ray of sunshine for the minstrels of that period. For the language of the region has never lacked workers, and especially at the time of *Bouillabaisse* (1841–46), there was a group around Marseille that deserves an accolade if it had done nothing but maintain the practice of writing in Provençal.

Besides, we must realize that the people loved poets like the valiant Désanat of Tarascon, like Bellot, Chailan, Bénédit, and Gelu—Gelu above all—who expressed in their fashion the broad, lusty laughter of Marseille, and have never been surpassed in that local comic vein. And Camihe Reybaud, a poet from Carpentras who was of that noble breed, sent a great epistle to Roumanille, despairing of the fate of Provençal abandoned by fools, who, he said,

> Laisson, pèr imita li moussu de la vilo,
> I sàgi segne-grand nosto lengo trop vilo
> E nous fan dóu francés, qu'estroupion que-noun-sai,
> De tóuti li patoues lou plus afrous, bessai.

> To imitate the city gentlemen,
> Leave our lowly tongue to wise elders,
> And beget a crippled bastard French,
> Perhaps the most hideous of all dialects.

He seemed to anticipate the eggs that were hatching when he wrote to the editors of *Bouillabaisse*:

> Quiten-nous; mai avans de nous dessepara,
> Fraire, contro l'óublid soungen de nous para;
> Fasen tóutis ensèn quauco obro couloussalo,
> Tourre de Babilouno en brico prouvençalo;
> A la cimo, en cantant, gravas pièi voste noum,
> Car vous-àutri, ami, sias digne de renoum.
> Iéu qu'un brisoun d'encèns m'entèsto e m'encigalo,
> Que cante pèr canta, coume fai la cigalo,
> E que vous adurriéu pèr voste mounumen
> Qu'un pessu de peireto e de marrit cimen,
> Cavarai pèr ma muso un toumbèu dins la sablo;
> E quand aurés fini vosto obro imperissablo,
> Se, d'apereilamount, de voste cèu tant blu,
> Regardas eiçavau, fraire, me veirés plu.

> Let us part; but before separating,
> Brothers, let us guard against oblivion;
> Let us build some colossal work together,
> A tower of Babel in Provençal brick;
> Then engrave your names on its peak in verse,
> For you, my friends, are worthy of renown.
> I, whom a grain of incense dazes and befuddles,
> I, who sing like the cicada only to sing,
> And who would bring to your monument
> Only a pinch of gravel and some bad cement,
> I will dig a grave in the sand for my Muse;
> And when you have finished your imperishable work,
> If you look down from the heights of your sky so blue,
> Brothers, you will see me no more.

However, those gentlemen, imbued with the false idea that the speech of the people was good only for treating comical or low subjects, did not care to clean it up or rehabilitate it.

Since the time of Louis XIV the traditional usage for writing our language had almost been lost. Either from carelessness or rather from ignorance, Southern poets had adopted the phonetics of the French language, and each one then added his whimsical spelling to that system—which was not made for it and which disfigured our charming spoken language—so as a result of being distorted in writing, the dialects of the *langue d'oc* seemed completely foreign to each other.

Roumanille, reading the manuscripts of Saboly in the library of Avignon, was struck by the good effect our language created when spelled according to the native genius and the practices of our old troubadours. Young as I was, he was willing to accept my advice in restoring Provençal to its natural spelling, and we boldly set out to change its skin, both in agreement on the plan of reform. Instinctively we felt we needed a light and newly sharpened instrument for the unknown task that awaited us in the offing.

Spelling was not the only problem. From a habit of imitation and bourgeois prejudice—which unfortunately is spreading more than ever—people had become accustomed to avoiding as "vulgar" the words most ingrained in Provençal speech, and consequently the precursors of the Félibres, even poets of renown, commonly and quite uncritically used the corrupt, bastardized, Frenchified forms that were spoken in the streets. Once we had made up our minds to write in the language of the people, Roumanille and I had to bring out and set off to advantage its characteristic bluntness, vigor, and richness of expression, and we agreed to write the language purely as it was spoken in places free of outside influence. That is what the Rumanians did, as the poet Alecsandri told us. When they wanted to revive their national language, which the bourgeois class had lost or corrupted, they sought it in the country and in the mountains among the least civilized peasants.

Finally to make the written language conform to the general pronunciation in Provence, we decided to eliminate several final letters or etymologically obsolete letters, such as the plural *s*, the participial *t*, the *r* of the infinitive, and the *ch* in several words like *fach, dich, puech*, etc.

But let no one think these innovations were introduced into

common use without conflict or opposition, even though they affected only a limited circle of "dialect poets," as they were then called. Disturbed in their old routine and challenged in their habits, all those who wrote or rhymed in the language, from Avignon to Marseille, suddenly rose up in arms against the reformers. The war of pamphlets and venomous articles between the youth of Avignon and our opponents lasted more than twenty years.

In Marseille the lovers of trivia, the white-bearded rhymesters, the envious, the grumblers all gathered in back of Boy's bookshop in the evening to bemoan bitterly the suppression of the *s* and to sharpen their weapons against the innovators. Roumanille, always in the breach, boldly hurled at the enemy the Greek fire we were each preparing bit by bit in the crucible of troubadour art. And since we had the faith, the enthusiasm, the spirit of youth, and several other things on our side, in addition to good arguments, in the end we remained masters of the battlefield, as you will see later.

One afternoon when we were playing triple jump with the fellows in the courtyard, a new boarder entered and approached our group, a boy with slender legs, a Henry IV nose, and his hat over one ear, who looked a little like an old man with a dead cigar butt in his mouth. And with his hands in the pockets of his short jacket, as casually as if he were one of us, he said, "Well now, what are we doing? Do you want me to have a try at triple jump?"

And immediately without further ado, he took a run, light as a cat, and went about three hands beyond the mark of the best who had just jumped. We all clapped and said to him, "Friend, where do you hail from like that?"

"I hail from Châteauneuf," he said, "where they have such good wine. Have you ever heard of Châteuneuf-du-Pape?"

"Yes, and what's your name?"

"Me? Ansèume Mathieu."

With that the little devil thrust his two hands into his pockets and took them out full of old cigar butts, which he politely offered us one after the other with an easy, smiling manner.

And we who for the most part had never dared smoke (unless

as children some mulberry roots) immediately formed a high opinion of this newcomer who did things in such a grand manner and who gave every indication of being acquainted with high living.

That's how we made the acquaintance of Mathieu, the gentle author of *The Farandole*, at the Dupuy boarding school. I once told the story to our friend Daudet, who was very fond of Mathieu, and it pleased him so much that in his novel *Jack* he credited his little Negro prince with the handsome offer of the cigar butts.

So with Roumanille and Mathieu there were already three of us who were to found the Félibrige a little later on. *Tres faciunt capitulum*. But good old Mathieu, I don't know how he managed, we hardly saw him except at the hour of meals or recreation. Since he already looked like a little old man, though he was then scarcely sixteen, and since he was somewhat behind in his studies, he had been given a room up under the rooftiles, supposedly to work more freely by himself. And there in his garret, where you saw pictures nailed to the walls or plaster nudes by Pradier on the shelves, he dreamed, he smoked, he wrote poetry all day long, leaning out his window most of the time to watch the people passing in the street or the sparrows bringing a beakful to their little ones in the nest. Then he told dirty jokes to Marieto the chambermaid, ogled the master's daughter, and when he came down to see us, told us all sorts of village nonsense.

The only time he was serious was when he spoke to us of his titles of nobility. "My ancestors were marquises," he would say in a solemn voice, "Marquises of Montredon. At the time of the Revolution my grandfather dropped his title, and afterward, finding himself ruined, he did not want to take it up again because he could no longer bear it properly."

For that matter there was always something misty and romantic in the life of Mathieu. Sometimes he disappeared like the cats when they go to Rome. We would call him: "Mathieu!" —No sign of Mathieu. Where was he? Up above on the roofs running in the gutters to a rendezvous, from what he told us, with a neighborhood girl who was pretty as a day is long.

It happened that on the feast of Corpus Christi we were

watching the procession at the Pont-Troué as usual. And Mathieu said to me, "Frederi, do you want me to show you my love?"

"Gladly."

"Well then, watch," he said, "when the group of choristers goes by, clouded in white with their veils of tulle, you will see that they all have a flower pinned in the middle of their breast,

Flour au mitan	Flower in the middle
Cerco galant.	Seeks a lover.

But you will see one, fair as spun gold, wearing the flower to one side.

Flour au coustat,	Flower on the side
Galant trouva.	Has found a lover.

"There, see her. That's the one."

"That's your girlfriend?"

"That's her."

"My friend, she's like the sun! But how the devil did you ever manage to win such a fine young lady?"

"I'll tell you," he said. "She's the daughter of the confectioner in the rue Carreterie. I used to go there from time to time to buy some 'gaiter-buttons' or 'rat-droppings,' and after a while I became friendly with that fine girl and passed myself off as the Marquis de Montredon. One day when she was alone behind the counter, I said to her, 'Pretty maid, if you had no more sense than I have, I would speak to you of going on an excursion.'

"'Where?'

"'To the moon,' I replied.

"The girl burst out laughing.

"'Here's the plan,' I said. 'Climb up to the roof on top of your house, sweetheart, when you wish or when you can, and I— who place my heart and my fortune at your feet—will come there every day under the sky to tell you sweet nothings.'

"And that's what happened. On top of my girl's house, as on many houses, there is one of those flat roofs where laundry is hung out to dry. And every day I had only to climb over the roofs from gutter to gutter to go meet my fair one, who was spreading or folding her little wash. And there, nice and peaceful, with lips against lips, hand pressing hand, always in courtly fashion like a knight and his lady, we were in heaven."

That's how our friend Ansèume, the future "Félibre of Kisses," completed his studies on the roofs of Avignon, taking his ease while studying the Breviary of Love.

Speaking of processions and before leaving the papal city, I must say a word about those religious ceremonies that put Avignon in a commotion for a whole fortnight in our youth. The cathedral of Notre-Dame-des-Doms and the four parish churches, Saint-Agricol, Saint-Pierre, Saint-Didier, and Saint-Symphorien, competed to see which would put on the most beautiful display.

As soon as the sacristan had rung his bell through the streets where God and His canopy were to pass, they were swept, sprinkled, strewn with palm fronds and draped with awnings. The rich spread tapestries of damasked and embroidered silk on their balconies. The poor hung their patchwork quilts and quilted bedspreads out their windows. At the Gate of Maillane and in the poor neighborhoods they decorated the walls with fragrantly laundered white sheets and scattered boxwood on the streets.

Then monumental altars arose at intervals, high as pyramids, loaded with candelabras and vases of flowers. The people awaited the procession, sitting outdoors on chairs in front of their houses, eating little meat pastries. The young people, the bachelors, workingmen and bourgeois, walked up and down swaggering, eying the girls and tossing them roses under the awnings in the streets all perfumed with incense.

When the procession finally came, marching slowly to the beat of drums, with the Swiss guard in front dressed all in red, with files of maidens in white, with religious orders, brothers, monks, priests, with choirs and musicians, you could hear the murmur of the devout saying their rosary as it passed.

Then in a great silence all those kneeling or bowing prostrated themselves, and there beneath a shower of golden broom flowers the priest elevated the dazzling Blessed Sacrament.

But most striking were the Penitents who made their appearance in the evening by torchlight. When the White Penitents, among others, marched slowly through the city like hooded ghosts with their long cowls, some carrying portable tabernacles, others reliquaries or bearded statues, others incense burners, some a huge open eye in a triangle, others a snake twisted around a tree, you would have said it was an Indian procession in honor of Brahma.

The leading nobles of Avignon were generally the superiors of that confraternity, which dated back to the Catholic League and even to the Great Schism. And the great Félibre Aubanel, who was a zealous White Penitent all his life, was shrouded in the gown of his confraternity when he died.

We had as a master of studies in Monsieur Dupuy's school a former sergeant from Africa named Monsieur Monnier who would gladly have been a *red* penitent, he told us, if they had existed in Avignon at that time. Blunt, brusque, and profane as an old soldier, with his mustache and his unruly beard, he was always waxed and polished from head to foot.

At the Royal College, where we learned history, there was never any question of the politics of the century. But Sergeant Monnier, an enthusiastic republican, took it upon himself to instruct us in that subject. During recreation periods he would walk up and down with a history of the Revolution in his hand. And as he became inflamed by reading it, gesticulating, swearing, and crying in his agitation, he would exclaim, "How fine that is! How fine! What men! Camille Desmoulins, Mirabeau, Bailly, Vergniaud, Danton, Saint-Just, Boissy-d'Anglas! By God, we are worms nowadays compared to the giants of the National Convention!"

"Ah yes, they were something pretty, your giants of the Convention!" Roumanille would answer when he happened to be there, "choppers of heads, defilers of God, unnatural monsters who ate one another, and when Bonaparte wanted them, he bought them like hogs at a fair!"

And then they would go on arguing until good old Mathieu reconciled them by telling some foolish tale.

In short, with one day following another in those friendly and familiar surroundings, I finished my studies in August of

1847. To increase his small salary, Roumanille had gone to work as overseer of the Seguin printing house, and thanks to this employment he printed at little cost his first collection of poetry, *The Daisies*, which delighted us when we saw the proofs. And happy as a colt let out to forage, I came home to our farm.

VIII

HOW I PASSED MY BACCALAUREATE EXAM

ell, have you finished now?" said my father to me. "I've finished," I replied. "Only I must go to Nîmes to take my baccalaureate exam—a difficult step that makes me apprehensive."

"Forward march! When we were in the army at the siege of Figueras, my son, we took worse steps than that."

And with that I got ready for the trip to Nîmes, where they gave the bachelor's degrees in those days. My mother folded two ironed shirts with my Sunday clothes in a checked handkerchief neatly fastened with four pins. My father gave me one hundred and fifty francs' worth of crowns in a little linen bag, saying, "Now take care not to lose them or waste them."

And I left the farm for the city of Nîmes with my little package under my arm, my hat over one ear, and a grape cane in my hand.

When I arrived in Nîmes, I found an antheap of schoolboys from the region who had come like me to take the baccalaureate exam. They were accompanied for the most part by their parents, fine ladies and gentlemen with their pockets full of recommendations. This one had a letter for his honor the rector, another for the inspector, another for the prefect, that one for the vicar-general. And all gave themselves airs and strutted proudly with a little expression that seemed to say, "We are sure of the outcome."

I, poor farm boy, was no bigger than a pea, for I knew nothing of nobody. And my only recourse, alas, was to say several silent prayers to Saint Baudile, the patron of Nîmes (whose votive ribbon I had worn when I was little), to put a little kindness for me into the heart of the examiners.

They shut us up in the Hôtel de Ville in a big room bare as my hand, where an old professor who spoke through his nose dictated a Latin text. And afterward, taking a pinch of snuff, he said to us, "Gentlemen, you have one hour to translate the dictation I have given you into French. Now get busy." And with that we all set to work feverishly. By looking up every word in the dictionary, we figured out the Latin hodgepodge. Then when the hour rang, our old tobacco-snuffer gathered up everyone's translation and let us out, saying, "Till tomorrow!"

That was the first test.

The gentlemen schoolboys scattered throughout the city. And there I was, alone with my package and my grape cane in hand, on the pavements of Nîmes, gaping at the Amphitheater and the Maison-Carrée.

"However," I said, "I must find a place to stay." And I set out in search of an inn that was not too expensive but still decent. And since I had the time, I went around the city of Nîmes about ten times, looking at the signs. But those hotels with their insolent servants dressed in black, who seemed to snub me at fifty paces, and the bowing and scraping and the grand manners all intimidated me.

As I walked in the suburbs, I caught a glimpse of a banner on which was written "Au Petit Saint-Jean."

That Little Saint John made me happy. All at once I seemed to be on familiar ground. Saint John is a saint from our village, you might say. Saint John brings the harvest, we have the bonfires of Saint John, there is Saint John's wort. So I went into Little Saint John. I had made the right choice.

In the courtyard of the inn there were covered carts, un-hitched wagons, and little groups of Provençal girls, chattering and laughing. I slipped inside and sat down at the table.

The dining room was already full and the big table, too, with nothing but gardeners: gardeners from Saint-Rémy, from Château-Renard, from Barbentane, who all knew each other, for they came to market once a week. And what did they talk about? Nothing but gardening.

"Say, Benezet, how much did you get for your eggplants?"

"I had no luck, my friend. There was a glut. I had to let them go cheap."

"And what do they say about leek seed?"

"Seems it will sell. They say we're at war. I've been assured they make gunpowder of it."

"And the forty-day beans?"

"They're a bust."

"And the onions?"

"They took off by themselves."

"And the squash?"

"They'll have to be fed to the pigs."

"And the melons, the carrots, the celery, the potatoes. . . ."

In short, for a whole hour there was a hubbub over nothing but gardening.

I emptied my plate without saying a word. When they had finished talking, one of them who sat across from me said, "And you, young man, if I'm not too inquisitive, are you in gardening? You don't seem to belong."

"I, no. I have come to Nîmes," I replied a bit shyly, "to take my bachelor's exam."

"Bachelor? Boatman?" said the whole tableful. "What did he say?"

"Oh yes," one of them ventured, "I think he said *boatman*. That's it, he must have come to take the ferry. However, there's no Rhone here in Nîmes."

"Go on, you have misunderstood," another said. "Can't you see that he's a conscript who has come to join the *battery*?"

I broke out laughing and did my best to explain what a *bachelor* was.

"When we finish school," I told them, "where our teachers have taught us everything—French, Latin, Greek, history, rhetoric, mathematics, physics, chemistry, astronomy, philosophy, what-have-you, everything you can imagine—then they send us to Nîmes where learned men examine us."

"Oh, like when we went to catechism and they asked us, 'Are you a Christian?'"

"That's it. Those learned men question us here about all the mysteries there are in books. And if we answer well, they designate us *bachelors*. And then we can become notaries, doctors, lawyers, tax collectors, judges, sub-prefects, whatever you wish."

"And if you answer poorly?"

"They send us back to the asses' bench. Today they started us out to get rid of the majority. But it's tomorrow morning that we pass through the strainers."

"Oh, you lucky fellow!" they all cried. "We'd like to be there to see if you pass or if you stay in the hole. And what will they ask you, tell us, to give some idea?"

"Well, I suppose they will ask us the dates of all the battles that have taken place in the world since men have fought: battles of the Jews, battles of the Greeks, battles of the Romans, battles of the Saracens, of the Germans, of the Spaniards, of the French, of the English, of the Hungarians, and the Polish. Not only the battles but also the names of the generals in command, the names of the kings, of the queens, of all their ministers, of all their children, even of their bastards."

"Oh, what in the name of thunder is the use of making you remember everything that's happened since Saint Joseph was a boy? It doesn't seem possible that such men can be so silly. You can see they don't have anything better to do. If they had to go every morning like us to turn over the soil with a spade, I don't think they would spend their time speaking of the Saracens or of the bastards of King Herod. But go on, continue."

"Not only the names of the kings but also the names of all the nations, of all the regions, of all the mountains, and of all the rivers. And speaking of rivers, you must say where they have their source and what they flow into."

"Let me interrupt you!" said the one who objected, a gardener from Château-Renard with a throaty voice. "They must ask you where the Fountain of Vaucluse has its source? That's some water! They say it has seven branches and they all carry water. I've heard tell that a shepherd let his staff fall into the gorge where it rises and they found it seven leagues from there in a spring at Saint-Rémy. Is that true or not?"

"All that may be. . . . Then we must know the names of all the seas there are under the sun."

"Excuse me for interrupting you!" said the Objector. "Do you know how come the sea is salty?"

"Yes, because it contains potassium sulfate, magnesium sulfate, chloride. . . ."

"Not at all. Look, a fishmonger from Martigues assured me that it came from ships loaded with salt that were wrecked there a long time ago."

"All right, if you will have it so. They ask us how the dew is formed, the rain, frost, storms, thunder. . . ."

"Excuse me for interrupting you," said the Objector. "The rain, we all know the clouds go and get it from the sea in a goatskin bag. But thunder, is it true that it's round as a basket?"

"That depends," I replied. "They also ask us where the wind comes from and how far it travels per hour, per minute, per second."

"Let me interrupt you, young man," said the Objector. "Then you must know where the mistral comes from. I have always heard that it came out of a big rock with a hole in it and if you plugged the hole, the damned mud-eater would never blow again. That would be some achievement, no matter what!"

"The government doesn't want it," said a man from Barbentane. "If there was no mistral, Provence would be the garden of France. And who would keep us down? We'd be too rich."

"They question us," I resumed, "on the species of animals, of birds, of fish, even on the harmless snakes."

"Wait, wait," said the Objector with his two hands in the air, "and what about the Tarasque? Don't the books mention it? There are some who say it's a legend. However, I have seen its den in Tarascon behind the castle along the Rhone. Besides, everyone knows it's buried under the Covered Cross."

"Finally, they interrogate us," I went on to finish, "on the numbers, the size, and the distance of the stars, how many thousands of leagues there are from the earth to the moon, how many millions of leagues from the earth to the sun!"

"That won't wash," cried the dull-witted Lout from Noves. "Who goes up there to measure off the leagues? Can't you see that the scholars are making fun of us? that they would have us believe that pigeons suckle their young! A fine science to want to count the leagues from the sun to the moon! Well, what does that matter to us? If you spoke to me of understanding the moon in order to plant celery or remove lice from beans or cure sick pigs, I would say to you, that's a science! But everything this boy here tells us is nonsense."

"Go on, be quiet, you big goat!" shouted the whole crowd. "This wide-awake boy has probably forgotten more than all you'll ever know. Anyhow, my friends, you have to have a powerful head to hold everything he has told us."

"Poor fellow," said the girls, "look how pale he is. You can certainly see that reading isn't good for you. If he'd spent his time at the handle of a plow, he'd surely have more color. So what's the use of knowing so much?"

"I only went to Monsieur Blockhead's school," said the Plump One. "I don't know A or B. But I promise you that if I had had to cram into my noodle one hundred-thousandth of what they ask them to pass the bachelor's exam, why, they could have taken a mallet and wedges and beaten my pate—in vain!—the wedges would have been blunted."

"Well then, good friends," said the Objector, "do you know what we should do? When we go to a festival where they have bullfights and fine wrestling matches, we often stay a day longer to see who will get the cockade or the prize. We are in Nîmes. Here's a boy from Maillane who's going to take his bachelor's exam tomorrow morning. Instead of leaving tonight, gentlemen, let's sleep in Nîmes, and tomorrow we will at least know if our fellow from Maillane has passed his baccalaureate."

"Agreed!" they all said. "Anyway, the day is wasted. Yes, we must see the outcome."

The following morning, with my heart aflutter, I went back to the Hôtel de Ville with all the candidates who were supposed to appear. But already a fair number were not as proud as the day before. In a big hall, in front of a long table loaded with inkstands, papers, and books, sat five professors in yellow gowns, five famous professors who had come specially from Montpellier, with their hoods trimmed in ermine at the shoulder and with mortar boards on their heads. And as chance would have it, one of them was Monsieur Saint-René Taillandier, who was to become the most ardent champion of our Provençal tongue a few years later. But at that time we were not acquainted, and the illustrious professor certainly did not dream that the little farm boy who stammered before him would one day become one of his good friends.

I was lucky. I passed. And I went out into the city transported by angels. But as it was hot, I remembered that I was thirsty. And passing by a café with my grape cane on high, I panted to see a good head of beer foaming in a glass. But I was so new to the ways of the world and so shy, poor fellow, that I had never set foot in a café and did not dare go in.

And then what did I do? I wandered around Nîmes, beaming and glowing, so that everyone looked at me, and some even said, "That one's a bachelor!" And every time I came to a fountain, I plunged my face into the cool water. And the king of Paris was no kin to me.

But the finest was at Petit Saint-Jean. My worthy gardeners were impatiently awaiting me, and when they saw me coming—looking as if I would have melted the fog—they cried, "He passed!"

The men, the women, the girls, all came out, and what a lot of hugging and handshaking! It was as if manna had just fallen on them.

Then the Objector (the one with the throaty voice) asked to speak. His eyes were full of tears. And he said, "Maillanais, we are very happy indeed. You have shown these little gentlemen that not only ants come from the soil. So do men! So do men! Come one, little ones, let's have a round of the farandole!"

And we took hands and danced the farandole for a long time in the courtyard of Petit Saint-Jean. Then we went in to dinner, ate a *brandade*, drank, and sang, and then we parted.

That was more than fifty years ago, yet every time I go to Nîmes and see the sign of Petit Saint-Jean from a distance, that moment of my youth comes back to me as vividly as ever, and I

have warm thoughts for all those good souls who first ac-
quainted me with the good-heartedness of ordinary people and
with popularity.

Now at last I was free on my father's farm in my beautiful
plain rich in grain and fruit, with the peaceful look of my blue
Alpilles, with their rocky ridge in the distance, their escarp-
ments, their cliffs, their rounded hills, so familiar yet seen
anew, the Hole Rock, the Mound of Wheat, the Hill That Was
Built, the Fat Woman. When Sundays came around, I was free
again to see the companions of my early childhood whom I had
missed and envied so much when I was incarcerated. As we
walked on the promenade after vespers dressed in our Sunday
best, we told each other with such pleasure and enthusiasm
what had happened to us since we had seen each other. Rafèu
had won the prize in the men's race. Nouvelet had snatched the
cockade from a bull. Giloun had hitched the finest mule in
Maillane to the cart they ran on the feast of Saint Eloi. Tounin
had hired out for the month of seedtime at the big Merleta
farm. And Paulet had been on a binge for three days and three
nights at the Beaucaire fair.

Then too, they all had a girlfriend, to say the least, or if you
prefer, "a promised one," whom they had been courting since
their first communion. Some even had "*intrado,*" that is, the
right to spend part of the evening at their girl's house on
Sundays.

I, who had been estranged, alas, by my seven years at school,
was the only one there without a girl. And when we met troops
of young girls who locked arms and barred our way, I noticed
that they were not familiar with me as they were with my
fellows. They understood each other in the slightest matters
and could make each other laugh over nothing. I had become a
"Monsieur" to them, and if I had made declarations to one of
them, she would certainly not have believed me.

What's more, those boys, brought up in a round of simple
ideas, marveled endlessly over things that meant little or no-
thing to me, I must say, such as a sowed field that had yielded
tenfold or twelvefold, a cart whose wheels grated against its

axle, a mule that pulled well, a well-loaded cart, or even a fine manure pile. Then in winter I fell back on the evening gatherings, where I could listen to our storytellers, the Bellower among others, a former grenadier of the Army of Italy, who swallowed cicadas and tree-frogs alive and had these creatures singing in his stomach. I can still hear him when he wanted to wake up his drowsy audience with a reminder of the barracks or of camping out in the country:

Cric!—Crac!	Crick! Crack!
De la m . . . dans ton sac.	Sh- -in your sack.
Du butin dans le mien.	Booty in mine.

Another one who knew no end of silly tales was old Pious, and how it pleases me to pay my debt here, for simple as it was, I owe him the gift of my poem *Nerto*.

And while we are on the subject of those evenings, let me say a word about them. In our village nowadays the peasants go to the café after supper to play a round of billiards, of cards, of what you will. And all that remains of the old evening gatherings is a vague semblance among a few craftsmen who work by lamplight, such as cabinetmakers or shoemakers.

But at that time the custom of those joyful gatherings was far from being lost. They generally took place in stables or sheepfolds because there with the livestock people were warm. It was the practice for every man or woman who participated to take a turn in providing the candle, and the candle had to last two evenings, so when they saw it was half consumed, they got up and went to bed.

But to keep the candle from burning down too quickly, you know what they put on the end of the wick?—a grain of salt. They placed the candle on the bottom of a wooden bucket or a washtub, and the women who spun or rocked their little ones (for mothers brought cradles to the gathering) sat around on the straw or on blocks of wood with their husbands and children.

When there were no places to sit, the spinners, carrying distaffs in a sling, distaffs covered and capped with hemp, circled slowly around the candle one after another in order to have light on their thread.

And then they told stories, often interrupted by the snorting or lowing or bleating of the animals.

One of those evening tales which was often told was the one I am going to tell you now, because one of my uncles, good Monsieur Jirome, played a role in it, and because it is a true story.

About 1820 or 1825, no matter exactly when, a certain Glaudihoun died in Maillane, and since he had no children, his house remained closed for about five or six months. However, a tenant finally came to live there, and the windows were opened.

But what in the name of fate! Several days later a rumor ran around Maillane that the house of Glaudihoun was haunted. The new lodger and his wife heard rooting and rummaging all night long, with one sound in particular, as if someone was shuffling paper or parchment. As soon as a light was lit, the shuffling was no longer heard; and as soon as it was extinguished, suddenly you heard teeth grinding mysteriously. In vain did the tenants search and poke and probe in all the corners, cleaning the cupboards, looking under the bed, under the stairs, on the boards of the sink. They saw nothing, but nothing, that could explain the rummaging at night.

And every day it began again at night, to such a point, I tell you, that those people took fright and moved out, saying to the neighbors, "Let anyone who wishes sleep in the house of Glaudihoun. There are mysterious noises all night long." And they went away.

The neighbors were quite frightened, but they also wanted to see what was going on there. And the braver ones, armed with pitchforks and rifles, took turns sleeping in the house of Glaudihoun. But no sooner had they extinguished the lamp than the hellish rummaging started up again. The parchment rustled, and they could never see anything of where it came from.

Crossing themselves, the watchers spoke the words that are used to exorcise ghosts:

Se siés bono amo, parlo-me!	If you are a good spirit, speak to me!
Se siés marrido, esvalis-te!	If you are a bad one, disappear!

But no, that had as much effect as bran on a cat, and the sound was still heard the same as ever. And at the oven, at the mill, at the washhouse, at the evening gathering, they spoke only of ghosts.

"If only we knew," said the people, "who the ghost is, we could have Masses said for him, and the poor soul could enter into rest."

"Well, who do you suppose it is?" said fat Aneto, "it could only be Glaudihoun. Poor Glaudihoun left no children to have Mass said for him, and his poor soul must surely be in purgatory."

"That's it," they said, "Glaudihoun must be in purgatory."

And immediately the women collected among their neighbors, a copper at a time, enough to have a Mass said for poor Glaudihoun. The priest said his Mass, prayed to God for Glaudihoun, and that night several Maillanais volunteered to go back and see if the house was still haunted.

It was haunted more than ever! The shuffling of paper and parchment made your hair stand on end! And everyone added his own story. They had found a boot at the top of the stairs, a polished boot! Others had seen through the sink hole a white man all in flames coming down the chimney! Eisabèu the Cooper's wife told how she had found bruises on her body—which were "pinches of the dead"—in the morning when hunting for fleas. And the Widow Nanoun insisted that they had dragged her by the feet at night.

On Sunday the men held a further discussion of the matter near the well on the Square and said, "Glaudihoun, poor Glaudihoun, yet he was a good man. It's unbelievable that he could be the one."

"But then who could it be?"

Big Charle, a joker everyone respected, for he dominated everyone by his self-assurance as well as his large physique, cleared his throat and said, "Isn't it clear? Since they're shuffling papers, it must be notaries."

"Big Charle is right," everyone exclaimed, "it must be notaries, since they're shuffling papers! It's notaries!"

"Say, now I remember," added old Master Ferrut, "in my

youth that house was sold by the court. It came from an inheritance that had been in litigation at Tarascon for about twenty years. And the notaries, the lawyers, the attorneys plucked so much that everything was eaten up. Why, of course, those people must be burning in hell. It's not surprising they come back as ghosts searching in their deeds and documents."

"It's notaries! it's notaries!" You heard nothing but that in the streets of Maillane. The people could no longer sleep at the thought, and when they spoke of it, they had gooseflesh.

"You'll soon see if it's notaries," said Monsieur Jirome, the silk weaver, with his imperturbable calm.

My Uncle Jirome had served in the dragoons as a corporal in the time of Bonaparte. And he proudly bore on top of his nose the glorious scar of a healthy saber cut that a German hussar had given him at the battle of Austerlitz, and not for fun. Driven back against a wall, he had fought alone against twenty cavalrymen who slashed him with sabers until he fell with his face cut in two by the blunt side of a blade. That had earned him a pension of seven sous a day, just enough for his tobacco.

Uncle Jirome was the finest bird-snarer I have ever known. When the season came, he went off every morning, regardless of business, family, and trade, with his fowling snare in one hand, carrying on his shoulders the big blind of greenery under which he hid. When he crossed the fields of stubble, he looked like a walking tree. And he never returned without three or four dozen fat round white-rumps. And afterward he feasted with Monsieur Chabert, who had been a surgeon in the Army of Spain and had seen Madrid with King Joseph. Then they drank to the health of the Spanish and Hungarian women.

Enough of that. Monsieur Jirome loaded his pistols and calmly, as if he were going hunting, came and snuggled up for the night in the house of poor Glaudihoun. He had brought, it should be said, a dark lantern, which he covered with his coat. And while waiting for the notaries to shuffle, he stretched out on two chairs.

Suddenly the papers rattled, frou! frou! cra! cra! My uncle quickly uncovered his lantern, and what did he see? Two rats! two big rats that ran up on the shutter.

For in that house, as in many houses, there was a shutter to cover the stairway. Monsieur Jirome climbed on a chair and up there on the floorboards found only dried grapeleaves.

It seems that before dying poor Glaudihoun had brought in some grapes and spread them out on a bed of grapeleaves over the boards of the shutter. When he died, the rats ate the grapes, and when there were no more grapes, those fellows came every night, ferreting under the leaves to gnaw the seeds that might still be there.

My uncle removed the leaves and went off to bed. The following morning, when he went to the Square, the peasants said to him, "Well, Monsieur Jirome, you look quite pale. Did the notaries come haunting?"

"Your notaries," said Monsieur Jirome, "were a pair of rats who shuffled leaves on the shutter, dried grapeleaves."

A tremendous laugh shook the citizens of Maillane. And since that day the people of my village have no longer believed in ghosts.

I X
THE REPUBLIC
OF 1848

hat winter the people were all united and peaceful and contented, for the crops sold quite well, and thank God, there was no more talk of politics. To entertain us a little, performances of tragedies and comedies were organized in our village, and as I have already said, I played my little part with all the enthusiasm of seventeen. But while that was going on, toward the end of February, farewell peace! the Revolution of 1848 broke out.

At the entrance to Maillane in a little clay house with a grape arbor over the door there lived at that time an old grandmother they called Riquello. Dressed in the style of the women of Arles of an earlier time, she wore a big flattened headdress and over that a flat hat of black felt with wide brims. Her cheeks were also framed with a headband, a kind of beige linen veil fastened under her chin. She lived off her spinning and off several little plots of land. But she was so neat, well groomed, and well spoken that you could tell she must have been a stylish woman.

At the age of seven or eight when I went to school carrying my bookbag, I passed the little house of Riquello every day. And the old lady, who sat spinning on a stone bench near her door, would call me and say, "Frederi, do you have any red apples at your house?"

"I don't know," I would answer.

"When you come again, sweetheart, bring me some."

And I always forgot to do as she said. And Dame Riquello always spoke to me of those apples when she saw me going by. So that finally I said to my father, "Old Riquello always asks me to bring her *red apples*."

"That damned old witch!" replied my father angrily, "if she speaks of it to you again, tell her: They aren't ripe yet, neither now nor for a long time."

Then when the old lady asked for her red apples, I shouted, "My father told me that they weren't ripe, neither now nor for a long time!"

And from then on Riquello spoke to me no more of her apples.

But the day after we in the country heard of the February Days and heard that Paris had proclaimed the Republic, when I came to the village to learn the news, the first person I saw at the entrance was Dame Riquello. Standing on her doorstep, all spruced up and excited, with a topaz ring sparkling on her finger, she said to me, "So this time the *red apples* are ripe! They say they are going to plant the trees of liberty. Sweetheart, we are going to eat some of those good apples of the earthly paradise. Oh, Saint Marianne, I thought never to see you again! Frederi, my child, become a republican!"

"But Riquello," I said, "what a beautiful ring you have!"

"Ah," she said, "indeed that ring is beautiful! Look, I hadn't worn it since Bonaparte left for the island of Elba. A friend of ours, a friend of the family gave it to me at the time—ah, what a time!—when we danced the carmagnole."

And taking hold of her skirts as if to dance, the old lady went into her house, bursting with laughter. When I went back home and told my parents the news of Paris during supper and laughed as I told them what old Riquello had said, my father spoke gravely, saying, "The Republic, I saw it once. Let's hope this one won't cause atrocities like the other. They killed Louis XVI and his wife the Queen. And beautiful princesses, priests, nuns, all kinds of good people—who knows how many?—were put to death in France. The other kings declared war on us all together. To defend the Republic there was requisitioning and universal conscription. Everyone went, the lame, the halt, the one-eyed. They sent them to the depot to make bandages. I remember when the Allobrogian troops went by on their way to Toulon: 'Who goes there?'—'Allobrogians!' One of them seized my brother, who was no more than twelve years old, and raising a naked saber over his neck, said, 'Shout "Long live the Republic," or you're dead!' The poor little boy shouted, but his blood curdled, and he died of it.

"The nobles, the good priests, and all those who were suspect had to flee to escape the guillotine. Father Riousset made his way to Piedmont dressed as a shepherd with the flocks of Monsieur de Lubières. We saved Monsieur Vitourin Cartier, the choir-master of Saint Martha in Tarascon, whose estate we farmed. We kept him hidden for three months in a wine cellar we had dug under the casks. And when the municipal officers or the gendarmes of the district came to the farm to count the lambs we had in our fold and the bread we had put by (on the strength of the so-called law of 'the maximum'), my poor mother would make a big bacon omelet in the frying pan. And when they had eaten and drunk their fill, they forgot to conduct their search and left carrying branches of laurel to celebrate the victories of the French armies.

"Dovecotes were destroyed. They pillaged castles, smashed crosses, and melted down bells. In the churches they raised 'mountains' of earth where they planted pines, broom plants, dwarf oaks. In our church in Maillane, the 'club' was held, and when you did not attend civic meetings, you were marked as 'suspect.' I remember that the parish priest, who was cowardly and foolish, said one day from the pulpit, '*Citizens*, until now we have told you nothing but lies.' He made the people quiver with indignation, and they would have stoned him if they hadn't been afraid of one another. He's the one who on another occasion said at the end of his sermon, 'I warn you, my broth-ers, if you know of any hidden émigré, you are bound in conscience under pain of mortal sin to come to the town hall without fail to report him.' Finally, Sundays and feast days were abolished, and every ten days there was the *Decadi*, when the goddess Reason was worshiped with great ceremony. Now, do you know who was the goddess in Maillane?"

"No," we all said.

"It was old Riquello."

"Is that possible?" we cried.

"Riquello," my honored father continued, "was the daughter of the shoemaker Jaque Riquel, who was the mayor of Maillane at the time of the Terror. Oh, the bitch! At that time, when she was about eighteen years old, she was fresh, lively, and one of the prettiest there was. We belonged to the same group of young people. Her father had even made the shoes I wore in the army when I enlisted, square-toed shoes. Well, what if I told you that I saw her, Riquello, dressed as a goddess, her thighs half naked, one breast bared, with a red cap on her head, sitting there on the altar of the church?"

That's what my father Master Francés told us at the table during supper toward the end of February 1848. Now see what follows.

About eleven years later, at the time I published my *Mirèio*, I happened to be in Paris, where I was invited by the banker Millaud, who founded *Le Petit Journal*, to one of the dinners that cordial philanthropist gave every week for artists, scholars, and writers. There were at least fifty of us, and Madame Millaud, a magnificent Jewish woman, had Méry on one side and myself, I believe, on the other. At the end of the meal an old man dressed simply in a long jacket with a skullcap on his head addressed me in Provençal from the far end of the table, "Monsieur Mistral, you are from Maillane?"

"It's the father," they told me, "of the banker who is our host."

And since the table was too long to permit conversation, I got up and went to talk with the good old man.

"You are from Maillane?" he said.

"Yes," I replied.

"Do you know the daughter of Jaque Riquel who was in his day mayor of your town?"

"Do I know her!" I said, "Riquello the goddess? Indeed, we are friends."

"Well," said the old man, "when we went to Maillane to sell

our colts—for at that time we sold horses and mules—we used to stay at Riquello's. I am speaking of fifty years ago at least."

"And by chance," I said to him then, "would it be you, Monsieur Millaud, who presented her with a topaz ring?"

"Oh, that Riquello!" said the old Jewish man, shaking his head, snickering, with his eyes shining, "she spoke to you of that? Ah, my good sir, who saw us and who sees us!"

At that moment the banker Millaud, who had risen from the table, came, as he did after all his meals, and bowed in front of his father, who placed his hands on his forehead like the patriarchs and gave him his blessing.

To get back to myself: that overflow of liberty and new ideas that bursts the dikes during a revolution found me all on fire and ready to follow the impulse, I must confess, in spite of the stories I had heard in my family. When the proclamations were signed by the illustrious name of Lamartine, my lyricism burst out in a fiery song in French that the little newspapers of Arles and Avignon published:

> Réveillez-vous, enfants de la Gironde,
> Et tressaillez dans vos sépulcres froids:
> La liberté va rajeunir le monde . . .
> Guerre éternelle entre nous et les rois!

> Awake, you children of Gironde,
> Stir and quicken in your cold tombs;
> Freedom will rejuvenate the world—
> Eternal war against the kings!

A mad enthusiasm had suddenly intoxicated me with those liberal and humanitarian ideas that I saw at their finest. And while my republicanism scandalized the royalists of Maillane, who regarded me as a "turncoat," it brought joy to the local republicans, who, being in the minority, were proud and delighted to have me singing the "Marseillaise" with them.

Now among those men, who were for the most part descendants of the populist demagogues they called "the bellowers" during the Revolution, all the prejudices and resentments and grievances of the former Republic were transmitted like yeast from father to son. Once when I tried to make them understand the generous dreams of the new Republic without concealing my horror at the crimes that had put so many innocent people to death at the time of the first, old Boor shouted at me in a voice of thunder, "Innocent people! then you don't know that the aristocrats had taken an oath—those monsters!—to go bowling with the heads of the patriots!"

When I smiled at that, old Rogue said to me, "Have you ever heard the story of the castle of Tarascon?"

"What story?" I replied.

"The story of the time Representative Cadroy came to spur on the counterrevolutionaries. Listen and you'll understand the reason behind the refrain the Whites sometimes sang to our faces:

De brin o de bran	Willy or nilly
Cabussaran	They'll take a dive
Dóu fenestroun	From the window
De Tarascoun	Of Tarascon
Dedins lou Rose:	Into the Rhone.
N'en voulèn plus,	We want no more
D'aquéli gus,	Of those beggars,
D'aquéli gus,	Of those beggars,
De sèns-culoto.	Of sans-culottes.

"You know—or you don't know—that at the fall of Robespierre the moderates fell upon the good patriots and filled the prisons with them. At Tarascon they made the prisoners climb to the top of the castle, naked as earthworms, and from there forced them at bayonet point to jump through a window into the Rhone. It's then that Liautard of Graveson, who is still alive, and who was then the last one to take a dive, took advantage of a moment when they had left him alone to take off his shirt and throw it on top of the others. Then he hid in a chimney flue, so when the cutthroats returned from up above and counted the shirts, they thought they had drowned everyone and went away. But when night came, Liautard climbed to the top of the castle, slid down as far as he could on a rope he had made of the others' clothes, dove into the Rhone, swam across it, and in Beaucaire he went and knocked at the door of a friend who gave him refuge."

"And poor Balarin!" said Little Bottle, a waspish little man who constantly hammered away at the priests, "poor Balarin was fishing for eels down there at Font-Mourguette in 1815 when they assassinated him because he would not shout 'Long live the King!'"

"And the master of the White Farm," said fat Tardieu, "they did him in about the same time with a rifle shot through the door."

"And Trestaillon!" added one. "And the Spike!" added another.

Such were the recriminations that the Republic had revived, on one side as well as the other, and that brought back quarreling and antagonism among the people here as elsewhere. The Reds began to wear red kerchiefs and sashes, and the Whites wore green ones. The former decked themselves with thyme, symbol of the "Mountain"; the latter hoisted the royal fleur-de-lis. The republicans planted trees of liberty; the royalists sawed them down to the ground at night. Then came brawls, then knifings. And those good people, those Provençaux of the same stock, who had played, joked, and dined together a month before, now would have eaten each other's livers for trifles that wouldn't sharpen a spindle.

All we young men of the same age group also divided into two camps on the issue. And unfortunately, every time there was a round of dancing on Sunday evenings, when we had drunk a little, we soon reached the point of fighting. On the last days of Carnival it's the custom for boys to go around to the farms to collect enough eggs and salt pork to make several omelets. As they go on those rounds, they dance the morris to the beat of a drum and usually sing couplets like these:

> Boutas la man, dono, au cledoun:
> De chasco man un froumajoun.
> Boutas la man au saladou:
> Dounas un tros dóu jougadou.
> Boutas la man au panié d'iòu:
> Pourgès n'en tres o sièis o nòu.

Place your hand, lady, on the cheese-tray;
With each hand give a small cheese.
Place your hand in the salt box;
Give a stub of the ham-joint.
Place your hand in the egg basket;
Give us three or six or nine.

But in gathering eggs that year we sang only of politics, like the foolish sheep that we were. The Whites sang:

S' Enri Cinq venié deman,
Oh! que de fèsto, oh! que de fèsto,
S' Enri Cinq venié deman,
Oh! que de fèsto que farian!

If Henry V came tomorrow,
Oh, what a party! oh, what a party!
If Henry V came tomorrow,
Oh, what a party we would have!

And the Reds replied:

Enri Cinq es is isclo
Que pelo de vergan,
Pèr n'en couifa li fiho
Qu'amon lou verd e blanc.

Henry V is on the islands,
Peeling willow wands,
To crown the girls
Who love the green and white.

At night, when our crowd had eaten the omelet and emptied a number of bottles, we left the cabaret in shirtsleeves with napkins around our necks, as village people do. And with lanterns in hand we danced the carmagnole to the beat of a drum, singing the song that was so popular at that time:

La ferigoulo, mis ami,	Thyme, my friends,
Vai embauma noste païs.	Will scent our land.
Planten la ferigoulo,	Let's plant thyme,
Republican, arrapara!	Republicans, it will grow!
Fasen la farandoulo	Let's dance the farandole,
E la Mountagno flourira!	And the Mountain will bloom again.

Then we burned Lent in effigy, crying "Long live Marianne!" and waving our red sashes in the air. In short, we raised the devil.

The following morning when I got up—and I was not among the earliest to rise that day—my father was waiting for me, serious and solemn as on grave occasions. He said to me, "Frederi, come here, I have to speak to you."

"Oh, oh!" I thought to myself, "this is the moment the boiling water hits the wash!"

And going out of the house, walking ahead, with me behind (not saying a word), he led me to a ditch about a hundred paces from the house, made me sit down near him on the bank, and said to me, "What did I hear? that yesterday you joined a gang of those worthless characters who yell 'Vive Marianne!' that you danced the carmagnole! that you waved your red sash? Ah, my boy, you are young! It's with that dance and with those cries that the revolutionaries celebrated the scaffold. As if it weren't enough to have put in the papers a song where you sneer at the kings. But tell me, what have they done to you, those poor kings?"

At that question I confess I found myself at a loss for an answer. And my father went on, "Monsieur Durand-Maillane was a very learned man, for he presided over the Convention, but being wise as he was learned, he did not want to sign the death warrant of the king. And one day when he was conversing with the younger Pélissier, who was his nephew—we had neighboring farms, and my father, Master Antòni, happened to be with him—one day, I say, when he was conversing with his nephew Pélissier, who boasted of having voted for the death sentence, Monsieur Durand-Maillane said to him, 'You are young, Pélissier, you are young! and some day you will see, the people will pay with millions of heads for that of their king'— which was borne out all too truly, alas, by twenty years of harsh war."

"But this Republic," I replied, "doesn't want to do any harm. They have abolished the death penalty for political grounds. They have the foremost men of France in the provisional government, the astronomer Arago and the great poet Lamartine. The priests bless the trees of liberty. Besides, Father, if you will allow me to say so, isn't it true that before 1789 the nobles oppressed the peasants a little too much?"

"Oh," said my good father, "I'm not denying there were abuses, great abuses. And I'll give you an example. One day—I was probably no more than fourteen—I was coming from Saint-Rémy with a cartload of bundles of straw. The mistral was blowing, and I didn't hear the voice of the gentleman who came behind me in his carriage and who, it seems, shouted at me to get out of the way. That lordly person, who was a noble priest called Monsieur de Verclos, finally passed my cart, and as he came alongside, he lashed me across the face with a whip, leaving me covered with blood. Several peasants who were digging nearby were so indignant, my dear boy, that although the nobility was sacred then, they threw clods of dirt at him as long as they could see him. No, I don't deny that there were bad ones among the aristocrats. And the Revolution quite seduced us at the very beginning. Only it deteriorated little by little, and as always, the good paid for the bad."

That's enough to let you see the effect produced on me and in our village by the events of 1848. From the very first you would have said everything was going smoothly. To represent them in the National Assembly the Provençaux had very wisely sent the best who were there: men like Berryer, Lamartine, Lamennais, Béranger, Lacordaire, Garnier-Pagès, Marie, and a stevedore poet named Astouin. But the troublemakers, the partisans of the devil, soon poisoned everything. The June Days with their slaughter and their massacres horrified the nation. The moderates turned cool, the mad dogs became enraged, and a thick fog spread over my dream of a Platonic republic. Fortunately, a break in the clouds bathed me in sunshine at that time: it was nature's wide open spaces, the peace and order of country life. It was the triumph of Ceres, as the Roman poets said, at the time of harvest.

Now that machines have invaded agriculture, the tilling of the soil is losing its idyllic quality, its character as a sacred art, more and more. Now at harvest time you see a species of monstrous spider or gigantic crab called a "reaper" agitating its horrible claws across the plain, sawing the ears of grain with its blades, binding the sheaves with wire. Then when the grain is harvested, other steam-driven monsters arrive, "threshers," a species of dragon that gulps down the sheaves in their hoppers, roughing the ears, chopping the straw, sifting the grain. All that in American style, cheerlessly, in haste, without any joy or singing, around a furnace of red-hot coal, in a whirlwind of smoke and dust, with the uneasy fear of being ground up or dismembered if you don't watch out. That's progress, that's the terrible, inevitable harrow against which nothing can be done or said, the bitter fruit of science, from the scientific tree of good and evil.

But at the time I speak of, all the ancient, traditional ways and rituals were still observed. As soon as the ripening wheat turned the color of apricot, a messenger would set out from the town hall of Arles, traveling from village to village through the mountains, crying out to the sound of a horn, "In Arles they announce that the wheat is ripe."

At once the mountaineers, in teams of three, with their wives, their daughters, their mules, and their asses, would go trooping down to reap the harvest. Each team was composed of a pair of reapers and a young fellow or a girl to bind the sheaves. The men hired out in gangs of so many teams, according to the amount of work they contracted for. At the head of the gang was the foreman, who parceled out the work in the wheatfields, and a boss who directed the progress of the work.

As in the time of Cincinnatus, Cato, or Virgil, they harvested with a sickle (*falce recurva*), with the fingers of the left hand covered with cane guards to protect them from injury while cutting the wheat. In Arles about the feast of Saint John, you saw thousands of those contract workers on the Place des Hommes, some standing with their sickles in a curved wooden sheath called the *badoco* hanging behind their backs, others lying on the ground, waiting to be hired.

In the mountains they said that a man who had never worked as a reaper in the land of Arles had great difficulty finding a wife. The epic poem by Fèlis Gras, *The Charcoal-Burners*, revolves around that saying.

On our farm we hired seven or eight teams in an average

year. What a bustle in the household when that crowd arrived!
All sorts of special utensils were taken out of storage for them:
little willow barrels, harvesters' platters, big wine pitchers, oil
jugs, a whole battery of rough earthenware made at Apt. It was
a continuous festival, above all on the feast of Saint John, when
they danced a brawl around the fire, singing the song of the
harvesters from Mount Ventoux:

L'autre dimècre à Saut	Last Wednesday at Sault
Erian bèn vue cent sóuco.	We had a good eight hundred teams.

At daybreak, after the foreman had opened the way in the big
wheatfields, where the dew glistened on the golden ears, the
reapers lined up cheerfully, unsheathing their blades, and down
went the bunches of wheat! The girls who bound the sheaves
set to work—there were so many pretty ones chattering and
laughing, it was a pleasure to see them. Then when the sun
burst through with its sheaf of brilliant rays in the pink eastern
sky, the foreman, raising his sickle in the air, would cry,
"Another one!" When they had all greeted the dazzling orb, to
it again! the wheat fell in big fistfuls. From time to time the
boss turned around toward the gang and cried, "Is the sow
coming?" And the "sow" (that was the name of the last of the
group) answered, "The sow is coming." Then after four hours
of valiant effort, the foreman cried, "Wash!" All straightened
up, wiped their brows with the back of their hands, went to a
spring to wash off the blades of their sickles, sat down on the
sheaves in the midst of the stubble, and took their first meal
with this merry saying:

Benedicité de Crau,	The blessing of Crau,
Bono biasso, bon bàrrau.	Good food and good drink.

It was I who brought them their food in saddle baskets on our
mule Babacho. The reapers had five meals a day: about seven
o'clock, breakfast, consisting of a pickled anchovy spread on a
slice of bread dipped in vinegar and oil and a very hot red onion;
about ten o'clock, the "big drink," consisting of a hard-boiled
egg in its shell with a chunk of cheese; at one o'clock, dinner,

consisting of soup and boiled vegetables; about four o'clock, tea, a big salad with a "capon" of bread rubbed with garlic; and in the evening, supper, pork or lamb or a so-called "harvester" omelet, with onions. In the field they took turns drinking at the keg, which the foreman tipped, holding it on a stick, with one end supported on the drinker's shoulder. They had a cup or a tin goblet for three, that is, one per team. Similarly, there was only one plate among the three, from which each one took food with his wooden spoon.

That reminds me of one of our reapers, old Master Igoulen of Saint-Saturnin-lès-Apt, who believed that a witch had "taken water from him" and who had not tasted water for thirty years nor been able to eat anything that had been boiled. He lived on bread, salad, onions, cheese, and undiluted wine. When they asked him why he did without cooking, the old man would become silent. But here is the story his companions told.

One day in his youth when Igoulen and some friends were eating outside a cabaret, a gypsy passed by on the road, and as a joke he raised his glass of wine to her, crying, "To our health, granny, to our health!" "Much good may it do you!" replied the gypsy, "much good! and, sweetheart, pray God never to shun water!" That was a spell the witch had just cast on him. It was all over. From then on Master Igoulen was never able to drink water. That case of psychological influence, which I saw with my own eyes, can be added to the most curious instances, I believe, that science nowadays explains by the word "suggestion."

Behind the reapers you finally had the gleaners, picking up the ears left in the stubble. In Arles there were troops of them who traveled all over the region for a month. They slept in the fields under little so-called "gleaners'" tents to protect themselves against the mosquitoes, and a third of their gleaning went to the hospital, according to the custom of Arles.

Reader, these good children of nature are the people who were my models, I can tell you, and also my masters in poetry. It was there, with them, in the full light of the sun, stretched out under a willow tree, that I learned, reader, to play the reed pipe in a poem of four cantos entitled *The Harvests*, which included the lament of Margai, now in my *Golden Isles.* That attempt at Georgics began like this:

> Lou mes de jun e li blad que roussejon
> E lou grand-béure e la gaio meissoun
> E de Sant Jan li fiò que beluguejon,
> Vaqui de que parlaran mi cansoun,

> The month of June and the ripening wheat
> And the big drink and the joyful harvest
> And the twinkling fires of Saint John,
> This is what my songs shall sing,

and ended with an allusion to the Revolution of 1848 in the style of Virgil:

> Muso, emé tu, despièi la Madaleno,
> Se d'escoundoun cantan coume d'ourgueno
> Despièi lou mounde a vira d'aut en bas;
> E d'aquéu tèms que, nega dins la pas,
> De-long di riéu nòsti voues se mesclavon,
> D'amount li rèi à bóudre barrulavon
> Souto li cop di pople trop gibla,
> E, marridoun, li pople se chaplavon
> Coume à l'eiròu lis espigo de blad.

> Muse, since the feast of Mary Magdalen,
> Since the world has turned upside down,
> Although in hiding, we sing in unison;
> And while our voices blended
> Along the streams, drowned in peace,
> The kings went rolling down from on high
> Under the blows of people too long oppressed,
> And the people struck themselves, poor wretches,
> Like ears of wheat on the threshing floor.

But that was not quite the tone I wanted, and that is why it was never published. A simple legend that our reapers told every year was certainly better than all those thousands of lines of verse, and it belongs here like a stone in a ring. Master Igoulen told the story.

"That year the wheat had ripened almost all at once. There was a risk that it might be chopped by a hailstorm, stripped by the mistral, or blighted by some fog. And men were hard to find that year.

"And there was a farmer, a rich, miserly farmer, who stood at the door of his house with his arms crossed, waiting anxiously.

"'No, indeed,' he said, 'I wouldn't begrudge a crown a day, a fine crown as well as food, for whoever would come to work.'

"As he spoke, the sun rose, and three men came walking toward the farm, three robust reapers, one with a blond beard, one with a white beard, one with a black beard. The dawn surrounded them with its rays.

"'Master, God give you good day!' said the foreman (the one with the blond beard). 'We are three reapers from the mountains who have been told that you have ripe wheat and plenty. If you are willing to give us work, either on contract or by the day, we are here to work.'

"'My wheat's in no great hurry' replied the master. 'However, so as not to deny you work, I'll give you thirty sous and food, if you wish. That's quite enough at the rate things are now.'"

"Now it was the Lord, Saint Peter, and Saint John.

"When it was about seven o'clock, the hired boy of the household went with a white she-ass to bring them breakfast, and on his return to the house, the master said to him, 'Boy, what are the reapers doing?'

"'Master, I found them lying on the bank, sharpening their sickles, but they haven't cut down a single ear of wheat.'

"When it was about ten o'clock, the hired boy of the household went with the white she-ass to bring them the big drink. And on his return to the house, the master said to him, 'Boy, what are the reapers doing?'

"'Master, I found them lying on the bank, sharpening their sickles, but they haven't cut down a single ear of wheat.'

"When it was about midday, the hired boy of the household went with the white she-ass to bring them their dinner. And on his return to the house, the master said to him, 'Boy, what are the reapers doing?'

"'Master, I found them lying on the bank, sharpening their sickles, but they haven't cut down a single ear of wheat.'

"When it was about four o'clock, the hired boy of the household went with the white she-ass to bring them their tea. And on his return to the house, the master said to him, 'Boy, what are the reapers doing?'

"'Master, I found them lying on the bank, sharpening their sickles, but they haven't cut down a single ear of wheat.'

"'Those are lazy fellows,' said the master, 'who look for work and pray God to find none. However, I must go and see.'

"And having said that, the miser went quietly to his field, hid in a ditch, and watched his men. But the Lord then spoke to Saint Peter, 'Peter, strike some fire.'

"'Yes, Lord,' said Saint Peter.

"And Saint Peter drew the key to paradise from his jacket, applied a bit of tinder to a stone, and struck fire with the key.

"Then the Lord said to Saint John, 'Blow, John!'

"'Yes, Lord,' said Saint John.

"And thereupon Saint John blew sparks in the wheat. And from one bank to the other a whirlwind of flame and a big cloud of smoke enveloped the field. And quickly the flame fell, and quickly the smoke blew away. And thousands and thousands of sheaves suddenly appeared, properly cut, properly bound, and properly piled in shocks.

"And that done, the team sheathed its sickles and slowly walked toward the house for supper.

"'Master,' said the foreman during supper, 'we have finished the field. Where do you want us to harvest tomorrow?'

"'Foreman,' answered the miserly master, 'I have inspected the rest of my wheat, and it isn't ripe. Here is your money. I can give you no more work.'

"And with that the three men, the three handsome reapers, said to the master, 'May you be with God!' and carrying their sickles sheathed behind their backs, they went quietly on their way, the Lord in the middle, Saint Peter on the right, Saint John on the left. The last rays of the setting sun accompanied them far off in the distance.

"Early the following morning the master got up and said to himself gleefully, 'Never mind, I earned my day's wages yesterday watching those sorcerers! Now I know as much about it as they do.'

"And calling his two hired men—one of whom was called John and the other Peter—he led them to his biggest wheatfield. As soon as they were in the field, the master said to Peter, 'You, Peter, strike some fire.'

"'Yes, Master,' replied Peter.

"And Peter then drew his knife from his breeches, applied a bunch of tinder to a flint, and struck fire with the knife. Then the master said to John, 'Blow, John!'

'Yes, Master,' replied John.

"And John blew sparks in the wheat. Oh! oh! oh! a wildfire enveloped the harvest in tongues of flame. The ears of wheat caught fire, the stubble crackled, the grain turned to charcoal. And when the smoke cleared, the bloodsucker was crestfallen when he saw instead of sheaves only embers and charred straw."

X

AT AIX-EN-PROVENCE

fter the wine harvest that year (1848), my parents, seeing me gaping at the owl—or at the moon, if you prefer—sent me to Aix-en-Provence to study law. For they had understood that my diploma as Bachelor of Letters was not sufficient proof of wisdom or learning. But before I left for the city of Sextius, a tender and touching adventure befell me that I want to include here.

In a house not too far from ours, a family from the city had come to live whose daughters we sometimes met on the way to Mass. Toward the end of summer those girls came with their mother to our house to see us. And my mother hospitably offered them clabber. For since we had a fine flock of ewes, we had milk in abundance. It was my mother herself who put rennet in the milk right after milking and she herself who made the little cheeses when the milk was ready, those fresh cheeses of the region of Arles that Bellaud de la Bellaudière, the Provençal poet of the Valois era, found so good:

> A la vilo di Baus, pèr uno flourinado,
> Avès de froumajoun uno pleno faudado
> Que coumo sucre fin foundon au gargassoun.

> In the town of Les Baux for a florin,
> You get cheeses to fill an apron,
> That melt in your mouth like fine sugar.

Like the shepherdesses that Virgil sang, my mother went into the storeroom every day with her skimmer and with her earthenware "curdler" on her hip, and there, drawing the white clabber from the pot in fine curds, she poured it into the little holes of the round cheese tray. And afterward, when the cheeses were made, she let them drain properly on rushes— which I myself liked to go and cut in the streams.

And there we were eating a pan of clabber with those young ladies, and one of them, who appeared to be about my age, was rather pale, with a profile like those medals that are found in the ravine of Les Antiques at Saint-Rémy, with black eyes, big, languorous eyes always looking at me. Her name was Louïso.

We went to see the peacocks spreading their tails like rainbows in the yard, the bees and their hives all in a row sheltered from the wind, the bleating lambs penned in the fold, the well with its arbor on stone columns, in short, everything on the farm that could interest them. Louïso seemed to walk in ecstasy.

In the garden, while my mother spoke with hers and picked some choice pears for her sisters, the two of us sat on the parapet of the old pulley well.

"I must tell you this," said Mademoiselle Louïso suddenly. "Do you remember, Monsieur, a little dress, a muslin dress that your mother brought you when you were in boarding school at Saint-Michel-de-Frigolet?"

"Yes, indeed, to play a role in *The Children of Edward*."

"Well, that dress, Monsieur, was my dress."

"But haven't they given it back to you?" said I, like a fool.

"Oh, yes!" she said, a bit disconcerted, "I merely mentioned it as a topic of conversation."

Then her mother called her, "Louïso!"

The girl held out her hand to me, cold as ice. And as it was growing late, they left for their house.

A week later toward sunset Mademoiselle Louïso appeared on our doorstep again, this time accompanied only by a friend.

"Good evening," she said, "we came to buy several pounds of those choice pears you let us taste in your garden the other day."

"Sit down, young ladies," my mother said to them.

"Oh, no," she said, "we're in a hurry because it will soon be night."

And I accompanied them, I alone this time, to go pick the pears.

Louïso's friend was a beautiful girl from Saint-Rémy called Courrado, with luxuriant black curls under her Arlesian ribbon, whom the young lady, nice as she was, was not wise to bring with her.

In the garden, while I lowered a rather high branch of the tree, Courrado began picking, displaying her bulging bodice and raising her bare arms, her round arms, out of her sleeves. But Louïso, who looked very pale, said to her, "Courrado, you pick. And choose the ripest."

And she moved away with me as if she wanted to tell me something—while I was already disturbed, without knowing too well by which girl. We went slowly down a cypress walk where there was a stone bench. There we sat down next to each other, I embarrassed, she drinking me in with her eyes.

"Frederi," she said, "the other day I spoke to you of a dress I lent you when I was eleven to act in a tragedy at Saint-Michel-de-Frigolet. Have you read the story of Deianira and Hercules?"

"Yes," said I, laughing, "and also of the robe the beautiful Deianira gave poor Hercules that burned his blood."

"Ah, me!" said the young girl, "now it's just the reverse. For when I put on again that little dress of white muslin that you had touched, that you had worn, I loved you from that moment. Don't be angry with me for this declaration—which must seem strange to you, which must seem mad to you—oh, don't be angry with me!' she continued, crying, "for that divine fire, that fire which came to me from the fateful dress, that fire, Frederi, which has consumed me for seven years, I have kept hidden in my heart until now!"

I kissed her feverish little hand and wanted to respond by embracing her. But she gently pushed me away, saying, "No, we cannot know, Frederi, if the poem whose first canto I wrote will ever have a second. I must leave now. Think of what I have told you. And since I am one who does not take back her word, whatever you may reply, you have in me a soul that has given itself for ever."

She rose, and running toward her friend Courrado, she said, "Come quickly, let's weigh and pay for the pears."

And with that we went back. They paid, they left, leaving me with my heart in turmoil, bewitched and agitated by that visitation of maidens, each of whom appeared desirable to me in her own way. For a long time I watched the turtle doves flying off in the distance among the trees in the last rays of the fading day.

But exhilarated and happy as I was, upon reflection I saw that I was in a muddle. It's all very well for the *Pervigilium Veneris* to say:

> Que deman ame, aquéu qu'amè jamai,
> E quau amè, que deman ame mai!

> May he love tomorrow who never loved,
> And he who loves still love tomorrow.

But love cannot be controlled. That brave girl, armed only with her virtue and her charm, could in her infatuation well believe that she had won the victory. Charming as she was and charmed by her long dreams of love, she could well believe that "love excuses no lover from loving" as Dante says (*"Amor ch'a null' amato amar perdona"*), that a young man like me, isolated on a farm, in the flower of youth, must immediately thrill to his first wooing. But love is the giving and abandonment of all our being, and the soul sometimes acts like a bird that flees when called, if it feels itself pursued and about to be captured. Or like the swimmer, who always experiences an instinctive fear at the moment of diving into a deep pool of water.

The fact is that I proceeded cautiously in the face of that chain of flowers and fragrant roses that opened up before me. And without willing it, I felt myself drawn toward the other one, the confidante, who out of her sense of duty as a devoted friend seemed to avoid my approach and my look. For, to tell the truth, I had formed my own particular idea of love and the beloved at that age. Yes, I had imagined that sooner or later somewhere in the region of Arles I would meet some magnificent farm girl, dressed like a queen in Arlesian costume, galloping on her mare with a trident in hand in the roundups of the Crau, who, after I had courted her a long time with my love songs, would allow herself to be brought to our farm one fine day, to reign there like my mother over a society of shepherds, cowboys, plowmen, and silkworm growers. It seemed that I already dreamed of my Mirèio, and although I neither could nor dared to admit it, that vision of a type of powerfully sensual beauty which I had already hatched in my mind did great harm to poor Louïso, who was too much of a young lady to fulfill my dream.

Then a correspondence began between her and me, or rather an exchange of love and friendship, which lasted more than three years (all the time I stayed at Aix), I politely going along with her attachment to dissuade her little by little if I could, she more and more painful and insistent, sending me despairing farewells in letter after letter. Here is the last of those letters that I received. I reproduce it word for word:

> I have loved but once, and I shall die, I swear to you, with the name of Frederi engraved all alone in my heart. How many sleepless nights have I spent dreaming of my unhappy fate! But yesterday, in reading your vain consolations, I made such a violent effort to restrain my tears that my heart grew weak. The doctor says that I have a fever, that it was an attack of nerves, that I need a rest.
>
> "A fever!" I cried out, "ah, if it were the right one!"
>
> And already I felt happy to die, to go and await you off there, where your letters offer to meet me. But listen, Frederi, since it is so. When they tell you—and it won't be long now—when they tell you that I have left the world, give me, I beg of you, a tear and a sigh of regret. Twelve years ago I made a promise to ask God every day to make you happy, perfectly happy. Well, I have never failed, and I shall be faithful till my last breath. But you, Frederi, I ask you out of kindness, when you are out walking, if you see yellow leaves rolling in your path, think a little of my life, stained with tears and withered with sorrow. And if you see a brook flowing gently, listen to its lamentation, and it will tell you how I loved you. And if some little bird brushes you with its wings, lend an ear to its warbling, and it will tell you that I, poor little thing, am always with you. Oh, Frederi, I implore you, never forget Louïso!

This was the crowning farewell, sealed with her blood, that the young virgin sent me, with a little medal of the Virgin Mary which she had covered with kisses, in a little case of crimson velvet, on whose cover she had embroidered my initials with her chestnut hair in the middle of a sprig of ivy.

| Iéu lou clot d'èurre me farai, | I shall become the shoot of ivy, |
| T'embrassarai. | I shall embrace you. |

Ah, poor little Louïso! some time after that she took the veil as a nun and died, poor thing, a few years later. After all these years I am still deeply moved by the melancholy of that blighted love, that love cut down before its time. Oh Louïso, I dedicate this pitiful remembrance to you and offer it to your shade, wandering perhaps around me.

The city of Aix, "capital of justice" (as they used to say), where I had come then to study the "written law," because of its past as the capital of Provence and as a parliamentary city, has a reputation for grave and haughty demeanor that would seem to contrast with the Provençal style. The grand air of its shaded Cours Mirabeau, its monumental fountains and noble town houses, plus the crowd of lawyers, magistrates, professors, members of the legal profession of every stripe that you meet in its streets, contribute much to its solemn, not to say cold, aspect. But in my time at least, that was only on the surface. And among the young men of Aix, as I recall, there was a brand of familiar humor, a native gaiety that derived, it would seem, from the traditions left by good King René.

You had learned counselors and presiding judges who entertained themselves in their drawing rooms and in their country houses by playing the little Provençal drum. At the Academy grave men like Doctor d'Astros, the brother of a cardinal, read their own writings in the language of Provence. This was one way to cultivate the regional spirit, and it never diminished in Aix, where Count Portalis, one of the great jurists of the Code Napoléon, wrote a comedy in Provençal. And in the reign of Louis XVIII, Monsieur Diouloufet, a librarian of the Athens of the South (as Aix is sometimes called), sang a poem about "Silkworms."

Monsieur Mignet, the illustrious historian and academician, came to Aix every year to play *boules* and had even laid down the following maxim: To put new life into a man nothing is better than walking in the sunshine, speaking Provençal, eating *brandade*, and playing a game of *boules* every morning.

Monsieur Borély, a former attorney general, used to enter the city on horseback, dressed in gaiters like a rich herdsman, proudly driving a herd of English pigs. And people said of him, "He who drives his own pigs is not a swineherd."

The day after Christmas we used to go to Saint-Sauveur to hear the *Lamentations of Saint Stephen* recited in Provençal (as they are to this day) by a canon of the chapter. And on the feast of Kings they performed the carol "This morning I met the retinue" in that cathedral with spectacular pomp (as they still do).

At the church of the Holy Spirit the ladies liked to listen to the sermons Father Emery preached in Provençal. And at Carnival time and the season of soirées people in high society had themselves carried in sedan chairs to keep from spoiling their elegant costumes and were accompanied by torch-bearers who put out their torches at the extinguisher on arrival at the entrance.

It was not unusual to have several big elopements in the course of a winter, like that of a beautiful Jewish woman with Monsieur de Castillon, who managed to spend a fortune lavishly as "Prince of Love" in the Corpus Christi Games.

Speaking of those games, during my stay in Aix I had the opportunity to see them come out for, I believe, the last or the second last time: the King of the Inkstand, the Abbot of Youth, the Slaughtered Innocents, the Devil, the Watch, the Queen of Sheba, above all the Hobby Horses with their rigadoon that Bizet took for Daudet's *Arlésienne*:

Madamo de Limagno	Madame de Limagne
Fa dansa lei Chivau-frus;	Makes the Hobby Horses dance;
Li douno de castagno,	She gives them horse chestnuts,
Dison que n'en vouelon plus:	They say they want no more:
E danso, o gus! e danso, o gus!	So dance, beggar! dance, beggar!
Madamo de Limagno	Madame de Limagne
Fa dansa lei Chivau-frus.	Makes the Hobby Horses dance.

I was deeply impressed by that revival of the Provençal past with its naive old games of long ago, as you can see in the tenth canto of *Calendau*, where I have described them just as I saw them.

Now just imagine that after I had been in Aix several months, as I was taking a stroll on the Cours one afternoon, what in the name of good fellowship did I see emerging to the right of the Fontaine-Chaude but the hooked nose of my friend Ansèume Mathieu of Châteauneuf.

"They weren't joking," said Mathieu in his unruffled way when he saw me, "that water's really hot, my friend, you can certainly say that one steams!"

"But how long have you been in Aix?" I asked, shaking his hand.

"Since, let's see," he said, "since night before last."

"And what good wind brings you here?"

"Well," he said, "I said to myself, Now that young Mistral is in Aix studying law, you must go there and study it too."

"What a good idea," I said, "Ansèume, you can't imagine how delighted I am. But did you pass your baccalaureate?"

"Oh," he said, laughing, "I passed like cheap wine when it's pressed."

"The fact is, my poor Ansèume, I believe you have to have your bachelor's degree to be admitted to the Law School."

"Why, you simple soul!" my good friend Mathieu said to me, "suppose they don't want to give me a diploma like the others, come now, could they prevent me from taking my degree in the Law of Love? Listen, just a short while ago, as I was strolling in a little valley called La Torse, I met a young laundress—who was a bit dark, perhaps, but who had a red mouth, the teeth of a little dog all set to bite, two little curly locks straying out from under her little white coif, a bare neck, a turned up nose, plump arms. . . ."

"Go on, you rogue, you seem to have eyed her pretty thoroughly."

"No, Frederi," he said, "you mustn't believe that I, a scion of the Marquises of Montredon, foolish as I am, would go and fall in love with a pretty little face from a laundry. I don't know if you're like me, but when I run into a pretty face, even if it's only a cat's, I can't help turning around to look. Anyhow, when I chatted with that little girl, we agreed that she would launder my linens and would come get them next week."

"Mathieu, you're a great scoundrel and a rake, and you smell like you're on fire."

"No," he said, "look, you're mistaken. Let me finish. As I made this arrangement with my laundress, while we were talking, I saw through the suds between her fingers that she was scrubbing a lace blouse, and I said to the girl, 'What devilishly fine linen! that blouse isn't meant to cover the bosom of an aging slut!' 'Far from it,' she replied, 'that's the blouse of one of the most beautiful ladies of the rue des Nobles, a baroness of thirty, married, unfortunately, to an old graybeard judge who's jealous as a Turk.' 'But she must be bored to death, poor thing.' 'Bored, indeed! She's constantly on her balcony looking as if she was waiting for a lover to keep her company.' 'And what's her name?' 'Ah, Monsieur, now you want to know too much. Look, I do laundry. But otherwise, I don't meddle in what doesn't concern me.' And I wasn't able to get more out of her for the moment. But," added Mathieu, "when she comes to my room to get my laundry, I may have to kiss her two or three times, but she'll have to be clever if I don't worm it out of her."

"And when you know the name of the baroness?"

"Then, my friend, I shall have bread on my table for three years. While you poor law students are going to punish yourselves, picking over the Code Napoléon, I am going to quietly study the gentle 'Laws of Love' under the balcony of my beautiful baroness like the troubadours of old Provence."

And the three years we spent in Aix went just as I tell you, and so did the quest and the study of the chivalrous Mathieu.

Oh, the outings to the bridge over the Arc on the Marseille highway, ankle-deep in dust! Oh, the parties at Le Tholonet, where we went to drink the spiced wine of Langesse! And the duels between students in the valley of Infernets, with pistols loaded with goat turds! And that lovely trip we made by stagecoach to Toulon, passing through the woods of Cuge and crossing the gorges of Ollioules!

Lord, we did more or less what students had done at the time of the Popes of Avignon and the time of Queen Jano. Listen to what the satirist Antonius de Arena wrote about it in the time of Francis I:

> Touti lis estudiant soun de galànti gènt
> E sèmpre an abitudo d'ama li bèlli chato;
> E sèmpre pèr braga, dintre li calignaire,
> La primo glori, bèu mignot, revèn à-n-éli;
> E banqueton e bragon e fan tripet-pelori;
> E quant à la bounta, vès, soun bon sènso fin.
>
> (*Di gentilesso dis Estudiant*)

> All the students are gallant fellows,
> And always in love with pretty girls;
> And always bragging among themselves
> That their sweetheart wins the prize;
> And they feast and swagger and raise the devil;
> And as for goodness, why, they are infinitely good.
>
> (*Of the Courtesy of Students*)

While we were thus affecting the art of the troubadours in the noble city of the Counts of Provence, Roumanille in Avignon was being more sensible and publishing in a polemical newspaper called *The Commune* those shrewd, hearty, pungent dialogues, such as "Thyme," "A Red and a White," and "The Priests," which displayed Provençal prose to advantage and made it popular. Then with that determination and authority which had already resulted in the successful publication of his *Daisies* and his bold pamphlets, he brought together on the ground floor of his newspaper all the troubadours of that time, young and old. And from that rallying came the anthology *Provençal Poems*, which a distinguished professor then at Montpellier, Monsieur Saint-René Taillandier, introduced to the public in a cordial and learned preface (published by Seguin in Avignon, 1852).

That first collection included poems by old Doctor d'Astros and Gaut of Aix; Aubert, Bellot, Bénédit, Bourrelly, and Barthélemy (the author of *Nemesis*) of Marseille; Boudin, Cassan, and Giéra from Avignon; Bonnet from Beaucaire; Gautier from

Tarascon; Reybaud and Dupuy, who were from Carpentras; Castil-Blaze from Cavaillon; Crousillat from Salon; Garcin, "the fiery son of the blacksmith of Alleins" (as I wrote in *Mirèio*); Mathieu from Châteauneuf; Chalvet from Nyons, and others. Plus a sampling from Languedoc: Moquin-Tandon, Peyrottes, Lafare-Alais, and a poem by Jasmin. But the greatest number were by Roumanille, then at the height of his powers, whose "Crèches" Sainte-Beuve had hailed as worthy of Klopstock. Here too, Teodor Aubanel, then in his twenty-second year, also contributed his first masterstrokes, "The 9th of Thermidor," "The Reapers," and "On All Saints' Day." Finally I, inflamed with the finest ardor, provided ten poems ("Bitterness," "The Mistral," "A Bullfight") with one, "Hello, Everybody," that took note of our beginnings:

> Atrouverian dedins li jas,
> Vestido em' un marrit pedas,
>   La lengo prouvençalo.
> En anant paisse lou troupèu,
> Lou caud avié bruni sa pèu,
> La pauro avié que si long pèu
>   Pèr curbi sis espalo.
> E de jouvenome, vaqui,
> En varaiant aperaqui,
>   De la vèire tant bello,
> Se sentiguèron esmougu:
> Que siegon dounc li bèn-vengu,
> Car l'an vestido à soun degu
>   Coume uno damisello.

> We found her in a sheepfold,
> Dressed in ugly rags,
>   The Provençal tongue.
> The heat had tanned her skin
> As she led her flock to graze;
> The poor thing had only her hair,
>   To cover her shoulders.
> Then along came some young men,
> Who as they happened by,
>   Seeing her so beautiful,
> Were overcome with feeling.

So may they be welcome here,
For they have dressed her properly
Like a young lady.

But I haven't finished the story of Mathieu's love affair with the baroness of Aix. Every time I ran into this student of the "Laws of Love," I said to him, "Well, Mathieu, how are we doing?"

"We are doing so well," he said, "that Leleto" (that was the name of his laundress) "finally pointed out the baroness' house to me. I have gone under the caryatids of her balcony again and again, my friend, so many times that—Lord, I give you thanks—I have been noticed. And the lady, a beauty such as you have never seen, the lady, enchanted with her courtly knight, deigned the other evening to let a carnation fall on me—from heaven!"

As he said that, Mathieu showed me a faded flower and, making sheep's eyes, sent a kiss flying into the blue.

A month passed, two months passed, and I no longer ran into Mathieu. I said to myself, I must go see him. So I went up to his little room, and what did I find? My friend Ansèume with his foot on a chair, who said to me, "Come right in, let me tell you about my accident. Just imagine, friend, I had found the way into the garden of my divine baroness one night at eleven o'clock. Everything was arranged. Leleto (my good laundress) gave us a hand. I planned to climb a rose bush—you know, one of those rose bushes growing on a trellis—up to a window where my lady was to reach out her arms to be kissed. I was already climbing. My heart, believe me, was beating pitapat. Dear God, all at once the window slowly opened halfway. The slats of the Venetian blind were raised. A hand, Frederi, a hand—I knew right away that it was not the baroness'—shook pipe ashes on my nose! As you can imagine, I didn't wait for anything more. I slid to the ground, ran, jumped over the garden wall, and crash! sprained my ankle, curse the luck!"

You can imagine how we laughed till our jaws ached.

"But have you called a doctor?"

"Oh," he said, "it's not worth the trouble. Leleto's mother

happens to be a conjuress. (Perhaps you know them. They have a tavern near the Porte d'Italie). They made me soak my foot in a bucket of salt water. The old woman muttered several spells and made three signs of the cross over me with her big toe. Then they bandaged me. And now I am reading Roumanille's *Daisies*, while waiting for God to heal me. But I'm not languishing," he said, "for Leleto brings me my meals twice a day. And for want of thrushes, as the proverb says, one eats little blackbirds."

Now, did my friend Mathieu, the well-named future "Félibre of Kisses," who was all his life the greatest daydreamer I ever knew, dream the story I have just told you? I was never able to find out. And I have told the story just as he told it to me.

XI

BACK TO THE FARM

nce I had my law degree, as indeed did so many others (and as you have seen, I didn't work too hard), I came home, proud as a young rooster that has found a worm. I arrived at the hour when they were about to have supper outdoors on the stone table under the arbor in the last rays of the setting sun.

"Good evening, everyone!"

"God give it to you, Frederi!"

"Father, Mother, all is well. This time, it's all over."

"And a fine deliverance!" added Madaleno, the young house servant from the Piedmont.

And when I had stood in front of all the farmhands and given an account of my last ordeal, my venerable father, without further question, only said to me, "Now, my fine lad, I have done my duty. You know far more than they ever taught me. It's up to you to choose your course. I leave you free."

"A great many thanks!" I replied.

Then and there—I was twenty-one at the time—with my foot on the threshold of my father's house and my eyes turned toward the Alpilles, I made a silent vow to myself: first, to raise and revive in Provence the traditional spirit that was being destroyed by all the schools and their false and unnatural education; second, to promote that revival by restoring the natural and historical language of the country, against which all the schools were waging a war to the death; third, to bring Provençal back into fashion through the benign influence and divine fire of poetry.

All that was rumbling vaguely inside me, but I felt it just as I tell you. And full of that rising tide, of that seething Provençal sap that filled me with vigor, open to all literary influence or mastery, strengthened with the freedom that gave me wings, confident that nothing more would disturb me, one evening during seedtime, as I watched the farmhands following the plow in the furrow, singing as they went—glory be to God!—I began the first canto of *Mirèio*.

That poem, a love child, grew very quietly, little by little, in a gentle breeze or in the heat of the sun or in the blasts of the mistral, during a time when I was managing the farm under the direction of my father, who on reaching his eightieth year had become blind.

All I wanted was first to please myself, then several friends of my early youth, as I wrote in one song in *Mirèio*:

> O dous ami de ma jouvènço,
> Alenas moun camin de voste sant alen.

> Oh, dear friends of my youth,
> Breathe a prayer on my journey.

We did not think of Paris in that innocent time. Enough if Arles—which was my horizon, as Mantua was Virgil's—would one day recognize its poetry in mine. That was my remote ambition. And that's why I could say, thinking of the country folk of Crau and Camargue:

> Car cantan que pèr vautre, o pastre e gènt di mas.

> We sing only for you, shepherds and people of the farms.

To tell the truth, I had only the rough outline of a plan and that only in my head. Here it is: I had decided to make love blossom between two beautiful Provençal children of different circumstances, and then to let the ball of yarn run its course, drifting before the wind at random in the unpredictable way of life.

Mirèio, that poetic name born under a lucky star, was predestined to be the name of my heroine. For I had heard it at home from the cradle, but only in our house. Dear Nanounet, my maternal grandmother, when she wanted to compliment one of her daughters, would say, "That's Mirèio, that's my love, my beautiful Mirèio!" And my mother, if she wanted to tease some girl, would say, "Now look at her, Mirèio my love!"

But when I asked about that Mirèio, no one knew more than that. The story was lost, leaving only the name of the heroine and an aura of beauty in a mist of love. That was enough to bring luck to a poem which was perhaps—who knows?—the reconstruction of a genuine romance by poetic intuition.

At that time the Judge's Farm was a breeding ground of limpid poetry, Biblical as well as idyllic. Living and singing all around me was that poem of Provence framed by the Alpilles with their azure background, which dazzled you as soon as you went outdoors. I could see Mirèio going by, not only in my youthful dreams but also in person, sometimes in those pretty girls of Maillane who came to pick mulberry leaves for the silkworms, sometimes in those happy girls with their white coifs and their half-opened bodices who came and went in the wheatfields, among the haystacks, the grapevines, and the olive trees, weeding or haying or gathering grapes or olives.

The actors in my drama, my plowmen, my harvesters, my cowherds and shepherds, came and went from dawn to dark, arousing my youthful enthusiasm. Could you want a finer old man, one more patriarchal, more worthy to be the model for my Master Ramoun than old Francés Mistral, whom everyone, even my mother, called "the Master"? Poor father, sometimes when the work was demanding, when they needed a hand to bring in the hay or direct the water of the pulley-well, he would shout from outdoors, "Where's Frederi?"

Even if I was stretched out under a willow tree at that moment, loafing in search of a rhyme, my dear mother would answer, "He's writing." And the good man would immediately soften his rough voice, and say, "You mustn't disturb him." For though he had never read anything but Holy Scripture and *Don Quixote* when he was young, writing was to him a sacred act.

And the beginning of a tale they used to tell at our house
(which I shall speak of again in connection with the word
"Félibre") demonstrates that respect for the mystery of writing:

> Mounsegne Sant Ansèume legissié, escrivié.
> Un jour de sa santo escrituro,
> A mounta au cèu sus lis auturo. . . .

> Monsignor Saint Anselm was reading and writing.
> One day from his holy writing,
> He rose to heaven on high. . . .

Another individual who had the unconscious knack of fasci-
nating my epic muse was my cousin Tourrette from the village
of Mouriès: a great big block of a man, lame but powerfully
built, with big leather gaiters on his shoes, known far and wide
on the plains of Crau by the name of "Major" because he had
been a drum major in the national guards recruited by the Duc
d'Angoulême in 1815 to oppose Napoleon on his return from
the island of Elba. In his youth he had gambled away his posses-
sions, and when he was old and in extreme need, he used to
come to the farm every winter to spend two weeks with us.
Then when he left, my father would give him several bushels of
wheat. In the summer he traveled around the Crau and the
Camargue, helping the shepherds when they sheared the
sheep, the farmers with the threshing, the marsh-dwellers in
making sheaves of reeds, or finally, the salt-makers in gather-
ing salt. That is why he knew the land of Arles and its agricul-
ture as no one else did, surely. He knew the names of the farms,
the pastures, the head shepherds, the ranches that bred horses
and wild bulls, the cowboys, and he spoke of everything with an
exuberant, picturesque, noble use of Provençal expressions
that was a pleasure to hear. For example, to say that Count de
Mailly was very rich in property with buildings on it, he would
say, "He owns seven acres of roofs."

The girls who picked olives—of whom there was a multitude
at Mouriès—would hire him to tell them stories in the evening.
They each gave him, I believe, one sou per evening. And he
made them die laughing, for he knew all the stories, indecent or

otherwise, that are transmitted by word of mouth among the people, such as "Jan and the Cow," "Jan and the Mule," "Jan and the Bear," "The Scavenger," etc.

Once the snow began to fall, we would say, "There now, our cousin will soon appear."

And he never failed.

"Hello, Cousin!"

"Cousin, hello!"

With that, when he had shaken hands and humbly placed his stick behind the door, he sat down at the table and ate a slice of bread with sharp cheese spread, then immediately launched forth on the olive harvest. And he said that there were so many olives down there in Mouriès that the mills could not keep up.

"How cozy you are in those olive mills when it's cold!" he used to say. "With your legs spread out over the nice warm squeezings, you watch by lamplight as the men, stripped to the waist and agile as cats, all push the bar to press the olives on the orders of the boss, 'Heave! that's it! another one! go on, another good one! ho, give it all you've got there!' "

Cousin Tourrette, who like all daydreamers was a bit lazy, had dreamed all his life of having a job that required hardly any work.

"And what job would you like, Cousin?" I would ask him.

"I'd like the job of codfish counter in one of those big warehouses in Marseille, where a man can earn his twelve hundred francs a year (I've been led to believe) sitting down and counting the dozens as they unload them."

That poor old Major! He died like so many others, without having fulfilled his dream of codfish.

Nor shall I forget the woodcutter Siboul among my collaborators or, to tell the truth, those who inspired the poetry of *Mirèio.* A good man from Montfrin, dressed in corduroy, he came at the end of autumn every year and neatly trimmed our willow branches with his big pruning hook. While he cut and matched the sticks into fagots, he made all kinds of precise observations to me on the Rhone, its currents, its whirlpools, its bays and its backwaters, its gravel bars and its islands, and on the wildlife that lives on its banks, the otters that den in hollow trees, the beavers that cut down trees big as your thigh, the titmice that hang their nests on the boughs of white poplars at Les Ségonnaux, and the willow-weavers and basket-makers of Vallabrègue!

Finally there was our neighbor Savié, a peasant herbalist who told me the names (in Provençal) and properties of the plants and of all the herbs of Saint John and Saint Roch. That's how I acquired my slight knowledge of literary botany—fortunately!—for without wishing to insult our teachers of high or low schools, I believe they would have been hard put to tell a thistle from a sow-thistle.

In the midst of this preamble to *Mirèio*, the new coup d'état of December 2, 1851, burst like a bomb. Although I was not one of those fanatics for whom the Republic took the place of religion, justice, and homeland, although the Jacobins had disillusioned and wounded me more than once with their intolerance, their rage for novelty, and their cold crude materialism, I was indignant at the government's crime in tearing up the law it had sworn to uphold. I was indignant, for it destroyed all my illusions that the French Republic could be the nursery of future federations.

Several friends from law school who had collaborated in politics took command of the insurgent bands that arose in the Var in the name of the Constitution. But the majority, in Provence as elsewhere, welcomed the change in regime, some disgusted with party strife, others flabbergasted at the similarity to the First Empire. Who could have guessed that the new Empire was to break down in a monstrous war and the nation's collapse?

To conclude, I want to quote what was said to me by Taxile Delord—although he was a republican deputy from Vaucluse—one day after 1870 when we were taking a walk together on the Place de l'Horloge in Avignon: "The most spectacular blunder that was ever made by the progressive party was the Revolution of 1848. For we had a fine governing family—French, patriotic, the most liberal of all, and even willing to compromise with the Revolution—from which we could obtain all the liberties progress allows without agitating. And we banished it.

Why? To make way for this infamous Empire which has caused the downfall of France!"

Anyhow, as a result I left inflammatory politics behind forever, like the baggage you abandon along the way to travel more lightly. And I gave myself over entirely to you, my Provence, and to you, Poetry, who have never given me anything but pure joy.

And one evening when I was in a state of meditation, walking in search of rhymes—for when I wrote poetry, I always hit upon my lines while walking around the countryside—I met an old man called "Gallant Jan" watching his sheep. It was a starry night, the owl was crying, and the following dialogue, which you may have read in my friend Daudet's translation, resulted from that encounter.

Shepherd: You are far from home, Monsieur Frederi.

I: I am taking a little stroll, Master Jan.

Shepherd: Are you going on a tour of the stars?

I: Master Jan, you have guessed it. I am so surfeited, disheartened, and disgusted with the things of this Earth that I would like to sail off into space tonight, up there in the kingdom of stars.

Shepherd: Look at me, I hardly spend a night without wandering there, and I can assure you it's a most beautiful voyage.

I: But how do you find your way in that vast emptiness of light?

Shepherd: If you want to follow me, I'll take you there at a gentle pace while my flock is feeding. And I'll show you everything.

I: Gallant Jan, I take you at your word.

Shepherd: Here, let's go up this path that is whitening the sky from north to south. It's Saint James's Way. It goes from France straight to Spain. When Emperor Charlemagne made war against the Saracens, Saint James of Galicia marked it in front of him to show him the way.

I: That's what the pagans named the "Milky Way."

Shepherd: That may be, but I tell you what I have always heard. Look, do you see that beautiful wagon with four wheels lighting up all the northern sky? That's the Chariot of Souls.

The three stars in front are the three Draft Animals, and the little one you see near the third is the Driver.

I: That's what the books call the Great Bear.

Shepherd: As you please. Look, look at the stars falling all around. Those are poor souls who have just entered heaven. Let's make the sign of the cross, Monsieur Frederi.

I: Beautiful angels (as they say), may God go with you!

Shepherd: Look, there's a beautiful star shining like fire up there not far from the Wagon. It's the Herdsman of the Sky.

I: Which astronomers call Arcturus.

Shepherd: Never mind. Now look there to the north, that star that just barely twinkles. That's the Star of the Sea or, if you prefer, the North Star. It's always visible and serves as a beacon to sailors, who consider themselves lost when they lose sight of the North Star.

I: So the Pole Star, as it is also called, is in the Little Bear. And since the north wind comes from there, the sailors of Provence, like those of Italy, say they are "going to the Bear" when they sail against the wind.

Shepherd: Let's turn around and see the Chicken Coop or, if you prefer, the Louse Bed, twinkling.

I: Which scholars call the Pleiades and Gascons call the Dog Cart.

Shepherd: That's right. A little lower down are the brightly shining Signs that mark the hours for the shepherds. Some call them the Three Kings, others the Three Staffs or the Rake or the Scythe Handle.

I: Exactly, it's Orion or Orion's Belt.

Shepherd: Right. Still to the south and lower yet is Jan of Milan.

I: I could be mistaken, but it looks like Sirius.

Shepherd: Jan of Milan is the stars' torch. One day Jan of Milan was invited to a wedding, they say, along with the Signs and the Chicken Coop, the wedding of the beautiful Magalouno, of whom we'll speak in a moment. The Chicken Coop, who was an early riser, left first, they say, and took the high road. The Signs, who are three bright girls, cut across lower down and finally caught up. Jan of Milan, who had gone on sleeping, took the short cut when he woke up, ran after the Signs, and sent his stick flying after them to stop them. Which is why the Scythe Handle has since been called Jan of Milan's Stick.

I: And that one away off there that has just poked its nose above the mountain?

Shepherd: That's the Cripple. He was invited to the wedding too, but since he's lame, poor fellow, he doesn't travel very fast. He gets up late and goes to bed early.

I: And that one going down there in the west sparkling like a bride?

Shepherd: Well now, there she is! the Shepherd's Star, the Morning Star, that gives us light at dawn when we turn the flock loose or in the evening when we enclose it again. She's the Queen of Stars, the Beautiful Star, Magalouno, the Beautiful Magalouno, pursued by Pèire of Provence, and every seven years they marry.

I: The conjuction, I believe, of Venus with Jupiter or sometimes with Saturn.

Shepherd: As you wish. But here, Shep!—while we were chatting, the sheep have strayed—here, here, bring them back! Oh, that bitch of a dog, she's a real strumpet! I see that I must go there myself. Well now, Monsieur Frederi, you take care not to get lost.

I: Goodbye, Gallant Jan.

Let us also, like the shepherd, return to our sheep. Beginning with *Provençal Poems*, the anthology on which young and old poets of that time had collaborated, some of us continued to correspond on the subject of the language and our work, and those increasingly enthusiastic exchanges gave birth to the idea of a gathering of Provençal poets. And at the summons of Roumanille and Gaut, who had written a joint invitation in the periodical *Bouillabaise*, the meeting took place in Arles on August 29, 1852, in a room of the old archbishop's palace, with the gentle Doctor d'Astros, eldest of the poets, presiding.

That's where we all became acquainted with one another: Aubanel, Aubert, Bourrelly, Cassan, Crousillat, Désanat, Garcin, Gaut, Gelu, Giéra, Mathieu, Roumanille, I, and others.

Thanks to the good artist from Carpentras, Bonaventuro Laurens, our portraits had the honor of appearing in *L'Illustration* (September 18, 1852).

Roumanille had written to Monsieur Moquin-Tandon, who was a professor at the Faculty of Science in Toulouse and a witty poet in his Montpellier idiom, asking him to bring Jasmin to Arles. But when Moquin-Tandon wrote to the illustrious singer of "Martha the Mad," do you know what he replied? "When you go to Arles," he said, "tell them that even if there are forty or a hundred at the gathering, they will never make as much noise as I've made all by myself."

"That's Jasmin from head to foot, isn't it?" Roumanille said to me. "Such a reply portrays him much more faithfully than the bronze they raised in his honor at Agen. Jasmin was what you call a proud bugger."

For that matter, in spite of his genius, the barber of Agen was always unpleasant to those who wanted to sing in our language like himself. Speaking of which, Roumanille had sent him his *Daisies* several years before, dedicating "Madaleno," one of his finest poems, to him. Jasmin did not deign to reply with thanks. But when the Gascon came to Avignon about 1848 to give a concert with the harpist Mademoiselle Roaldès, Roumanille went up with several others after the reading to greet the poet who had made everyone cry when he recited "My Memories":

Ount bas, pairi?—Moun fil, à l'espital. . .
Acò 's aqui que lous Jansemins moron.

"Where are you going, grandfather?" "To the hospital, my boy.
That's where the Jasmins go to die."

"And who are you?" the man from Agen asked the one from Saint-Rémy.

"One of your admirers, Jóusè Roumanille."

"Roumanille? I remember that name. But I thought it was that of a dead author."

"Monsieur," replied the author of *Daisies*, who never let anyone step on his corns, "you can see that I am still young enough to write your epitaph some day, God willing."

One who was much more gracious toward the gathering in

Arles was that good fellow Reboul, who wrote to us: "May God bless your table! May your contests be festive, may the rivals become friends! He who made the heavens made those of our country big enough and blue enough so that there is room for all the stars."

And another writer from Nîmes, Jùli Canonge, added: "My friends, if some day you must defend your cause, don't forget that your first meeting was held in Arles, that you were guided by the stars in that proud, noble city, whose coat of arms and motto are 'The sword and the lion's wrath.' "

I don't remember what I said or sang. I only know that I was there in a trance when I saw the next day dawning. And as Roumanille said in his speech at Montmajour in 1889, it appears that I was "daydreaming, lost in thought, and the seven rays of the Star already gleamed in my young eyes."

Our gathering at Arles had been too successful not to be repeated. The following year, on August 21, 1853, the Poets' Festival met at Aix-en-Provence on the initiative of Gaut, the jovial poet of Aix, with twice as many present as the first time. There the great Breton bard Brizeux welcomed us with a greeting in which he said:

> Le rameau d'olivier couronnera vos têtes,
> Moi je n'ai que la lande en fleurs:
> L'un, symbole riant de la paix et des fêtes,
> L'autre, symbole des douleurs.
>
> Unissons-les, amis! Les fils qui vont nous suivre
> De ces fleurs n'ornent plus leurs fronts;
> Aucun ne redira le son qui nous enivre,
> Quand nous, fidèles, nous mourrons. . .
>
> Mais, peut-elle mourir, la brise fraîche et douce?
> L'aquilon l'emporte en son vol,
> Et puis, elle revient légère sur la mousse:
> Meurt-il le chant du rossignol?
>
> Non, tu ranimeras l'idiome sonore,
>   Belle Provence, à son déclin;
> Sur ma tombe longtemps doit soupirer encore
>   La voix errante de Merlin.

The olive branch will crown you;
I have only the moors in bloom:
One, a smiling symbol of peace and joy,
The other, a symbol of suffering.

Let us unite them, friends, for our sons
Will no longer flaunt these flowers,
Nor utter the sounds that bewitch us,
When we, the faithful, have died.

But can this gentle breeze die?
The north wind bears it away,
But then it comes back lightly to rest.
Can the song of the nightingale die?

No, you will restore the sounding tongue
From its decline, fair Provence;
And the wandering voice of Merlin
Will sigh over my grave long after I am gone.

In addition to those I mentioned as participants at Arles, here are the new names that began to appear at the gathering in Aix: Alègre, Father Aubert, Autheman, Bellot, Brunet, Chalvet, Father Emery, Laidet, Mathiéu Lacroix, Father Lambert, Lejourdan, Peyrottes, Ricard-Bérard, Tavan, Vidal, etc., together with three women poets, Mesdemoiselles Rèino Garde, Leounido Constans, and Ourtènsi Rolland.

In the afternoon all the fashionable society of Aix attended a literary session held in the great hall of the Hôtel de Ville, which was gaily decked out in the colors of Provence and the arms of all the Provençal cities, with a crimson velvet banner listing the principal Provençal poets of the last few centuries. The mayor of Aix, who was a deputy as well as mayor, was then Monsieur Rigaud, the same who later translated *Mirèio* into French verse.

A choir sang the overture with the words of Jan-Batisto Gaut:

Troubaire de Prouvènço,	Poets of Provence,
Pèr nàutri que bèu jour!	What a fine day for us!
Vesèn la reneissènço	We see the renaissance
Dóu parla dóu Miejour.	Of the speech of the South.

After that the chairman, D'Astros, talked pleasantly in Provençal, then each of us in turn produced his piece. Roumanille, who was much applauded, recited one of his stories and sang "The Blind Girl"; Aubanel reeled off his piece on "Twins"; and I, "The Reaper's Death." But what pleased people most was the peasant Tavan with his little song, "Marieto's Curls," and the mason Mathiéu Lacroix, who made everyone shudder with his "Poor Martino."

Emile Zola, then a schoolboy at the College of Aix, was present at that session, and here is what he said about it forty years later in a speech he gave at the literary banquet of the Félibres at Sceaux in 1892:

> I was fifteen or sixteen, and I can see myself again, an escapee from school, in the great hall of the Hôtel de Ville at Aix attending a poetic celebration somewhat like the one I have the honor of presiding over today. Mistral was there reciting "The Reaper's Death," no doubt Roumanille and Aubanel were there, and still others, all those who were to become the Félibres several years later and who were then only troubadours.

Finally at dinner that evening, where we recited, narrated, and sang all manner of things, we had the pleasure of raising our glasses to the health of old Bellot, who had earned a well-deserved reputation in Marseille and all Provence as a comic poet. Amazed to see that abundance of new growth, the poor fellow said in reply:

> Siéu qu'un pasto-mourtié;
> Dins ma vidasso ai proun mascara de papié.
> Gaut, Mistrau, Crousihat, que n'an pas la castagno,
> De noueste prouvençau desbuiaran l'escagno.

> I am only a botcher;
> I have soiled enough paper in my poor life.
> Gaut, Mistral, Crousillat, who aren't lazy,
> Will unravel the skein of our Provençal.

XII

FONT-SÉGUGNE

e now had a group of young men in the region who were close friends in perfect agreement about the sacred task of the Provençal renaissance. And we went at it wholeheartedly.

We would get together almost every Sunday, sometimes in Avignon, sometimes on the plains of Maillane or in the gardens of Saint-Rémy, sometimes on the heights of Châteauneuf-de-Gadagne or of Châteauneuf-du-Pape, for convivial gatherings, young men's parties, Provençal banquets, with poetry more delicious than the food, with enthusiasm and feeling more intoxicating than the wine. There Roumanille sang his *Carols* to us. There he read us his recent work, *The Dreamers*, or his very latest, *God's Share*. There Aubanel, a believer who always gnawed at the restraints of his faith, recited *The Slaughter of the Innocents*. And there *Mirèio* came from time to time to reel off her newly written stanzas.

The "poets" (as people already called us) came to Maillane every year at the feast of Saint Agatha, who is the patron of the village, to spend three days, like the gypsies. Agatha was a young Sicilian virgin and martyr whose breasts were cut off. In the treasury of the church of Saint Trophime in Arles there is even an *agate* plate which is traditionally supposed to have held the breasts of the young saint. But how could that devotion for a saint from Catania have come to the people of Arles and Maillane?

I would explain it in the following fashion. According to history, a lord of Maillane who came from Arles, Guilhèn des Porcellets, because of his rectitude and virtue, was the only Frenchman spared at the Sicilian Vespers. Couldn't he or his descendants have introduced the veneration of the virgin from Catania? Whatever the explanation, in Sicily Saint Agatha is invoked against the volcanic fires of Mount Etna and in Maillane against fire and lightning. An honor sought by our young women of Maillane before they marry is that of being "prioresses" (or priestesses, you might say) of the altar of Saint Agatha for three years. And according to a charming custom, on the eve of the feast, before the dancing begins, couples and young people all come together in front of the church to serenade Saint Agatha.

We too came to offer our respects to the patron saint of Maillane, along with the young gallants, following the fiddlers by the light of wandering lanterns, to the noise of firecrackers, squibs, and rockets. I have sometimes asked myself what is our worldly glory as poets, artists, scholars, or soldiers, slightly known to a few admirers, compared to the saints honored at the altar for centuries and centuries, in cities and villages, here and there, north and south. Victor Hugo himself will never be venerated like the least saint in the church calendar, not even Saint Gent, who for seven hundred years has seen thousands of the faithful come to pray to him every year in his lost valley. And that is why, when some flatterers once asked the author of *Contemplations*, "Is there any greater glory in this world than the poet's?" he replied, "That of the saint."

So we went to the dance on the feast of Saint Agatha to watch our friend Mathieu dancing with my beautiful cousins Gango, Vileto, and Lali. We went to the meadow by the mill to watch the men and youths wrestling to the beat of the drum:

> Quau voudra lucha, que se presènte,
> Quau voudra lucha
> Que vèngue au prat!

> Whoever wants to wrestle, step forward,
> Whoever wants to wrestle,
> Come to the meadow.

There Master Jesèto was in charge, going around and around the naked wrestlers, who were struggling one against the other, with their knees straining, occasionally reminding them in a stern voice, "No tearing flesh!"

"Oh, Jesèto, do you remember when you threw Quequino?"

"Yes, and when I floored Bèl-Aubre of Aramon," the old athlete would reply, delighted to tell us again of his former victories. "You know what they called me? The Little Maillanais, alias the Flexible One. No one could ever say he had thrown me on my back, and yet I tangled with the famous Meissounié, the Hercules of Avignon who threw everyone, with Rabassoun, and Creste from Apt. But we couldn't beat each other."

In Saint-Rémy we used to stay with Roumanille's parents, Jan-Danis and Peireto, hearty market-gardeners who cultivated a garden near the Gate of the Hole. There we dined outdoors in the mottled shade of a grape arbor on painted plates they brought out in our honor, together with pewter spoons and steel forks. And our friend's sisters, Zino and Touneto, two smiling brunettes in their twenties, served us the lamb *blanquette* they had prepared.

That old Jan-Danis, Roumanille's father, was a tough man. As a soldier under Bonaparte (as he scornfully called the Emperor), he had been through the battle of Waterloo, and he was fond of saying that he had won the croix de guerre. "But in the defeat," he said, "it was forgotten." So when his son received the decoration in the time of MacMahon, Jan-Danis had the satisfaction of saying proudly, "The father won it, but the son has it."

Here's the epitaph that Roumanille wrote for the tomb of his parents in the cemetery of Saint-Rémy:

TO JAN-DANIS ROUMANILLE,
GARDENER, A GOOD AND WORTHY MAN (1791–1875).

AND TO PEIRETO DE PIQUET, HIS WIFE,
GOOD, PIOUS, AND STRONG (1793-1875).
THEY LIVED AS CHRISTIANS AND DIED
IN PEACE. MAY THEY BE WITH GOD.

Crousillat, who was from Salon and devoted to the language
and muses of Crau, often came to those little parties. On the
day after a reading in Saint-Rémy, he congratulated me with
the following sonnet:

Ausiguère un ressouen de ta puro armounié,
Lou jour que pousquerian encò de Roumaniho,
Cinq troubaire galoi, franc de ceremounié,
Manja, turta lou got, canta, rire en famiho.

Mai quouro auras fini de trena toun panié,
Quouro de nous lisca ta bello jouino-fiho?
Que m'escride countènt e jamai façounié:
Ta *Mirèio*, o Mistrau, es uno meraviho!

Se coumo l'auro adounc que soun noum te counvèn,
Fouert es lou sant alen que t'ispiro, o jouvènt,
Auto! au mounde abrama largo lèu ta musico!
A tei flàmeis acord lei baus van ressauta,
Leis aubre trefouli, lei gaudre s'aplanta,
Coumo à de souen dinda subre la liro antico.

I heard your harmony resound
The day we spent at Roumanille's,
Five happy, carefree troubadours,
Eating, toasting, singing, laughing together.

But when will you be done with your weaving?
And stop touching up your fair young maid?
I am satisfied and will never find fault:
Mistral, your *Mirèio* is a marvel!

Like the wind whose name becomes you,
Strong is the holy breath that inspires you,
Go, pour forth your music to an eager world!
To your blazing harmonies the mountains will resound,
The trees will throb, the torrents stop,
As to the ringing of an antique lyre.

In Avignon we used to go to the house of Aubanel in the rue Saint-Marc (which now bears the name of the glorious Félibre), a townhouse with towers, formerly a cardinal's palace, since destroyed to make way for a new street. On entering you saw in the vestibule a wooden press that looked like a wine press with its screw and had been used for two hundred years to print the books of the parishes and schools of the Comtat. There we sat down at the table, somewhat intimidated by the ecclesiastical aroma in the walls and above all by Janetoun, the old cook, who always seemed to be saying, "Here they are again!"

But Aubanel's good-natured father, who was the official printer to our Holy Father the Pope, and his jolly uncle, the canon, soon put us at ease. And as we clinked glasses, the good old priest told us a story:

"One night they called me to bring the last sacraments to an unfortunate woman in one of those houses of ill repute in the Square of Mary Magdalen. When I had administered the last rites to the poor dying woman and started back down with the sacristan, the ladies lined up along the stairway in their low-cut dresses and carnival frippery to greet me as I passed, looking so contrite with their heads bowed that you would have forgiven their sins, as they say, without hearing their confessions. And the madame, who accompanied me, tried to offer pretexts to excuse her way of life. But as soon as she had opened the door for me, I turned around and said to her, 'You old sow, if there weren't so many bawds, there would be fewer harlots!'"

We also had good times dining at the homes of Brunet and Mathieu (of whom I shall speak later). But the place chosen by a lucky star was Font-Ségugne, a country house near the village of Gadagne where we were invited by Giéra's family: his mother, a gracious lady; the eldest son named Pau, a notary in Avignon who was keen on the art of poetry; the second son, Jùli, who dreamed of reforming the world through the work of the White Penitents; and finally, two pleasant and charming young ladies, Clarisso and Fefin, who were the sweetness and joy of that nest.

Font-Ségugne, on the slopes of the plateau of Camp-Cabel,

faces Mount Ventoux in the distance and the gorge of Vau-
cluse, which can be seen several leagues away. The estate takes
its name from a little spring that rises at the foot of the cha-
teau. A delightful cluster of oaks, acacias, and plane trees shel-
ters it against the sun and wind.

"Font-Ségugne," said Tavan (the Félibre of Gadagne), "is the
place where village lovers still come on Sunday. There they
have shade, coolness, silence, and places to hide. There are fish
ponds, benches covered with ivy, paths winding up and down
through the woods, and beautiful views. There you can hear
birds singing, leaves rustling, fountains burbling. Wherever
you go, you can sit on the lawn and dream of love if you are
alone, or make love if there are two of you."

That is where we came to enjoy ourselves, Roumanille,
Giéra, Mathieu, Brunet, Tavan, Crousillat, myself, and oth-
ers—Aubanel most of all, for he was betwitched by Zani's eyes.
Jenny Manivet, to give her real name, was a girl from Avignon
who was a friend and companion of the young ladies of the
family.

> Emé soun jougne prim e sa raubo de lano
>   Coulour de la mióugrano,
> Emé soun front tant lisc e si grands iue tant bèu,
> Emé si long péu negre e sa caro brunello,
> Tout-aro la veirai, la douço vierginello,
> Que me dira: Bon vèspre!—O Zani, venès lèu!

> With her slim figure and her woolen dress
>   The color of pomegranates,
> With her smooth forehead and big, beautiful eyes,
> With her long black hair and her dusky face,
> I shall see her soon, that sweet young maid,
> She will wish me good night. Oh, Zani, come quickly.

Thus Aubanel himself portrayed her in his *Book of Love*. But
listen to him now as he remembers Font-Ségugne after Zani
had become a nun.

> Veici l'estiéu, li niue soun claro;
> A Castèu-Nòu lou vèspre es bèu;
> Dedins li bos la luno encaro

Mounto la niue sus Camp-Cabèu.
T'ensouvèn? dins li clapeirolo,
Emé ta fàci d'espagnolo,
De quand courriés coume uno folo,
De quand courrian coume de fòu,
Au plus sourne, e pièi qu'avian pòu?

E pèr ta taio mistoulino
Iéu t'agantave, e qu'èro dous!
Au canta de la sóuvagino,
Dansavian alor tóuti dous,
Grihet, roussignòu e reineto
Disien tóuti si cansouneto;
Tu, i'apoundiés ta voues clareto. . .
O bello amigo, aro ounte soun
Tant de brande e tant de cansoun?

A la fin pamens, las de courre,
Las de rire, las de dansa,
S'assetavian souto li roure,
Un moumenet pèr se pausa;
Toun long péu que se destrenavo,
Moun amourouso man amavo
De lou rejougne, e tu, tant bravo,
Me leissaves faire, plan-plan,
Coume uno maire soun enfant.

Summertime and the nights are clear;
At Châteauneuf the evening is fair;
In the woods the moon still climbs
The night sky over Camp-Cabel.
Do you remember? When you ran
Like a mad thing among the stones
With your dark Spanish face,
When we ran like two mad things
In the dark of night and were afraid?

How sweet it was when I caught you
And held you by your slender waist!
Then we danced together
To the music of the woods.

Crickets, nightingales, and tree-frogs
All sang their little songs;
And you sang with them in your sweet voice.
Ah, dear one, where are they now,
All those songs and dances?

But at last, tired of running,
Tired of laughing, tired of dancing,
We sat down under the oaks
To rest a while;
Then my amorous hand
Loved to smooth
Your long tangled hair,
And you let me, sweet and gentle,
Like a mother with her child.

And the lines he wrote in the little chateau of Font-Ségugne are on the walls of the room where Zani used to sleep:

O chambreto, chambreto,
Siés pichoto segur, mai que de souveni!
Quand passe toun lindau, me dise:—Van veni!
Me sèmblo de vous vèire, o bèlli jouveineto,
Tu, pauro Julia, tu, pecaire, Zani!
E pamens es fini!
Dins aquelo chambreto, ah! vendrés plus dourmi!
O Julia, siés morto! o Zani, siés moungeto!

Dear little room,
You may be small, but what memories you hold!
When I enter, I tell myself, "They are coming!"
I seem to see those lovely girls,
You, poor Julia, and you, my dear Zani.
But it's all over.
You will never come and sleep here again.
For you died, Julia, and, Zani, you took the veil.

Could you want a more favorable place to cradle a glorious dream and foster a blossoming ideal than this hilltop with a view of the surrounding countryside serene and blue in the distance? In this discreet court of love a group of young men worshiped Beauty in three forms, all identical for them, "Poetry, Love, Provence," with several happy, gracious young ladies to keep them company.

The stars decided that on a flowery Sunday, the 21st of May, with the spring of the year and life at its fullest, seven of those poets were to gather at the little chateau of Font-Ségugne: Pau Giéra, a satirist who signed his work Glaup (an anagram of Paul G.); Roumanille, an unobtrusive promoter who constantly stirred the sacred fire among his friends; Aubanel, whom Roumanille had won over to our language and who at that very moment was opening his bright coral *Pomegranate* in the sunshine of his love; Mathieu, lost in his cloudy visions of a Provence restored to chivalry and love as of yore; Brunet, with the face of Christ in Galilee and his utopian dream of an earthly paradise; the peasant Tavan, bent over his hoe, singing in the sun like a cricket on a clod; and Frederi, all ready to hurl the rallying cry to the mistral, to "halloo" (as the shepherds of the mountains say), and to plant the banner on Mount Ventoux.

As usual at dinner we spoke again of what was needed to raise our language from the neglect in which it lay ever since the bourgeois had betrayed the honor of Provence and reduced it to a menial condition. Then considering that nothing had come of the two meetings at Arles and Aix that would lead to an agreement to rehabilitate the Provençal tongue, that on the contrary the reforms proposed by the young members of the school of Avignon had been badly received and rejected by many, the seven of Font-Ségugne unanimously decided to form their own party, taking the mark and throwing it where they wished.

"Only we need a new name for our new blood," said Glaup. "For all rhymesters call themselves *trouvères*, even those who find nothing at all. On the other hand there is the word *troubadour*. But that name, used to designate poets of a certain period, has lost its freshness through overuse. And a new enterprise needs a new sign."

Then I spoke up and said, "My friends, the common people of Maillane recite an old poem that has been transmitted by word

of mouth and that contains, I believe, the predestined word."
And I began:

>   Monsegnour sant Anséume legissié,
>   Escrivié.
>   Un jour de sa santo escrituro,
>   Es mounta au cèu sus lis auturo.
>   Auprès de l'Enfant Jèsu, soun fiéu tant precious
>   A trouva la Vierge assetado.
>   En meme tèms l'a saludado.
>   Elo i'a di: Sigués lou bèn-vengu, nebout!
>   —Bello coumpagno, a di soun enfant, qu'avès vous?
>   —Ai soufert sèt doulour amaro
>   Que vous li vole counta aro.
>
>   La proumiero doulour qu'ai souferto pèr vous,
>   O moun fiéu tant precious,
>   Es quand entendeguère iéu messo de vous,
>   Qu'au tèmple iéu me presentère,
>   Qu'entre li man de sant Simoun vous meteguère.
>   Me fuguè 'n coutèu de doulour
>   Que me tranquè lou cor, me travessè moun amo,
>   Emai à vous,
>   O moun fiéu tant precious.
>
>   La segoundo doulour qu'ai souferto pèr vous, etc.
>
>   La tresèimo doulour qu'ai souferto pèr vous, etc.
>
>   La quatrèimo doulour qu'ai souferto pèr vous,
>   O moun fiéu tant precious,
>   Es quand vous perdeguère,
>   Que de tres jour, tres niue, iéu noun vous retrouvère,
>   Que dins lou tèmple erias,
>   Que vous disputavias
>   Emé li tiroun de la Lèi,
>   Emé li sèt felibre de la Lèi. . . .
>
>
>   Monsignor Saint Anselm was reading
>   And writing.
>   One day from his holy writing,
>   He rose to heaven on high.

Near the Infant Jesus, her precious son,
    He found the Virgin sitting
    And hailed her at once.
"Welcome, nephew!" she said to him.
"Dear mother," said her child, "what's the matter?"
    "I have suffered seven bitter sorrows
    That I want to tell you now."

"The first sorrow I suffered for you,
    Oh, my precious son,
When I went to Mass to be churched,
    And presenting myself at the temple,
I placed you in the hands of Saint Simeon.
    For me then a sword of sorrow
Pierced my heart right through my soul,
    And for you, too,
    Oh, my precious son.

"The second sorrow I suffered for you, etc.

"The third sorrow I suffered for you, etc.

"The fourth sorrow I suffered for you,
    Oh, my precious son,
    Was when I lost you,
When for three days and three nights I could not find you,
    When you were in the temple,
    Where you were disputing
    With the doctors of the Law
    With the seven Félibres of the Law. . . ."*

   "The seven Félibres of the Law, why, that's us!" everyone at
the table cried out. "Let it be *Félibre!*"

*This folk poem is also recited in Catalonia. Here is the Catalan parallel to the
Provençal I have just quoted:

Lo ters fou quan lo tinguèreu	The third was when you'd lost
Part de tres dies perdut;	Your son nearly three days;
Lo trobàreu à 'nél temple	You found him in the temple
Disputant ab los sabuts,	Disputing with the doctors,
Predicant à l'arboleda	Preaching heavenly doctrine
La celestial doctrina.	Under the arches.

And Glaup poured into our crystal glasses a bottle of Châteauneuf-du-Pape that had been aging for seven years, saying solemnly, "To the health of the Félibres! And while we are christening our Renaissance, let us adapt the name to all the shoots that are bound to sprout. First I propose *Félibrarié* as a name for every school of Félibres that includes at least seven members in memory, gentlemen, of the *Pléiade* of Avignon."

"I," said Roumanille, "propose the nice word *Félibreja*, meaning 'to hold a gathering of Félibres,' as we are doing here."

"I," said Mathieu, "contribute the word *Félibrejado*, meaning 'a fellowship of Provençal poets.' "

"I," said Tavan, "believe that the adjective *Félibren* would not be a bad way of describing whatever concerns the Félibres."

"I," said Aubanel, "confer the name of *Félibresso* on the ladies who will sing in the Provençal tongue."

"And I," said Brunet, "find that the word *Félibrihoun* would suit the children of the Félibres."

"And I," said Mistral, "conclude with this patriotic cry to designate the work of our association: *'Félibrige, 'Félibrige!'* "

Then Glaup spoke again: "That's not all, my fellow poets. We are the Félibres of the Law. But who is going to establish the Law?"

"I will," said I, "and I swear to you that if it takes me twenty years to demonstrate that our language is a language, I will draw up the articles of law that govern it."

How funny! It sounds like a story, and yet that pledge made on a holiday, a day of poetry and intoxication, resulted in the enormous, absorbing task of my *Tresor dóu Felibrige* or dictionary of the Provençal tongue, which consumed twenty years of a poet's career.

And anyone who doubts it need only read the prologue Glaup (P. Giéra) wrote in the *Provençal Almanac* of 1855, where the following is clearly recorded: "When the 'Law' that a Félibre is preparing has been completed, stating why this and why that better than you can imagine, our opponents will be silenced."

At that truly memorable and now legendary meeting we decided to publish a small annual anthology in the form of an almanac which was to be the ensign of our poetry, the battle flag of our ideas, the link among Félibres, and their means of communicating with the people.

When all that was settled, we noticed that the date of our meeting, the 21st of May, was the feast of Saint Estelle, and like the Magi recognizing the mysterious influence of some conjunction of the spheres, we hailed the Star that presided over the cradle of our redemption.

The Provençal Almanac for the Fine Year of Our Lord 1855 appeared the same year, 112 pages long. At the very front, like a frame for athletic prizes, our "Song of the Félibres" announced the program of that vigorous popular revival.

> Sian tout d' ami, sian tout de fraire,
> Sian li cantaire dóu païs!
> Tout enfantoun amo sa maire,
> Tout auceloun amo soun nis:
> Noste cèu blu, noste terraire,
> Soun pèr nous-autre un paradis.
>
> Sian tout d'ami galoi e libre,
> Que la Prouvènço nous fai gau;
> Es nàutri que sian li felibre,
> Li gai felibre prouvençau!
>
> En prouvençau ço que l'on pènso
> Vèn sus li bouco eisadamen:
> O douço lengo de Prouvènço,
> Vaqui perqué fau que t'amen!
> Sus li frejau de la Durènço
> N'en fasèn vuei lou sarramen!
>
> Sian tout d'ami, etc.
>
> Li bouscarleto, de soun paire
> Jamai óublidon lou piéuta;
> Lou roussignòu l'óublido gaire,
> Ço que soun paire i' a canta;
> E lou parla de nòsti maire,
> Poudrian nautre l'óublida?
>
> Sian tout d'ami, etc.

Enterin que li chatouneto
Danson au brut dóu tambourin,
Lou dimenche, souto l'oumbreto
D'uno figuiero vo d'un pin,
Aman de faire la gousteto
E de chourla 'n flasquet de vin.

Sian tout d'ami, etc.

Alor, quand lou moust de la Nerto
Sautourlejo e ris dins lou got,
De la cansoun qu'a descuberto
Tre qu'un felibre a larga 'n mot,
Tóuti li bouco soun duberto
E la cantan tóutis au cop.

Sian tout d'ami, etc.

Di chatouno escarrabihado
Aman lou rire enfantouli;
E se quaucuno nous agrado,
Dins nòsti vers achatourli
Es pièi cantado e recantado
Emé de mot mai que poulit.

Sian tout d'ami, etc.

Quand li meissoun saran vengudo,
Se la sartan fregis souvènt;
Quand chaucharés vòsti cournudo,
Se lou rasin moustejo bèn,
E que vous faugue un pau d'ajudo,
I' anaren tóuti en courrènt.

Sian tout d'ami, etc.

Di farandoulo sian en tèsto;
Per Sant Aloi turtan lou got;
Quand fau lucha, quitan la vèsto;
Vèngue Sant Jan, sautan lou fiò;
E pèr Calèndo, la grand fèsto,
Pausan ensèn lou cacho fiò.

Sian tout d'ami, etc.

Quand au moulin se vèn desfaire,
Li sa d'óulivo, se vesès
D'agué besoun d'un barrejaire,
Poudès veni, sian toujour lèst:
Atrouvarés de galejaire
Qu'en ges de part n' i' a panca dès.

Sian tout d'ami, etc.

Se 'n-cop fasès la castagnado,
Apereiça vers Sant Martin,
S'amas li conte de vihado,
Apelas-nous, bràvi vesin,
E vous n' en diren talo astiado
Que n'en rirés jusquo au matin.

Sian tout d'ami, etc.

Vous manco un priéu pèr vosto voto?
Quouro que fugue, sian eici . . .
E vous, nouvieto cafinoto,
Un gai coublet vous fai plesi?
Counvidas-nous: n'avèn, mignoto,
N'avèn pèr vous cènt de chausi.

Sian tout d'ami, etc.

Quouro que sagatés la trueio,
Manquessias pas de nous souna!
Quand s'atrouvèsse un jour de plueio,
Tendren la co pèr la sauna:
Un bon taioun de fricassueio,
I' a rèn de tau pèr bèn dina.

Sian tout d'ami, etc.

Fau que lou pople se satire;
Toujour, pecaire, acò 's esta . . .
Eh! se jamai falié rèn dire,
N' i' aurié, bon goi, pèr ié peta!
Fau que n' i' ague pèr lou fai rire,
Fau que n' i' ague pèr ié canta!

Sian tout d'ami galoi e libre
Que la Prouvènço nous fai gau:

Es nàutri que sian li felibre,
Li gai felibre prouvençau.

We are all friends, all brothers,
We are the singers of the land!
As all children love their mothers,
And all nestlings love their nests,
So we love our blue sky and our land,
To us they are a paradise.

We are all friends, joyful and free,
All enamored of Provence;
We are the Félibres,
The merry Félibres of Provence!

In Provençal your thoughts
Come readily to your lips.
Oh, sweet tongue of Provence,
That's why we love you!
On the pebbles of Durance
We swear this oath today!

We are all friends, etc.

Warblers do not forget
The warbling of their father;
Nightingales do not forget
What their father sang to them;
So how could we forget
The language of our mothers?

We are all friends, etc.

On Sundays while the girls are dancing
To the beat of the little drum,
We like to sit in the shade
Of a fig tree or a pine
And have ourselves a snack
And swig wine from the flask.

We are all friends, etc.

Then as the new wine sparkles,
Bubbles, and laughs in the glass,
If a Félibre utters a word

Of a song he has heard,
All burst into song at once
And all together we sing.

We are all friends, etc.

We love the innocent laughter
Of bright and sprightly girls;
And if we find one pleasing,
We sing her again and again
In our love poems
With the prettiest words we know.

We are all friends, etc.

When the harvest season comes
And the frying pan is busy,
When you're pressing out the vintage
And the grapes are in a ferment,
And you need a little help,
Count on us to all come running.

We are all friends, etc.

We always lead the dance;
To Saint Eloi we raise a toast;
At a wrestling match, we strip;
On Saint John's we leap the fire;
And for the great feast of Christmas
We bring in the Yule log together.

We are all friends, etc.

When you open the sacks in the olive mill
And find you need help with the pressing,
Some fellows to push that heavy bar,
Call us, we're always ready;
You will find us jolly fellows—
There aren't ten like us in the world.

We are all friends, etc.

When it's time for roasting chestnuts
In the season of Saint Martin,
If you want to hear good stories,
Call us, neighbors, for the evening,

And we'll tell you such an earful
It will make you laugh till morning.

We are all friends, etc.

If you need us for your saint's day,
Here we are, no matter when.
And you, newlyweds,
Would a jolly couplet please you?
Invite us, sweethearts, and we'll have
Hundreds for you to choose from.

We are all friends, etc.

When you slaughter the hog,
Don't fail to call on us!
Even on a rainy day,
Count on us to hold the tail:
Nothing's so tasty for dinner
As a morsel of liver or lights.

We are all friends, etc.

People need to work like slaves;
Alas, it's always been that way.
But if you could never speak,
It would be enough to kill you!
You need someone to make you laugh,
You need someone to make you sing!

We are all friends, joyful and free,
All enamored of Provence:
We are the Félibres,
The merry Félibres of Provence!

As you can see, the Félibrige did not spawn melancholy or pessimism. Everything was done in high spirits, without any thought of profit or fame. Those who contributed to the first *Almanac* had all taken pseudonyms: the Félibre of the Gardens (Roumanille), the Félibre of the Pomegranate (Aubanel), the Félibre of Kisses (Mathieu), the Playful Félibre (Glaup), the Félibre of the Farm or of Belle-Viste (Mistral), the Félibre of the Army (Tavan, who had drawn an unlucky number), the Félibre of the Rainbow (J. Brunet, who was a painter); then all those who gradually came to swell the ranks: the Félibre of Glass (D. Cassan), the Félibre of Acorns (T. Poussel), the Félibre of Sainte-Braise (E. Garcin), the Félibre of Lusène (Crousillat, who was from Salon), the Félibre of Garlic (J.-B. Martin, nicknamed "the Greek"), the Félibre of Melons (V. Martin, from Cavaillon), the Félibresso of the Little Pod (daughter of the former), the Sentimental Félibre (B. Laurens), the Félibre of Documents (Achard, the archivist of Vaucluse), the Félibre of Pontias (B. Chalvet), the Félibre of Magalouno (Moquin-Tandon), the Félibre of the Tour-Magne (Roumieux), the Félibre of the Sea (M. Bourrelly), the Félibre of Incense (Father Bayle), the Félibre of Pencils (Father Cotton), and the Myopic Félibre (the first pseudonym used as a signature for the jests and naive folktales of Roumanille and Mistral, later changed to "The Whimsical One").

The Judge's Farm.

Five of the original Félibres, and friends, 1854. Seated from left to right: Mistral, Roumanille, Jules Giéra. Standing: Aubanel, Paul Giéra, Tavan, and Chastel, a painter.

ARMANA PROUVENÇAU

PÈR LOU BÈL AN DE DIÈU

1855

ADOUBA E PUBLICA DE LA MAN DI FELIBRE

MARCO LI LUNO, LIS ESCLUSSI, LI FÈSTO, LI VOTO, LI BOUMAVAGE, LI LICEN
E LI PROUVÈRBI DE CHASQUE JOUR DOU MES

TAN PÈR LA PROUVÉNÇO QUE PÈR LA COUMTAT

SE JES APOUNDU TAMBÈN PROUN D'AUTRI POELIDI CAUSO QUE FAI GRAND CAU DE LI LEGI.

Costo : 50 centimo,
Voulounta-dire, dès sòu.

EN AVIGNOUN

VÈS LI FRAIRE AUBANEL, EMPRIMAIRE, CARRIÈRO SANT-MARC.

Title page of the first *Provençal Almanac*.

MIRÈIO   MIREILLE

POUÈMO PROUVENÇAU   POÈME PROVENÇAL

de   de

FREDERI MISTRAL   FREDERIC MISTRAL

AVÉ LA TRADUCIOUN LITERALO EN REGARD   AVEC LA TRADUCTION LITTÉRALE EN REGARD

PARIS   PARIS
ENCÒ DE CHARPENTIER, LIBRAIRE-EDITEUR   CHARPENTIER, LIBRAIRE-EDITEUR

AVIGNOUN ENCÒ DE ROUMANILLO, LIBRAIRE   AVIGNON, ROUMANILLE, LIBRAIRE

1861   1861

Bilingual edition of *Mirèio*. This is the second edition, which includes the dedication to Lamartine.

Mistral in 1863, studio portrait by Nadar. (*Photothèque Hachette*)

Opposite, top:
Mistral reading his poem *Calendau* to a group of Félibres in 1866.
From left to right: Gras, Mathieu, William Bonaparte-Wyse, Crousil-
lat, Aubanel, Mistral, Grivolas, Brunet, Roumieux, Victor Balaguer,
Roumanille. (*Photothèque Hachette*)

Opposite, bottom:
Daudet and Mistral. (*Roger-Viollet*)

Mistral in 1913. (*Roger-Viollet*)

XIII
THE PROVENÇAL ALMANAC

elcomed by peasants, relished by the faithful, esteemed by the discriminating, sought out by artists, *The Provençal Almanac* soon won public favor, and its printing quickly went from 500 copies the first year to 1,200 to 3,000 to 5,000 to 7,000 to 10,000, which has been the average figure for fifteen or twenty years.

And given that it's a book for the family and for evening gatherings, that represents 50,000 readers, more or less. I cannot tell you what care, devotion, and pride Roumanille and I constantly gave this little book during its first forty years. And the quantity of stories, legends, nursery tales, jests, and jokes gathered here, all harvested from the soil, makes this venture and collection unique—to say nothing of the innumerable poems it published nor of the chronicles that contain the history of the Félibrige. All the tradition, all the humor, all the wit of the common people are crowded into its pages, and if the people of Provence were one day to disappear, their spirit and style could be recovered exactly as they were in the Félibres' almanac.

Roumanille has published the choicest stories and jokes in a separate volume (*Provençal Tales and Whimsicalities*) that he selected at random from our popular almanac. I could easily have done the same. But I shall limit myself here to a sampling of several pieces that had the greatest success and were in fact translated and circulated everywhere by our good friends Alphonse Daudet and Paul Arène.

The Good Pilgrim

A Provençal Tale

1

Master Archimbaud was almost a hundred years old. In his day he had been a tough soldier, but now crippled and cramped by old age, he always kept to his bed and could no longer get around.

Old Master Archimbaud had three sons. One morning he called the eldest and said to him, "Come here, Archimbalet. In turning and tossing in my bed—for you have plenty of time to reflect in bed—I remembered that one day in a battle, when I found myself in danger of dying, I promised God that I would make a pilgrimage to Rome. Alas, I am old as the earth now and can no longer go to war. I would like you to go make that pilgrimage in my place, for it grieves me to die without fulfilling my vow."

The eldest replied, "What in the name of a thousand thunders put in your head a pilgrimage to Rome and who knows what other pilgrimages besides? Father, eat, drink, and say your prayers in bed as much as you like. We have plenty of other things to do."

The next morning Master Archimbaud called his second son, "Son, listen," he said. "In reflecting and daydreaming—for you have plenty of time to muse in bed—I remembered that one day in a massacre, when I found myself in mortal danger, I promised God that I would make the big pilgrimage to Rome. Alas, I am old as the earth now and can no longer go to war. I would like you to go make the pilgrimage in my place."

The second son replied, "Father, the good weather is coming in two weeks, and we'll have to plow the wheatfield, cultivate the vineyard, and cut the hay. Our eldest must lead the flock to the mountains, and the youngest is only a child. Who will direct the men if I go off to Rome, loafing along the roads? Father, eat, sleep, and leave us alone."

The next morning good Master Archimbaud called his youngest son, "Esperit, my child, come near," he said to him. "I promised the Lord to make a pilgrimage to Rome. But I am old as the earth now and can no longer go to war. Poor boy, I would send you in my place. But you are a bit young, you don't know the way, Rome is very far away, and dear Lord, what if you came to harm. . . ."

"I will go, Father," answered the youngest.

But his mother cried out, "I don't want you to go there! That old dotard gets on your nerves with his war and his Rome. It's not enough that we have to listen to him grumble, whine, and complain without letup all year long, now he wants to send that sweet innocent boy off to get lost!"

"Mother," said the youngest, "a father's wish is an order from God. When God commands, I must go."

And without saying anything more Esperit went and drew some wine in a little gourd, put a loaf of bread and some onions in his knapsack, put on a new pair of shoes, looked in the woodshed for a good oak staff, put his coat on his shoulder, embraced his old father, who gave him much advice, said goodbye to all his family, and left.

2

But before setting out he piously attended Holy Mass. And what do you know, on leaving the church he found a handsome young man on the threshold who said to him, "Friend, aren't you going to Rome?"

"Yes, yes," said Esperit.

"So am I, comrade. If it suits you, we could travel together."

"Gladly, my fine friend."

Now that beautiful youth was an angel sent from God.

So Esperit and the angel took the road to Rome and traveled quite cheerfully, sometimes in sun, sometimes in shade, begging their bread and singing hymns, with their little gourds at the end of their staffs, until they finally arrived in the city of Rome.

When they had rested, they prayed at the big church of Saint Peter; visited all the basilicas, chapels, oratories, sanctuaries, and reliquaries one after another; kissed the relics of the apostles Peter and Paul, of the virgins, the martyrs, and the True Cross; and finally before leaving, they went to see the Pope, who gave them his blessing.

Then Esperit and his companion lay down on the porch of Saint Peter's, and Esperit fell asleep.

And behold while sleeping the pilgrim saw in a dream his brothers and his mother burning in hell, and he saw himself seated with his father in the eternal glory of God's heaven.

"Oh, my God!" he cried out. "I would like to pull my poor mother and my brothers out of the fire!"

"For your brothers, it can't be done," God replied, "for they have disobeyed my commandment. But for your mother, perhaps, if you can make her perform three acts of charity before she dies."

And Esperit woke up. The angel had disappeared. In vain he waited and searched and asked, he could not find him anywhere, and he had to return from Rome all alone.

Then he made his way to the seashore, gathered up some seashells, put some on his clothes and on his hat, then slowly, by road and by way, by valley and mountain, begging and praying, he returned home.

3

So he arrived at his village and at his house. He had been gone for two years. He had grown thin, poor fellow, and was sunburned, dusty, ragged, and barefoot, with his little gourd at the end of his pilgrim's staff, his rosary and his shells, so that he was unrecognizable and no one knew him. And he went straight to his parents' door and said gently, "Alms for a poor pilgrim, in the name of God!"

"Hey!" cried his mother, "this is getting tiresome! Every day some of these rogues, vagabonds, and beggars come around."

"Have pity, wife," said good old Archimbaud from his bed, "give him something. Who knows if our boy is not at this very hour in the same need!"

And indeed, though she grumbled, the woman cut a crust and took it to the poor man.

The following day the good pilgrim returned to the door of his father's house and started to say, "In the name of God, mistress, give a bit of alms to a poor pilgrim!"

"Are you here again?" cried the old woman. "Don't you know that we gave you something yesterday? These gluttons would eat up the poorhouse!"

"Have pity, wife," said good old Archimbaud, "didn't you eat yesterday, yourself? And aren't you eating again today? Who knows if our boy is not in the same wretched poverty!"

And at that the wife's heart again softened, and she went and cut another crust and took it again to the poor man.

Finally, the day after that, Esperit returned to his parents' door and said, "In the name of God, mistress, could you give hospitality to a poor pilgrim?"

"No!" cried the old harridan. "Go away and sleep in the poorhouse."

"Have pity, wife," said good old Archimbaud, "give him hospitality. Who knows if our child, our poor Esperit, is not at this very hour wandering about at the mercy of bad weather!"

"Yes, you're right," said the mother. And she went at once and opened the door to the stable. And poor Esperit lay down on the straw in a corner behind the animals.

At daybreak the following day Esperit's mother and Esperit's brothers came to open the stable. The stable, my friends, was flooded with light. The pilgrim was dead, white and stiff with cold, with four big tapers burning around him. The straw where he lay sparkled. The cobwebs hung from the ceiling in shining strands like the screen of a mortuary chapel. The beasts in the stable, the mules and the oxen, pricked up their ears in alarm, with their big eyes full of tears. A fragrance of violets perfumed the stable. And the poor pilgrim, his face radiant, his hands joined, held a paper on which was written, "I am your son."

Then bursting with tears, they all crossed themselves and fell on their knees. Esperit was a saint.

(*The Provençal Almanac of 1879*)

Jarjaio in Heaven

Jarjaio, a stevedore of Tarascon, died and fell into the other world with his eyes shut. And he wandered and wandered. Eternity was vast, black as pitch, huge, and so dark it was frightening. Jarjaio didn't know where to turn, he wavered, his teeth chattered, and he shivered. But finally by dint of wandering he saw a little light far off in the distance, far, far away. He made his way there. It was the Lord's gate.

Jarjaio knocked at the gate: bang! bang!

"Who's there," shouted Saint Peter.

"It's me."

"Who are you?"

"Jarjaio."

"Jarjaio of Tarascon?"

"That's right."

"Why, you rogue," said Saint Peter, "how do you have the gall to ask to enter heaven, you who have never said your prayers for twenty years!—who, when they told you, 'Jarjaio, come to Mass,' answered, 'Whoever piled the mass, let him remove it!'—who scoffed and called thunder 'the snails' drum'!—who ate meat on Friday when you could and Saturday when you had any and said, 'I hope there is some! Meat makes flesh, and what enters the body does no harm to the soul!'—who when the angelus rang, instead of crossing yourself as a good Christian should, said, 'There, they're hanging a pig in the belfry!'—who to your father's warning, 'Jarjaio, the Lord will punish you!' usually retorted, 'The Lord? who has seen Him? When we're dead, we're very dead!' Finally, you who blaspheme and renounce your faith, is it possible, I say, is it possible that you dare present your Godforsaken self?"

Poor Jarjaio replied, "I don't deny it. I am a sinner, a miserable sinner. But who could have known there were so many mysteries after death? Well, I have sinned, and the wine is drawn. If I must drink it, I'll drink it. But great Saint Peter, let me at least see my uncle a little while to tell him what's happening in Tarascon."

"What uncle?"

"My Uncle Matèri, who was a White Penitent."

"Your Uncle Matèri? He got a hundred years of purgatory."

"Curses! A hundred years! What did he do?"

"You remember that he used to carry the cross in processions. One day some jokers plotted together, and one of them started saying, 'Look at Matèri carrying the cross!' A little farther on, another said it again, 'Look at Matèri carrying the cross!' Finally another one spoke to him like this, 'Look, look at Matèri, what's he carrying?' Matèri lost his patience, and they say he replied, 'I'm carrying a fool like you!' And he had a stroke and died in his wrath."

"Then let me see my Aunt Douroutèio, who was so very, very pious."

"For shame! She must be with the devil. I don't know her."

"Oh well, it doesn't surprise me if that one's with the devil, for whenever she was outdone in piety, she was a very devil for spite. Just imagine that she. . . ."

"Jarjaio, I don't have time to waste. I must go open the door for a poor sweeper whose donkey has just sent him to heaven with a kick."

"Oh, great Saint Peter, since you have done so much and since a look costs nothing, let me take a look at heaven, which they say is so beautiful!"

"Oh, yes, of course, I'll do it right away for you, you ugly sinner!"

"Come now, Saint Peter, remember that my father, who's a fisherman down there, carries your banner in procession, walking barefoot."

"Oh well," said the saint, "for your father I'll grant it, but look, you scoundrel, it's understood that you'll only show the tip of your nose."

"That's enough."

So the heavenly gatekeeper slowly opened the gate and said to Jarjaio, "Take a look."

But the fellow suddenly turned around and walked into heaven backward.

"What are you doing?" Saint Peter asked him.

"The brilliant light dazzles my eyes," replied the man from Tarascon, "and I must go backward. But don't worry, when my nose is in, as you said, I'll go no farther."

Well now, thought the saint, I've put my foot in the nosebag.

And the man from Tarascon was in heaven. "Oh!" he said, "how fine you feel here! How beautiful it is! What music!"

After a little while the keeper of the keys said to him, "When you've gawked enough, please leave, because I don't have time to keep you company."

"Don't trouble yourself," said Jarjaio. "If you have something to do, go do your work. I'll leave when I leave. I'm in no hurry."

"Oh, but that's not what we agreed."

"Good Lord, holy man, you're quite wrought up! It would be different if there were no space to move around, but thanks to God, there's plenty of room."

"And I beg you to leave, for if the Lord were to come. . . ."

"Then do as you please. I've always heard the saying, 'If you're well off, don't move.' I'm here, and I'm staying."

Saint Peter shook his head and stamped his foot. He went off to find Saint Ives.

"Ives," he said, "you're an attorney. You must give me a piece of advice."

"Two, if you need them," answered Saint Ives.

"You know, I'm in a fix. I'm in such and such a case. . . . Now what should I do?"

"You must get a good lawyer," said Saint Ives, "and have a summons served by a bailiff on the said Jarjaio to appear before God."

They looked for a lawyer, but no one ever saw a lawyer in heaven. They asked for a bailiff, and they were even scarcer. Saint Peter no longer knew which way to turn.

Saint Luke happened to pass by. "Peter, you look very worried. Did Our Lord give you another scolding?"

"Oh, be quiet, my friend," he said. "I'm in a devilish difficulty. A certain Jarjaio has tricked his way into heaven, and I don't know how to put him out."

"And where is that fellow from?"

"From Tarascon."

"From Tarascon?" said Saint Luke. "My Lord, how simple you are! Getting him out is child's play. I am the bulls' friend and the patron of herdsmen, so I hang around the Camargue, Arles, Beaucaire, Nîmes, Tarascon, etc. I know those people and where they itch and how to catch them. Look, I'll show you."

At that moment a flock of chubby angels fluttered by.

"Little ones," Saint Luke called them, "pst! pst!"

The cherubs descended.

"Sneak out of heaven, and when you're in front of the gate, go out running and shouting, 'The bulls! the bulls!' "

Which the cherubs did. They went out of heaven, and when they were in front of the gate, they dashed forward, shouting, "The bulls! The bulls! Come on! Come on! Jab them!"

Good Lord in heaven! Jarjaio turned around with astonishment and said, "What in the name of thunder! Do they have bullfights here? Let's go!"

And he rushed toward the gate like a whirlwind and left heaven, poor fool! Saint Peter quickly barred and bolted the gate, then putting his head out the wicket, said with a laugh, "Well, Jarjaio, how are you now?"

"Oh, it doesn't matter," replied Jarjaio. "If those had been bulls, I wouldn't have missed my share of heaven."

And having said that, he dove head first into the abyss.

(*The Provençal Almanac of 1864*)

The Frog of Narbonne

1

One afternoon in the month of June, young Pignoulet, a journeyman carpenter nicknamed "The Flower of Grasse," came home in high spirits from his tour of France. The heat was overwhelming. Carrying his cane, decorated with ribbons, in his hand, and his tools—chisels, planes, and mallet—folded in his linen apron on his back, Pignoulet walked up the highway to Grasse, which he had left some three or four years before.

As is the custom of the Journeymen of the Guild, he had just gone up to Sainte-Baume to pay his respects at the tomb of Master Jacque, the founder of the Guild. Then after having carved his nickname on a rock, he had gone down to Saint-Maximin to take his "colors" from Master Fabre, the smith who initiates the Sons of the Guild. And proud as a Caesar, with his kerchief around his neck, his hat sporting a multicolored cascade of ribbons, and two little silver compasses hanging from his ears, he walked quickly in the thick dust. He was covered with it.

Oh, what heat! From time to time he looked at the fig trees to see if there were any figs, but they weren't ripe yet. The lizards gasped in the withered grass, and the cicadas sang madly in the dusty olive trees, the bushes, and the scrub oaks.

"Good God, what heat!" Pignoulet kept saying. He had drunk all the brandy in his gourd some time before, he was panting with thirst, and his shirt was soaking wet.

"But ever onward!" he said. "Soon we shall be in Grasse. Oh, what devilishly good luck, what joy, what happiness, to embrace my father and mother, and to drink the good water of Grasse from a pitcher, and to tell about my tour of France, and to kiss the fresh cheeks of Mïoun, and to get married on the feast of Mary Magdalen, and never to leave home again! On you go, Pignoulet, only a little stretch farther!"

And at last, here he was at the entrance to Grasse and in four strides at his father's workshop.

2

"My boy! Oh, my fine boy!" cried old Pignòu, leaving his workbench. "You have arrived safely! Margarido, it's the boy! Quick, go draw some wine, get out the frying pan, the tablecloth. Oh, what a blessing! How are you?"

"Not bad, thanks be to God. And you here, are you all in good health?"

"Oh, like poor old folks. But how big he's grown!"

And they all embrace him, his father, mother, neighbors, friends, and the girls, and they take off his pack, and the children finger the beautiful ribbons on his hat and on his long, thin cane. With tears in her eyes old Margarido lights the fire briskly with a handful of wood shavings, and while she is dusting flour on several pieces of cod to give the boy a treat, the father, Master Pignòu, sits down at the table with Pignoulet, and clinking glasses, they begin to wet the spigot.

"Look at you!" said old Pignòu, clinking with his glass. "In less than four years you have completed your tour of France, and you tell me you have already passed and been accepted as a Journeyman of the Guild.

"How all that has changed, I must say. In my day we needed a good seven years to win our colors. It's true, my child, that you had already done enough rough planing here in the shop, and for an apprentice you were not bad at wielding the plane and the jointer. But the main thing is that you know your craft, and I believe you have seen and learned all that a fine fellow must know who is the son of a master."

"Oh, Father, as far as that goes," the boy replied, "without bragging, I don't think anyone in the carpenter's trade can put one over on me."

"Well then," said the old man, "while the cod is singing in the pan, tell me what fine things you saw while traveling around the country."

3

"First, Father, you know that in leaving Grasse here I took off for Toulon, where I went into the Arsenal. No need to point out everything that's in there, since you've seen it like me."

"Yes, it's well known."

"On leaving Toulon I went and hired out in Marseille, a fine, big city, as you know, a good place for a craftsman, where the fellows took me to see, Father, a carved sea-horse on the sign of an inn."

"That's good."

"From there, well, I went up to Aix, where I admired the sculptures on the front of Saint-Sauveur."

"We've seen all that."

"Then from there we went to Arles and saw the vaulting of the city hall."

"So well designed that you can't understand how it holds up."

"From Arles, Father, we traveled to the town of Saint-Gilles, and there we saw the famous Spiral Staircase."

"Yes, a marvel for its design and for its size, which makes you realize, Son, that there were good craftsmen in former times as well as now."

"Then from Saint-Gilles we made our way to Montpellier, and there they showed us the famous Seashell. . . ."

"Yes, which is in the Vignoles quarter and which the book calls 'the horn of Montpellier.' "

"That's right. Then we walked to Narbonne."

"That's what I was waiting for."

"What's that, Father? In Narbonne I saw the Three Nurses and the archbishop's palace and the woodwork of the big church of Saint Paul."

"And then?"

"And then? The song doesn't tell of anything else.

Carcassone et Narbonne	Carcassone and Narbonne
Sont deux villes fort bonnes	Are two right good towns
Pour aller à Béziers;	On the way to Béziers;
Pézénas est zentille,	Pézénas is quite nice,
Mais les plus zolies filles	But the prettiest girls
N'en sont à Montpellier.	Are in Montpellier."

"Then, you bungler, you didn't see the Frog?"

"What Frog?"

"The Frog that's at the bottom of the holy water font in the church of Saint Paul! Oh, no wonder you made your tour of France so quickly, you lazy lout! The Frog of Narbonne, the masterpiece of masterpieces, that people come from all over to see! And this whippersnapper," cried old Pignòu, growing more and more agitated, "this brook-jumper who has just become a journeyman hasn't even seen the Frog of Narbonne! Oh, but it won't be said, sweetheart, that the son of a master had to hang his head in the house of his father. Eat, drink, sleep, and tomorrow morning, if you want us to be partners, you will return to Narbonne to see the Frog."

4

Poor Pignoulet knew that his father wasn't joking and that once he had made up his mind about something, he didn't relent, so he ate, drank, went to sleep, and at dawn the following day, without further argument, filled his knapsack and set out again for Narbonne.

With his feet bruised and swollen, with the heat and thirst, by road and by way, he walked and walked.

After seven or eight days he arrived at the city of Narbonne, whence, as the saying goes, "no good wind nor good person ever comes." Immediately Pignoulet, who was not singing this time, I assure you, went straight to the big church of Saint Paul, without taking time to eat a bite or have a drink at a cabaret, and went right to the holy water font to see the Frog.

And indeed, there at the bottom of the marble basin, under the clear water, crouched a frog with reddish stripes, so well carved that you would have said it was alive, looking with its two golden eyes and its quizzical expression at poor Pignoulet, who had come all the way from Grasse to see it.

"Oh, you damned slut!" the carpenter let out a sudden fierce cry, "you're the one who made me walk two hundred leagues in the burning sun! Now you'll remember Pignoulet of Grasse, Pignoulet, the Flower of Grasse!"

And behold, the rascal took his mallet and chisel from his pack, and whack! with one blow he made one of the Frog's legs jump. They say the holy water suddenly turned blood red. And the basin of the font has been reddish ever since.

(*The Provençal Almanac of 1890*)

The Girl from Monteux

1

Once upon a time in Monteux, which is the village of the good Saint Gent and of Micoulau Saboly, there was a girl blonde as gold. They called her Roso. She was the daughter of a café owner. And because she was good and sang like an angel, the parish priest of Monteux placed her at the head of the choir of his church. Now it happened that the father of little Roso hired a singer for the feast of Saint Gent, who is the patron of Monteux. The singer, who was young, fell in love with the fair young maid, and indeed, the fair young maid fell in love too. Whereupon the two children got married without further ado, and little Roso became Madame Bordas.

Farewell, Monteux! They went away together. Oh, how delightful it was to be free as the air and young as water, to have nothing to worry about but making love and singing for a living.

The very first saint's day for which little Roso sang was Saint Agatha, the feast day of Maillane. I remember it as if it were yesterday. It was at the café on the Square, and the room was full as an egg. Little Roso, who was no more frightened than a sparrow in a willow, was standing there in back on a platform, with her blonde hair, her pretty arms bare, and her husband at her feet accompanying her on his guitar.

What a lot of smoke there was! It was full of peasants, from Graveson, from Saint-Rémy, from Eyragues, and from Maillane. But not a dirty word was heard. They only said, "How pretty she is! What a charming manner! She sings like an organ! And she's not from far away, only from Monteux!"

It's true that little Roso sang pretty songs. She sang only of country, flag, battles, liberty, glory, and with a passion, a fire, a thundering spirit that thrilled all those masculine breasts. Then when she had finished, she cried out, "Long live Saint Gent!"

The applause would have destroyed the room. The little girl got down and cheerfully took up a collection around the table. Two-sou pieces rained into the bowl, and laughing happily as if she had a hundred thousand francs, she poured the money into her husband's guitar, saying, "Look, if this lasts, we shall soon be rich."

2

When Madame Bordas had done all the saints' days in our neighborhood, she wanted to try the cities.

There as in the villages, the girl from Monteux was a success.

She sang of Poland with its flag in her hand and put so much soul into it and such feeling that it made you shiver.

In Avignon, in Sète, in Toulouse, and in Bordeaux, she was adored by the people—to such a point that she said, "Now only Paris is left."

So she went up to Paris. Paris is the funnel that sucks in everything. There as everywhere and even more so, she was the idol of the crowd.

We were then in the last days of the Empire. The chestnuts were beginning to smoke, and Madame Bordas sang the "Marseillaise." Never had a singer performed that hymn with such enthusiasm and such frenzy. The workmen at the barricades believed they saw Liberty incarnate, and Tony Révillon, a Paris poet, wrote in the newspaper:

> Elle nous vient de la Provence
> Où soufflent les vents de la mer,
> Où l'on respire l'éloquence
> Tout enfant, en respirant l'air.
> Tous les bras sont tendus vers elle . . .
> Nous te saluons, ó beauté!
> Pour suivre tes pas, Immortelle,
> Nous quitterons notre cité:
> Tu nous mèneras aux frontières.
> A ton moindre geste soumis;
> Car tous les peuples sont nos frères,
> Et les tyrans nos ennemis!

> She comes to us from Provence,
> Where the sea winds blow,
> Where they breathe eloquence,
> Every child that breathes.
> All arms reach out to her—
> Immortal Beauty, we hail you!
> We will leave our city
> To follow in your footsteps.
> You will lead us to the frontiers,
> To your least wish submissive.
> For all people are our brothers
> And all tyrants our foes.

3

Alas, only too soon did she have to go to the frontiers. The war, the defeat, the revolution, the siege piled up one on top of the other. Then came the Commune with its devilish uproar.

The girl from Monteux went mad, bewildered like a bird in a storm. Intoxicated with smoke, with the upheaval, and with popularity, she sang "Marianne" for them like a little fiend. She would have sung in the water and better still in the fire!

One day the mob surrounded her in the street and carried her off like a straw to the Tuileries Palace.

The sovereign populace was having a party in the imperial drawing rooms. Arms black with powder seized Marianne—for Madame Bordas was Marianne to them—and placed her on the throne in the midst of red flags.

"Sing to us," they cried, "the last song the rafters of this cursed palace will hear!"

And the little girl from Monteux, wearing a red cap over her blonde locks, sang "The Rabble" for them.

A tremendous shout followed the last refrain, "Long live the Republic!" Only a voice lost in the crowd replied, "Long live Saint Gent!"

The eyes of the girl from Monteux misted over, two tears glistened in her blue eyes, and she turned pale as death.

"Stand back, give her some air!" shouted the crowd on seeing that she was fainting.

Oh, no, poor little Roso, it was not air that you needed. It was Monteux, it was Saint Gent in the mountains and the innocent joy of the saints' days of Provence.

But the mob rushed out through the open doors with its red flags, yelling. In Paris cannon fire thundered more and more, ominous rumors ran in the dark streets, sustained rifle fire could be heard in the distance, the smell of gas made you gasp for air, and several hours later, the fire of the Tuileries rose to the clouds.

Poor little girl from Monteux! No one ever heard of her again.

(*The Provençal Almanac of 1873*)

The Popular Man

A few years ago, the mayor of Gigognan invited me to his village's saint's day. We had been schoolmates for seven years in Avignon but had not seen each other since.

"God bless you!" he cried on seeing me, "you're still the same, fresh as a catfish, pretty as a penny, straight as a ramrod. I would have recognized you in a thousand."

"Yes, I'm still the same," I replied. "Only my sight is dimming a little, my temples are thinning, and my hair is getting white. And when the crests are white, the valleys are seldom warm."

"Go on, fellow," he said, "an old ox plows a straight furrow, and you're as old as you wish. Come, let's have dinner."

You know how they eat at village feasts, and at my friend Lassagne's house I can assure you it isn't cold. That was a dinner that demanded respect: coquilles of crayfish, fresh trout from the Sorgue, nothing but fine dishes and choice wines, a shot of brandy in the middle, and all sorts of liqueurs afterward, and to serve us a fetching girl of twenty who . . . I say no more.

As we were having dessert, we heard a sound in the street: "Vounvoun! vounvoun!" It was the beat of little drums. The youth of the village had come, as was the custom, to serenade the Consul.

"Open the door, Françouneto," cried my friend Lassagne," go get the cakes, and quick! wash the glasses."

Meanwhile the drummers were beating their tattoo. When they had finished, the Abbots of the Revels, with bouquets on their jackets, entered the room, along with the village beadle, who proudly carried the pole with the athletic prizes, the drummers, the dancers, and all the girls.

The glasses were filled with good wine from Alicante. All the young gallants in turn cut a slice of cake. The health of His Honor was toasted profusely. Then when they had drunk and joked a while, His Honor spoke to them: "My children, dance as much as you wish, enjoy yourselves as much as you can, always be polite to strangers. You are free to do everything as you please, except fighting and throwing things."

"Long live Monsieur Lassagne!" cried the young people. And with that they went out, and the dancing began. When they were all outside, I said to Lassagne, "How long have you been mayor of Gigognan?"

"Fifty years, my friend."

"You're not joking? Fifty years?"

"Yes, yes, it's been fifty years. I have seen eleven governments come and go, my fine fellow. And I don't expect to die, if the Lord helps me, without burying another half-dozen."

"But how have you managed to keep afloat through so much chaos and revolution?"

"Well, my dear friend, it's an ass's trick. The people, the good people, only ask to be governed. But not everyone knows how to govern them. There are those who say you must govern them strictly. Others say you must govern them gently. And you know what I say? *You must govern them cheerfully.*

"Take a look at the shepherds. The good shepherds are not those who always have their sticks raised. Nor are they those who lie down under a willow or sleep on embankments. The good shepherds are those who walk quietly in front of their flock playing the flute. The sheep feel free and are in effect free, so they readily browse on the grass and weeds. Then when their bellies are full and it's time to go home, the shepherd plays a retreat on his fife, and the flock is content to wend its way to the fold. That's how I do it, my friend. I play the flute, and my flock follows."

"You play the flute! That sounds fine, but come now, you have Reds, you have Whites, you have fools, you have stubborn people in your community like everywhere else, and when an election comes around for a deputy, say, how do you manage?"

"How do I manage? Well, my friend, I let things be. For to tell the Whites to vote for the Republic would be to lose your pains and your prayers, and to tell the Reds to vote for Henry V would be like spitting at that wall."

"But the straddlers, those who have no opinions, the poor innocents, all those good souls who shift as the wind blows them?"

"Oh, those? Sometimes when they ask my advice in the

barber shop, I tell them, 'Look, Bassaquin is no better than Bassacan. If you vote for Bassaquin, you'll have fleas this summer, and if you vote for Bassacan, you'll have fleas this summer. You see, a good rain is better for Gigognan than all the candidates' promises. Oh, it would be different if you nominated peasants. So long as you don't nominate peasants for deputy, as they do in Sweden and Denmark, you won't be represented. The lawyers, the doctors, the journalists, and the petit bourgeois that you send up there only want one thing, to stay in Paris as long as possible in order to feed at the public manger and milk the cow. They don't give a damn for Gigognan. But if you sent peasants, as I tell you, they would think about saving money, they would reduce the big salaries, they would never declare war, they would build canals, they would abolish the centralized tax system, and they would settle matters quickly in order to get back in time for the harvest. To think that there are more than twenty million dirt farmers in France and they don't have the wit to elect three hundred of their number to represent the land! What would they risk in trying? It's against the odds that they would do worse than the others.'"

"Oh, that Monsieur Lassagne!" they all answer, "he's joking, but he may be right."

"But let's get back to the point," I said. "How have you personally, you, Lassagne, managed to maintain your popularity and your authority in Gigognan for fifty years' time?"

"Oh, there's nothing to it. Look, let's get up from the table and go for a walk, and when you've gone around Gigognan with me once or twice, you'll know as much about it as I do."

And we got up from the table, lit a cigar, and went to see the games.

As we were going out, there was a game of *boules* in the road. The bowler struck the mark, and his ball stayed put, giving two points to the others.

"Damned lucky hit!" cried Monsieur Lassagne. "That's what you call shooting! Congratulations, Jan-Glaude. I've seen plenty of games, but I assure you I've never seen a mark removed like that. You're a great bowler!"

And we went on. After a little while we met a couple of girls out for a walk.

"Take a look at that," said Lassagne audibly. "Don't they look like two queens? What charming figures! What pretty faces! And those earrings in the latest fashion! That's the flower of Gigognan."

The two girls turned around and greeted us with a smile.

In crossing the Square we passed by an old man who was sitting in front of his door.

"Well now, Master Guintrand," Monsieur Lassagne said to him, "are we wrestling with the men or with the youths this year?"

"Ah, my dear sir, I'm not wrestling at all," answered Master Guintrand.

"Do you remember, Master Guintrand, that year when Meissounié, Quequino, and Rabassoun, the three proudest wrestlers of Provence, turned up at the meadow, and you threw all three of them on their backs?"

"You think I don't remember?" said the old wrestler, his face lighting up. "It was the year they took the citadel of Antwerp. There was a prize of a hundred crowns and a sheep for the youths. The prefect of Avignon shook my hand. The people of Bédarride thought they were fighting those of Courtezon, for they were on my side against the others. Ah, what times! It's not that way now when they fight, it's better not to speak of it, for you don't see men any more, no, sir, not any more. Why, they have an understanding among themselves."

We shook his hand and went on just as the village priest came out of the rectory.

"Hello, gentlemen."

"Hello, Father. Oh, say, Father," said Lassagne, "now that I see you, I must speak to you of something. This morning at Mass I thought our church was getting very crowded, especially on saints' days. Don't you think it would be a good idea to consider enlarging it?"

"Oh, there, Your Honor, I'm entirely of your opinion. Why, on holy days, we can't even turn around."

"I shall see to it, Father. At the first meeting of the town council I shall raise the question, we shall make a study of it, and if they are willing to help us at the prefecture. . . ."

"I'm delighted, Your Honor, and I can only thank you."

A while later we bumped into a young fellow who was going into the café with his jacket on his shoulder.

"It's all right," Lassagne said to him. "It seems you're not feeble. They say you threw a punch at that guy who was trying to beat your time with Madeloun."

"Did I do wrong, Your Honor?"

"You're a good man, Jóuselet. Don't let anyone steal your bacon. Only look, another time don't hit so hard."

"Now I begin to understand," said I to Lassagne. "You use soft soap."

"Wait another moment," he said.

As we were going outside the walls, we saw a flock coming that filled the whole road, and Lassagne shouted to the shepherd, "Just at the sound of the sheep-bells I said, 'It must be Jòrgi,' and I was not mistaken. What a pretty flock of sheep! What healthy ewes! But what do you feed them? I'm sure you wouldn't let any of them go for less then ten crowns."

"Oh, I don't think so," answered Jòrgi. "I bought them this winter at the Cold Fair. Almost all have lambed, and I believe they'll lamb again in the fall."

"Not only will they lamb again, but animals like those are likely to produce twins."

"May God hear you, Monsieur Lassagne!"

We had just finished talking with the shepherd when we saw a carter named Sabatoun come swaying along.

"Say, Sabatoun," Lassagne said to him, "you may or may not believe it, but I recognized the sound of your whip when you and your cart were still half a league away."

"Is it possible, Monsieur Lassagne?"

"My friend, you're the only one who can make a whip crack like that."

At that Sabatoun, to prove it was true, gave us a crack of the whip that rang in our ears.

Next as we walked on we came upon an old woman who was gathering chicory along the ditches.

"Say, is it you, Berenguiero?" Lassagne asked. "Well, from behind, with your red scarf, I took you for Cacha's daughter-in-law Teresoun. You look exactly like her."

"Me? Oh, Monsieur Lassagne, just remember that I'm seventy!"

"Believe me, if you could see yourself from behind, you show no sign of misery. One could harvest grapes with worse baskets."

"Oh, that Monsieur Lassagne, he's always joking," said the old woman as she burst out laughing.

Then turning to me, the old crone said, "You see, sir, it's not just a manner of speaking, but that Monsieur Lassagne is the cream of mankind. He's pleasant with everyone, you see, and he would speak with the last person in the country, even a one-year-old child! That's why he's been mayor of Gigognan for fifty years and will be all his life."

"Well now, friend," Lassagne said to me, "you see that I didn't make her say it. We all like good things to eat, we all like compliments, and we all take pleasure in good manners. Whether it's with women, or with kings, or with the people, whoever wishes to govern must please. And that's the secret of the Mayor of Gigognan."

(*The Provençal Almanac of 1883*)

XIV

THE JOURNEY TO THE SAINTES-MARIES-DE-LA-MER

ll my life I had heard of the Camargue and of the Saintes-Maries and of their pilgrimage. But I had never been there. In the spring of that year (1855), I wrote to Mathieu, who was always ready to go gadding, "Do you want to come with me to the Saints?"

"Yes," he replied, and we made a rendezvous in the Condamine quarter of Beaucaire, from which a caravan left for the Saintes-Maries every year on the 24th of May. We got under way a little after midnight with a crowd of common people, women, girls, children, and men, all piled in carts. You can imagine how crowded the carts were: there were fourteen of us in ours.

The worthy driver, a certain Lamouroux, was one of those men of Provence who have the gift of gab and are never at a loss. He placed us in front, seated on the shaft with our legs dangling. Half the time he walked alongside us to the left of the animal, with his whip around his neck, striking fire to light his pipe. And sometimes when he was tired, he sat in a seat that carters call "the lazybones-carrier," suspended in front of the wheels.

Behind me, wrapped in a woolen mantle with a hood, was a young girl called Alardo, snuggled up with her mother on a mattress, with her feet against my back. But since our neighbors were chattering among themselves and we had not yet made their acquaintance, Mathieu and I talked with the driver.

Lamouroux began the conversation, "So where are you from, if I am not being too inquisitive?"

"We are from Maillane," we said.

"Oh, then you're not from far away. I could tell that by the way you talked. 'A carter from Maillane,' they say, 'tips over on level ground.' "

"They're not all like that, my good fellow."

"Come now," said Lamouroux, "that's just a joke, And look, when I traveled the roads, I knew a teamster from Maillane who was built like Saint George. They called him the Ortolan."

"That was a few years ago."

"Ah, gentlemen, I am speaking of the days of the teamsters, before the big shots ruined us with their railroads. I am speaking of a time when the Beaucaire fair was at its height, when the first ship to arrive at the fair won the sheep, and when the sailors had skinned it, they hung the skin at the end of the mainmast. I am speaking of a time when there weren't enough tow horses to haul the heaps of merchandise sold at Beaucaire up the Rhone, and when the carters—you're too young to remember them—the teamsters and the drivers of carioles who traveled the highways and thought they owned them made their whips crack from Marseille to Paris and from Paris to Lille in Flanders."

And once launched on the subject of the teamsters, Lamouroux kept at it till sunrise, while his animal plodded quietly in the moonlight.

"Oh," he said, "you should have seen those lines of loaded wagons, covered carts, tightly strapped drays, all touching one another, on the bridge of Bon-Pas or on the plateau overlooking Marseille, on that highway twenty-four paces wide. You should have seen those rows of magnificent teams and wagons, teams of three, four, six animals, going down to Marseille or going up to Paris, hauling grain, wine, sacks of oats, bales of dried cod, casks of anchovies, or slabs of soap, jolting, groaning, and in God's keeping, as the waybills then said.

"And when we went through a village, gentlemen, a swarm

of children would hang on the bar of the cart and let themselves be dragged along behind, while others cried, 'Carter, carter, look behind you!' For dinner, for supper, or for sleeping on the road there was from time to time a famous inn with a handsome, laughing hostess, with a big kitchen and a big fireplace, where whole pigs turned on the spit, with its door wide open, with stables vast as churches, where two rows of mangers stretched off in the distance, and where colored pictures of Saint Eloi were stuck to the walls. The names of those inns were The Rook, Saint Martin, The Golden Lion, The White Horse, The Black Mule, The Red Hat, The Beautiful Hostess, The Big Lodging, and who knows what else, and people talked of them for a hundred leagues around.

"From time to time along the road there were harness-makers with a new collar on display, blacksmiths with smudged faces who had a horseshoe for a sign, little shops where packages of whipcords and caps for pipes hung behind the window, and little bars with a grape arbor over the door white with dust, where the teamsters came to drink their drop of brandy for a sou.

"And swaggering from side to side at the unhurried pace of their wagons, saluting everyone they knew with their whips, the famous teamsters walked arrogantly, one hand on the lead rope and the whip in the other, wearing a blue blouse, corduroy breeches, a multicolored cap, a cape against the wind, and gaiters on their legs, shouting from time to time 'Gee up!' or 'Gee!' or 'Haw!' And when the road was smooth and the journey was going well and the wheels were creaking away, they sang the teamsters' song in step with the animals and the jingling of their bells:

Un roulié qu'es bèn mounta,	A teamster who's well mounted
Fau qu'ague de rodo	Must have six-inch wheels
De sièis pouce à la Mabrou,	In the style of Marlborough,
Acò 's à la modo,	That's the fashion now,
Em' un eissiéu de dès pan,	With an axle of ten spans
Em' un pichot bidet blanc	And a little white nag
Pèr lou gouvernage	To help him manage
De soun equipage.	His equipage.

Why shouldn't they sing? Transportation was well paid: seven francs a hundredweight from Arles to Lyons, and barring accidents, a driver and his pair could easily earn a *louis d'or* a day.

"Besides, they did things in style on the roads of France. For our teamsters were proud. What big, handsome horses! What mules! What spirited animals! It was a pleasure to see them all harnessed and outfitted, the shaft horses, the off-wheelers, the lead horses, and the others, their nosebands with fringes, their halters with little bells, their bits with tassels of every color. The collars rose up in a pointed horn; the collar hames, like big feathers, held up the traces in blue glass rings; the sheepskins curled on the backs of the horses; the embroidered horse-blankets had fly-netting; the saddle bands, the bellybands, the crupper-straps, the harnesses, all were quilted and fitted by a master hand. Why shouldn't they sing?

En arribant à Lioun,	When we arrive in Lyon,
Nous cercon rancuro	They try to pick a quarrel
E nous fan passa dessus	And make us go over
De la basso-culo:	The drawbridge.
Acò n'es d'aquéli gènt	Those people are the sort
Que demandon que d'argènt	Who only ask for money
Pèr fai de dentello	To give lace
A si damisello.	To their ladies.

"From Marseille to Lyon the teamsters walked to their animals' left, or as they say, 'on the haw hand side,' because at that time the lead rope was on the left side of the horse. They called the other side of the team 'the off side.'

"But the custom of Provence went only as far as Lyon. At Lyon the climate, the speech, everything changed. So you had to change hands and hold the lead rope to the animals' right. Then came the rain, the continual downpour with mud and ruts, which you had to straddle if you didn't want to get bogged down. Then the weighmasters who tried to pick quarrels by speaking French. Then you wanted dirty words, thunderations, goddams! They swore and cursed like teamsters: 'Gee up, Black! gee up, Bay! gee up, you bag of bones! hey there, you old nag! Oh, you fiendish crook!' The cart was stuck!

"But reinforcements came with their drivers. The team was doubled and tripled, and with shoulders to the wheel, they extricated the cart. Then they went to the inn. To the sound of whipcracks the hostess, the chambermaid, and the stablehand came out, lantern in hand, to meet the mud-spattered teamsters. The team was brought in, unhitched, and fed, and then they went in to supper.

"Thanks be to God, on the road they served a meal fit for Mardi Gras for thirty sous a head. The teamsters ate with their elbows on the table. Under the table a nine-pint demijohn lurked in the dark, and when they had drunk, they threw the last drop in the glass over their shoulders. In the middle of the meal it was the custom to get up to go water the animals and give them grain. Then they sat down again to eat the roast. And here we are, fellows! Why shouldn't they sing?

Lou matin à soun leva,	In the morning at sunrise
La soupo au froumage:	A soup made with cheese:
Acò 's un friand manja,	That's a tasty dish,
Qu'amo lou latage.	Fresh from the dairy.
Pièi, pèr s'escarrabiha,	Then to wake us up,
Un vèire de ratafia;	A glass of cordial;
E, long de la routo,	And along the road
Béuran mai la gouto.	We drink another drop.

"They called that the 'worm-killer.' Then they struck the flint, lit their pipes, chucked the cheerful chambermaid under her delicate chin with their rough hands—she was waiting at the door for a tip—gave a twist of the crank to the lashing of the load, and off they went again!

"Now, to tell the truth, the days on the road were not always easy. Without counting the holes with mud up to the hubs, the uphill climbs with the team pulling with all its might, the downhill runs on the brakes, the spokes that gave way, the hubs that broke, the gendarmes with their mustaches who spotted the plates of drivers who had fallen asleep and made out tickets, sometimes you had to 'skip Mass,' that is, pass right by the inn without stopping and skip dinner in order to save time or make up time.

"At other times two drivers would run afoul of each other on the road. 'Out of the way, you!' 'Out of the way, yourself!' 'You won't get out of the way, you capon?' Suddenly a blow of the whip on the muzzle blinded the shaft horse and tipped over the cart against a pile of stones. Then they ran for posts and blocks of yew. There were horrible fights on the road in which a man was often struck by a crank handle and brained.

"Among the rules of the road, however, there was one old custom that was respected by everyone. The teamster whose lead horse had four white feet had the right of way, gentlemen, whether going uphill or downhill. Hence the saying, 'He who has four white feet can go anywhere.'

"Finally the teamsters arrived in Paris and went to the stables in the Grand'-Pinte, a quarter so populous, my grandfather said, that the government could raise a hundred thousand men there whenever it wished with one blast of a whistle.

En arribant à Paris,	On arriving in Paris,
Usanço nouvello:	We find new customs:
De taiolo n' i' a plus gis,	No more sashes to hold up your pants,
Culoto à bretello.	Instead they wear suspenders.
Acò n' es de franchimand	Only the French
Qu'atalon deforo man	Harness on the off side
E fan tout au burre. . .	And cook everything in butter.
Que lou tron te cure.	May lightning strike them!

"But when they entered the Big Town, they really worked at making the whip crack. They would let off a volley of repeated whipcracks, a crashing and clashing that sounded like thunder.

"'Watch out!' the Parisians would say, with both hands blocking their ringing ears. 'Here come the Provençaux with their "Go, in the name of thunder, are you afraid you don't have enough room?"'

"It must be said that the teamsters of Provence were the champion whipcrackers at that time. Meat-Eater of Tarascon once used up four pounds of whipcord in the space of a league by doing the quadruple whipcrack. Master Imbert of Beaucaire could trim a candle with one crack of the whip without putting it out. The Plant-Louse of Château-Renard could uncork a bottle without knocking it over. And, they say that Fat Charloun of Pierre-Plantade took the four shoes off a mule with a single flick of the whip.

"Anyhow, when the teamsters had unloaded their wagons, tucked their pay in their leather belts, loaded up again for Marseille, and taken a walk in the Palais-Royal, they joyfully struck up this last verse:

Tè, *garçon*, vaqui pèr tu,	Hostler, here's something for you,
Vai metre en caviho. . .	Go harness the horses.
Mai l'oustesso a respoundu:	Then the hostess spoke up:
Iéu que siéu *zolio*,	I am so pretty,
Iéu que te fau tant de bèn,	I did so much for you,
Tu jamai me dounes rèn?	Why don't you ever give me anything?
Fai-me 'no brassado,	Give me a kiss,
Sarai soulajado.	And I'll be satisfied.

"And they put on the collars and the harness. And in twenty, twenty-two, or twenty-four days, they returned to Provence to the jingle-jangle of the harness bells, to parade in triumph with the 'Leafy Cart' on the day of Saint Eloi. And then in the cabaret you had no end of story-telling and bragging and lies as big as Mount Ventoux. One traveling at night had seen Saint Elmo's fire glowing, and the fantastic fire had sat on his wagon for some two hours as he traveled. Another had found such a heavy suitcase by the road! There must have been at least a hundred thousand francs inside. But just as he was about to pick it up to put it in his cart, a masked horseman had come riding at full tilt and claimed it. Another had been held up. Fortunately for him, he had tied his *louis d'or* in the curl of his pigtail—for at that time they wore pigtails—and the robbers with their big beards, their stilettos, and their double-barreled pistols had rummaged and ransacked the wagon box in vain. They found only the demijohn.

"Another had dwelt in the distant land of the Manichees, who are not Christians at birth. Another had traveled in the country of the Wooden Shovels. 'Some people suppose that wooden shovels are made like wooden shoes or spoons,' he said. 'But that's nonsense. Wooden shovels, which are used to shovel wheat, grow on trees ready-made, the way almonds and carobs do here. When we went there, gentlemen, the harvest had been brought in, and we could not see them. But we were told by the people of the country that when they are ripe, and when the mistral blows while they are on the trees, they make a racket like the rattles during Tenebrae services.'

"Another insisted that he had seen in Paris a beautiful princess who had a pig's snout. Her parents took her around from one big city to another and showed her, poor thing, in a magic lantern and offered millions to anyone who would marry her.

"'Holy name of names!' said old Baggy Britches, 'that's something, but that's nothing. Let me tell you what surprised me most and amazed me most in Paris. Here in our region if someone speaks French, it's someone educated, a bourgeois, a lawyer, a police commissioner, who has spent maybe ten years and more in school. But good Lord! up there they all talk French. You see kids not yet seven years old, children no higher than that, with snotty noses, who speak French like grownups! I don't know how the devil they do it.'"

That good fellow Lamouroux would have told us more stories to the jogging of the cart if we had not arrived at the bridge of Fourques, and as the sun rose, the immense plains of the Camargue stretched out before us in the delta of the two Rhones.

But what pleased us more than the sunrise (for we were twenty-five) was that girl who huddled with her mother behind us, as I said before, and who as she smiled and removed the hood of her mantle, appeared in the dawn like a queen of youth. With a reddish-purple ribbon tied prettily over the ash-blonde hair that burst out of her coif, with the look of a somewhat distraught Sibyl, with her fine, clear complexion and her lovely lips all set to smile, she looked like a tulip emerging from the morning dew. Enchanted, we greeted her. But Alardo spoke as if she had not seen us, "Mother, are we far from the holy Saints?"

"We are probably nine or ten leagues away, my girl."

"Will he be there, will my young man be there?"

"Hush, sweetheart!"

And with a yawn that showed all her teeth, her milky teeth, her white teeth, the girl said, "I'm tired of waiting. I'm so hungry I can see it running. What if we had breakfast?"

And she quickly spread a towel of unbleached linen on her knees. Her mother took some bread, some figs, an orange, some dates, and bit of sausage out of a basket. And without further ado they began to eat.

"Enjoy your food!" we said to them.

"At your service, gentlemen," said Alardo sweetly, sinking her teeth into a chunk of bread.

"On condition that we share our food, Mademoiselle."

"Gladly."

And Mathieu, who had brought two bottles of good wine from La Nerthe in his knapsack, uncorked one, and after eating a bite, we all drank in turn, Alardo, her mother, me, Mathieu, and the driver, one after the other, all from the same cup, down the hatch! And now we were friends.

Then when we climbed down from the wagon for a moment to stretch our legs, we asked Lamouroux, "Who's that girl with such a fine manner?"

"To look at her," the driver answered in a low voice, "you wouldn't say she's a bit cracked, would you? And yet, gentlemen, it seems she's not right in the head since her young man left her three months ago."

"That pretty girl? Her suitor ran out on her?"

"He had eloped with her, the villain! Then he left her in the lurch for another, ugly as sin, but with lots of money. And Alardo, who's the flower of Condamine, her mother is bringing her to the Saints to distract her or cure her, if possible."

"Oh, the poor thing!"

We arrived at the sheepfolds of Albaron, where we stopped to let the animals eat from a feed bag in front of the wheels. During that time the girls of Beaucaire who were on the cart, wearing ribbons of all different colors on their heads, gathered about Alardo to dance a round:

Au brande de ma tanto,
Lou roussignòu ié canto:

> Oh! que de roso! Oh! que de flous!
>   Bello, bello Alardo, viras-vous.
>
> La bello s'es virado
> Soun bèu l'a regardado:
> Oh! que de roso! Oh! que de flous!
> Bello, bello Alardo, embrassas-vous.
>
> The nightingale was singing
>   As we danced at my aunt's.
> Oh, so many roses! Oh, so many flowers!
>   Pretty, pretty Alardo, turn around.
>
> The pretty girl turned,
>   Her beau looked at her.
> Oh, so many roses! Oh, so many flowers!
>   Pretty, pretty Alardo, kiss each other.

And the poor girl went off with her arms raised, laughing like a madwoman and crying, "My young man! My young man! My young man!"

Now the weather, which had been cloudy since dawn, grew more and more overcast. The sea wind blew, driving heavy storm clouds up toward Arles that gradually darkened the whole expanse of the sky. In the marshland, the frogs and toads sang. Our long wagon train stretched out, lost in the vast fields of saltwort, in the whitish salt flats, on a road of shifting sand lined by tamarisks covered with pink blossoms. The earth smelled musty. And flights of young ducks, flights of teal and goldeneye, flew overhead quacking.

"Lamouroux," cried the woman, "is it going to rain?"

"Hmm!" the man replied, looking quite anxiously at the sky. "When there are clouds, it's likely to rain."

"Well, we'll be sitting pretty if a downpour catches us in the middle of the Camargue!"

"My poor girls, you'll have to put your skirts up over your heads."

A cowboy on horseback with his trident in hand, who was rounding up his black bulls scattered in the salt fields, shouted at us, "You're going to have a bath!"

It began to drizzle. Then gradually the rain began in earnest.

And down came the water! In no time those low-lying plains were covered with pools of water. Sitting on the shaft of the cart, we saw herds of wild horses off in the distance, shaking their manes and their long, flowing tails, climbing the levees and the sand dunes. And down came the water! The road, submerged in the flood, made pulling harder and harder. The wheels got stuck. The animals stopped. Finally you saw only a vast lake as far as the eye could see. And the drivers said, "Come on, you have to get down—women, girls, everyone on the ground!—unless you want to sleep among the tamarisks."

"But then we'll have to walk in the water."

"By walking barefoot, pretty ladies, you'll earn the Great Pardon—which you need, for your sins are mighty heavy."

And the women and girls, young and old, got down. With shrieks and laughter they all took off their shoes and tucked up their skirts to go wading. The drivers carried the children on their shoulders like Saint Christopher. And Mathieu, offering his back to the mother of the pretty girl who was in our cart, said, "Here, get on there, good woman, I'll carry you piggy-back."

The fat woman, who found it hard to walk, did not refuse.

"And you," he said, winking at me, "take care of Alardo, won't you? Then to ease the burden, we'll change from time to time."

Then without any further alleluias, we each took our passengers on our backs. And when all the young fellows who were on the pilgrimage did like us, each taking up his burden, you can imagine the comedy!

Mathieu and his fat woman laughed themselves silly. As for me, I felt those cool round arms about my neck, as Alardo held the umbrella over our heads. When I held that girl's tender calves on my hips, which out of modesty she did not dare squeeze, I would not have given anything—to this day I confess it—in exchange for our journey in the Camargue amid the rain and mud.

"My God, if my young man could see me," Alardo kept saying, "my young man who doesn't want me any more, my handsome young man, my handsome young man."

In vain I spoke to her and paid her sly little compliments. She didn't hear me, she didn't see me. But she breathed on my neck and on my shoulder, and I only needed to turn my head a little to kiss her; her hair brushed against mine; the warm fragrance of her soft body perfumed me; her trembling breast heaved against me; and deluding myself like her—though she belonged entirely to her young man—I believed I was like Paul carrying my Virginie.

At the height of my dream, Mathieu, whose back was breaking under the fat mama, said to me, "Let's change for a while. I can't go on, my friend!" And after we had both rested at the foot of a "blind" (that's the name they give in the Camargue to tamarisks that have grown into trees), Mathieu took the girl and I, alas, the mother. And thus we waded at least a good league with water halfway up our legs—which didn't bother us—taking turns, as I tell you, exchanging our pains for the fantasy of a fairy's love.

In time, however, as we came in sight of the Château of Avignon, the downpour ceased, the weather cleared, and the road became dry again. We climbed back into the carts, and about four o'clock we suddenly saw the church of the Saintes-Maries rising against the blue of the sea and sky with the three bays of its Romanesque belfry, its reddish crenelations, and its massive walls.

All cried out as one, "Oh, holy Saints!" For that sanctuary, lost off there at the far end of the Vaccarès Lagoon, amid the sands of the seashore, is the Mecca, as they say, of the whole Gulf of the Lion. And there you are struck by the harmonious grandeur and the measureless arc of that flat expanse of land and sea, where the eye can embrace the circle of the terrestrial horizon, the *orbis terrarum* of the ancients, better than anywhere else.

"We'll arrive just in time to take down the shrines," Lamouroux said, "for you know, gentlemen, that we of Beaucaire have the right before all others to turn the winch that brings the Saints down."

To understand that remark, you must know that the sacred relics of Mary, the mother of James, of Mary Salome, and of their servant Sara are kept locked in a high chapel under the vault of the choir and the apse, and on the eve of the feast they are slowly lowered by a cable through an opening to the fervent crowd in the church.

We unhitched in the middle of the dunes that surround the little town, dunes covered with whitish shrubs and tamarisks, and immediately ran to the church.

"Light up those dear Saints!" cried some women from Montpellier who were selling candles, tapers, medals, and pictures in front of the door.

The church was full as an egg of people from Languedoc, women from around Arles, invalids, and gypsies, all on top of one another. In fact, it was the gypsies who burned the biggest tapers, but only at the altar of Saint Sara, who they believe belonged to their nation. These nomads hold their annual assemblies at the Saints and from time to time the election of their queen.

We had quite a time getting in. Some old crones in black coifs from Nîmes, who had brought twill cushions to sleep on in the church, fought over the chairs. "I had it before you!" "But I rented it!" A priest held out "the sacred arm" from mouth to mouth to be kissed. The sick were given glasses of brackish water from the well of the Saints, which is in the nave of the church and which they say becomes sweet on that day. Some people scraped with their fingernails the old marble "Saints' Pillow" sculptured and enshrined in the wall, in order to use the marble dust as a remedy. The odor and stifling heat of burning wax, of incense, of human bodies, and the smell of dogs made you gasp for breath. And each group sang its hymn loudly amid the confusion.

But oh, what cries when the two pointed shrines appeared suspended in the air: "Holy Saints! Holy Saint Marys!" And as the cord unreeled in space, the shrieks and spasms grew more and more intense. With faces and arms raised, the palpitating crowd waited expectantly for a miracle. Suddenly from the end of the church a girl leaped forward as if she had wings, a magnificent girl, blonde and disheveled, and treading with her feet on the heads of the crowd, she flew like a ghost through the nave toward the floating shrines, crying in a piercing voice, "Holy Saints, for pity's sake, give me back the love of my young man!"

Everyone rose up. "It's Alardo!" cried the people from Beaucaire. "It's Saint Mary Magdalen who has come to visit her sisters!" said others with consternation. And everyone wept.

To conclude, the following day there was the procession on the sands of the beach to the roar and the blast of the breaking, splashing whitecaps. In the distance, on the horizon, two or three boats beat against the wind and seemed to make no progress. And people showed each other the dazzling "trail" that the action of the waves extended on the sea. "It's the path," they said, "that the Holy Marys took in their skiff to reach Provence after the death of Our Lord." There on that vast shore, in the midst of those visions illuminated by a bright sun, it seemed to us that we were in heaven. The beautiful Alardo, now a bit pale, carried "the Saints' skiff" on her shoulders with the other women of Beaucaire, and everyone said, "What a pity! She's a poor madwoman whose young man has left her."

But since we wanted to go and see Aigues-Mortes, and a carriage that stopped there was leaving, as soon as the Saints had gone back up into their chapel (about four o'clock), we left with a flock of old women from Montpellier and Lunel, market women and tripe-sellers wearing coifs layered like cabbages, who began to sing again at the top of their lungs as soon as we were under way:

Courons aux Saintes Maries	Let us run to the Saint Marys
Pour leur donner notre foi;	To give them our faith;
Que nos coeurs se multiplient	May our hearts increase
Pour Jésus et pour sa Croix,	For Jesus and for his Cross,

and this other hymn, which was all the rage at the festival:

Désarmez le Christ, désarmez le Christ
  Par vos prières!
Désarmez le Christ, désarmez le Christ,
Et soyez au ciel nos bonnes mères!

Disarm Christ, disarm Christ
  With your prayers!

Disarm Christ, disarm Christ
And be our holy mothers in heaven.

"Dame Roca wrote that pretty song with her husband," said a fishwife as she finished her lunch, "and all night long they sang only that. Those women of Provence could only remember the old hymns in *The Pious Soul*:

J'ai vu sous de sombres voiles	Under dark sails
Onze étoiles,	I saw eleven stars,
La lune avec le soleil. . . .	The moon and sun together. . . .

Our songs of Montpellier are so much more beautiful!"

And they talked of this and that. We crossed the Little Rhone on a ferry at Sylve-Réal. At that time there was a fort there, a pretty little fort built by Vauban and gilded by the sun, which the Corps of Engineers has stupidly destroyed since. We crossed the wasteland and the pine woods of Le Sauvage. And finally in the evening we saw the gigantic towers, crenelations, and ramparts of Aigues-Mortes rising from amidst the marshes, looming fierce and black against the purple sunset.

"Never mind," said one of the women, "if there were a few too many funerals while the carriage was taking us to the Saints, the undertakers probably had plenty of work at Montpellier."

"Well, then they carried them by hand."

"Oh, come now, I think they have two carriages for the dead."

Realizing as we heard these words that the horrible old rattletrap was painted black, we asked, "But would this vehicle happen to be. . . . ?"

"The coach, gentlemen, of the funeral establishment of the city of Montpellier."

"Curse the luck," we cried. And opening the door with a kick, we jumped out on the road in a panic, paid the driver, quickly shook out our clothes in the air, and slowly made our way to Aigues-Mortes on foot.

A veritable stronghold out of Syria or Egypt is that silent city of the "Blue-Bellies" (as they sometimes call the fever-ridden people of Aigues-Mortes), with its awesome rectangle of ramparts baking in the sun, looking, you would say, as if it had just been abandoned by Saint Louis, and with its Tower of Constance, where forty Protestant women and girls were imprisoned after the dragonnades under Louis XIV and rotted there until the end of his reign, forgotten and condemned to misery for some forty years.

One day, long after that excursion, when we returned to visit the great tower of Aigues-Mortes with two beautiful Protestant ladies from Nîmes, as we read the names those prisoners had carved on the stones of the dungeon, they said to me, choking with emotion, "Poet, don't be surprised to see us crying. For us Huguenots those poor women martyred for their faith are our Saint Marys!"

X V

JAN ROUSSIÈRE
AND MAGALI

"Hello, Monsieur Frederi."

"Oh, hello."

"They tell me you need a hired man."

"Yes. Where are you from?"

"From Villeneuve, the town of the 'lizards,' near Avignon."

"And what can you do?"

"A bit of everything. I've worked in an olive mill, I've been a mule-driver, a quarryman, a plowman, a miller, a shearer, a reaper when necessary, a wrestler on occasion, a pruner of poplars, which is quite a lofty trade, and a cleaner of wells, which is the lowest of all."

"And they call you?"

"Jan Roussière. Rousseyron or Seyron for short."

"Well then, how much do you want to earn? The job is driving a team."

"About fifteen *louis d'or*."

"I'll give you a hundred crowns."

"Agreed on a hundred crowns!"

And that's how I hired the plowman Jan Roussière, who taught me the song of "Magali." A jolly, strapping fellow, built like Hercules, he was the cheerful companion who kept me from becoming despondent during our long, solitary evening watches with my father, who had gone blind the last year I spent on the farm.

A fine plowman, he always had some merry song to enliven his team:

L'araire es coumpausa	The plow is constructed
De trento-uno pèço.	Of thirty-one pieces.
Aquéu que l'a 'nventa,	The one who invented it
Falié que n'en sachèsso:	Must have known a lot.
Segur,	Oh yes,
Es quauque moussur.	He was some inventor!

Naturally adept or artistic, if you prefer, he knew how to give a harmonious line and style, as they say, to whatever he did, whether putting the top on a strawstack, piling manure, or loading a cart. But unfortunately, he had the failings of his master: he was rather fond of sleeping and loved to take a siesta.

But for conversation, he had a gift. You should have heard him talk of the time when he drove teams of tow horses on the riverbanks, the big horses that hauled the Rhone barges one after another to Valence and Lyons.

"Would you believe I drove," he said, "the finest team on the banks of the Rhone at the age of twenty? A team," he said, "of eighty stallions, hitched by fours, pulling six boats. How fine it was when we set out in the morning on the levees of that great river, with that flotilla moving slowly and silently upstream!"

And Jan Roussière named all the places from Arles to Le Revestidou, from La Coucourde to L'Ermitage, the inns, the hostesses, the rivers, the dikes, the paved roads, and the fords.

But his joy and his triumph came to my good Rousseyron at the time of Saint Eloi.

"I will show your people of Maillane," he said, "if they haven't seen it yet, how to ride a little mule."

Saint Eloi is, as you know, the festival of the farmers in Provence. Throughout Provence the priests bless the animals on that day, asses, donkeys, mules, and horses. And people give the animals a taste of the blessed bread, that good blessed bread they call "twists," perfumed with anise and gilded with eggs. Now in our region on that day they run the "Leafy Cart," a carriage covered with green boughs and hitched to forty or fifty animals, caparisoned as in the days of tournaments, accoutered with backstays, embroidered horse-cloths, ostrich plumes, colored glass mirrors, and brass moons. And "the whip is auctioned," that is, they publicly auction the office of Prior. "Thirty francs for the whip! a hundred francs! two hundred francs! Going, going, gone!"

The one who makes the highest bid reigns over the festival. The Leafy Cart goes on parade with its cavalcade of lively plowmen marching proudly alongside their animals and making their whips crack. The Priors are seated in the carriage, accompanied by a fife and drum. Fathers put their children astride the mules, where they like to hang onto the hames of the collars. The horns on top of the collars all have "twists" on them with little paper banners of Saint Eloi. And the Saint, borne on the shoulders of former Priors, the great Saint Eloi, proceeds in glory like a golden bishop with his crozier in hand.

Then after the procession, the Cart, drawn by the fifty mules and jennies, goes roaring in a whirlwind of dust, with the young plowmen running recklessly beside their animals, all in shirtsleeves, with caps over their ears, thin shoes on their feet, and sashes on their hips.

Jan Roussière amazed the spectators that year, mounted on Falèto, our jenny with an "almond rump." Nimble as a cat, he leaped on the animal, jumped off, got on again, sometimes sitting sidesaddle, sometimes astride, sometimes standing on Falèto's rump, sometimes on her back, hopping on one leg, doing a headstand, or hopping like a frog, in other words performing the "fantasia" the way Arab horsemen do.

The nicest part—and that's what I wanted to get to—was at the dinner of Saint Eloi, for after the procession, the Priors pay for the feast. When we had eaten and drunk our fill, and everyone was having his say, Roussière stood up and said, "Friends, here you are, a whole bunch of clods and clodhoppers who have been observing Saint Eloi for maybe a thousand years, and I'm sure you don't even know the history of your powerful patron!"

"No," they all said. "Wasn't he a blacksmith?"

"Yes. But I'm going to tell you how he was converted."

And dunking a "twist" in his glass of Tavel wine, my plow-man began as follows: "One day in heaven, Our Lord God the Father was worrying. The child Jesus asked Him, 'Father, what's the matter?'

"'I have a problem,' replied God, 'that's bothering me. Take a look down there.'

"'Where?' said Jesus.

"'Down there in Limousin, right in front of my finger. Do you see a blacksmith's shop near the outskirts of that village, a fine, big shop?'

"'I see it, I see it.'

"'Well, there, my son, there's a man I would have liked to save. They call him Master Eloi. He's a stout-hearted man who observes my commandments faithfully, is charitable to the poor, helpful to everyone, honest in his dealings, and hammer-ing from dawn to sunset without cursing or swearing. Yes, he seems to me worthy of becoming a great saint.'

"'And what's preventing it?' said Jesus.

"'His pride, my son. Because he's a first-class craftsman, Eloi believes there's nothing above him on earth. And presumption leads to perdition.'

"'My Lord Father,' said Jesus, 'if you will permit me to go down to earth, I will try to convert him.'

"'Go, my dear son.'

"And the good Jesus went down. Dressed as an apprentice with his bundle on his back, the divine artisan arrived right in the street where Eloi lived. Over Eloi's door there was the usual sign, and the sign bore the inscription, 'Eloi the blacksmith, master of all masters, forges a horseshoe by tempering it twice.'

"So the little apprentice put his foot on the threshold, and tipping his hat, said, 'God give you good day, Master, and all the company. Do you need a little help?'

"'Not at present,' replied Eloi.

"'Then God be with you, Master, until some other time.'

"And Jesus, the good Jesus, continued on his way. Now there was a group of men talking in the street, and in passing them Jesus said, 'I wouldn't have thought they would refuse me work in such a shop, where there must be so much work.'

"'Wait a moment, sweetheart,' one of the neighbors said to him, 'what greeting did you give when you entered Master Eloi's?'

"'I said what is usually said, "God give you good day, Master, and all the company."'

"'Aha! you shouldn't have said that. You should have called him "Master of all masters." Here, look at the sign.'

"'That's true," said Jesus, 'I'll try again.'

"And he went back to the shop at once and said, 'God give you a good one, Master of all masters! Don't you need workers?'

"'Come in, come in,' answered Eloi, 'I've been thinking that we could give you work. But listen here once and for all: when you greet me, you must call me "Master of all masters," for, not to brag, but there are not two men like me in Limousin who can forge a horseshoe by tempering it twice.'

"'Oh,' replied the apprentice, 'where I come from we only forge it once.'

"'Only one tempering? Go on, be quiet, boy, because that's not possible.'

"'All right, you shall see, Master of all masters.'

"Jesus takes a piece of iron, throws it in the forge, blows and pokes the fire, and when the iron is red, when it's red and glowing white-hot, he goes to take it in his hand.

"'Oh, you poor fool!' the first journeyman cries out, 'you're going to burn your fingers!'

"'Don't be afraid,' answers Jesus. 'My God, thanks to you, we don't need tongs where I come from.' And the little artisan takes the red-hot iron in his hand, carries it to the anvil, and with his hammer, bing! bang! rat-a-tat-tat! in the blink of an eye he draws it out, flattens it, rounds it off, and stamps it so well it looks as if it had been cast in a mold.

"'Oh well,' said Master Eloi, 'I could do that too if I wanted to.'

"Quickly he takes a piece of iron, puts it in the forge, blows and pokes the fire, and when the iron is red, he goes to take it in his hand like his apprentice and carry it to the anvil. But he burns his fingers. In vain he hurries, in vain he blusters, he has to let it go and run for the tongs. Meanwhile the horseshoe cools off. And then bang! bang! a few sparks fly. Poor Master Eloi! In vain he struck and wore himself out. He would never be able to finish in one tempering.

"'Listen!' said the apprentice, 'I thought I heard a horse galloping.'

"Master Eloi promptly goes to his door and sees a horseman, a splendid horseman, who stops in front of the shop. Now this was Saint Martin.

"'I come from far away,' he said, 'my horse has lost a couple of shoes, and it took me a long time to find a blacksmith.'

"Master Eloi swaggers and speaks to him as follows, 'Truly, my lord, you could not have come upon a better place. You have come to the foremost blacksmith of Limousin and even of France, who can call himself Master of all masters and who forges a horseshoe by tempering it twice. Boy, hold the horse's foot.'

"'Hold the foot?' replied Jesus. 'Where I come from we don't find that necessary.'

"'The idea!' cried the master smith, 'now that's altogether too funny! And how do they shoe a horse where you come from without holding the foot?'

"'My God, nothing could be easier. You shall see.'

"And with that the boy takes the knife, goes up to the horse, and slice! cuts off its foot. He brings the foot into the shop, tightens it in the vise, trims its hoof well, puts on the new horseshoe he has just forged, and drives in the nails with a shoeing hammer. Then he loosens the vise, brings the foot back to the horse, spits on it, fits it, and making the sign of the cross, says only, 'My God, may the blood clot!' The foot is restored, shod and solid as it has never been before nor will ever be again.

"The first journeyman opened two eyes wide, and Master Eloi, my friends, began to sweat.

"'Good Lord!' he said then, 'I could shoe a horse just as well if I did it that way.'

"And Eloi goes to work. He goes up to the horse with the knife, and slice! cuts off its foot. He brings it into the shop, tightens it in the vise, and shoes it at his ease as the boy had done. Then—here's the rub!—he has to put it back in place. He comes up to the horse, spits on the shoe, and does his best to stick it on the fetlock. But, alas, the ointment won't hold, the blood runs, and the foot falls off.

"Then the proud spirit of Master Eloi saw the light. He went back into his shop to prostrate himself at the feet of the apprentice. But the boy had disappeared and the horse and the horseman as well. Tears poured from the eyes of Master Eloi, and he recognized that there was a master above him, poor man, and above everyone. And he took off his apron and left his shop and went away to travel about the world preaching the word of Our Lord Jesus."

Oh, what a round of applause there was for Saint Eloi and Jan Roussière! Finally, I feel obligated to remember that good fellow Jan in this book of memoirs because he was the one who sang me that popular tune to which I set the aubade of "Magali"—with different words, which I shall give in a moment—a tune so melodious, sweet, and pleasing that many regretted not finding it in Gounod's *Mireille*.

What luck there is in the way things happen! The only person in my life I heard singing that popular song was Jan Roussière, who was apparently the very last to remember it, and he happened by chance to come and sing it to me at the moment I was searching for a Provençal note for my love song, so that I caught it right at the moment it was about to be swallowed in oblivion, like so many other things.

Here then is the song, or rather the duet, that gave me the rhythm and melody of "Magali":

> —Bon-jour, gai roussignòu sóuvage,
> N'en fugues lou bèn-arriba!
> Cresiéu qu'aguèsses pres daumage
> Dins lou coumbat de Gibarta.
> Mai dóu moumen que t'ai ausi,
>   Pèr toun ramage,
> Mai dóu moumen que t'ai ausi,
>   M'as rejouï.
>
> —Avès, moussu, bèn souvenènço
> De vous enrapela de iéu.

Aurés toujour la preferènço,
Eici vendrai passa l'estiéu
N'en respoundrai à voste amour
        Pèr moun ramage;
N'en cantarai, la niue, lou jour,
        Eici à l'entour.

—Te dounarai la jouissènço,
L'avantage de moun jardin;
Au jardinié farai defènso
De te douna gens de chagrin.
Pèr toun nis trouvaras un liò
        Dins lou fuiage;
Te mancara pas de fricot
        Pèr ti pichot.

—Moussu, counèisse à vosto mino
Qu'amas fort li pichot aucèu:
Farai veni la cardelino
Que vous cantara d'èr nouvèu.
La cardelino a 'n poulit cant,
        Quand es souleto;
N'en canto d'èr sus lou plan-cant
        Que soun charmant.

Enjusquo eiça au mes de setèmbre,
Saren toujour vòsti vesin.
Aurés lou plesi de m'entèndre
Autant la niue que lou matin.
Mai quand faudra prene soun vòu,
        Quinto tristesso!
Tout lou bouscage sara 'n dòu
        Dóu roussignòu.

Aro, moussu, sian de partènço,
Sabès qu'acò 's noste destin;
Quand nous fau quita la Prouvènço,
N'es pas segur sènso chagrin.
Tóuti lis an, fau qu'ivernen
        Dedins lis Indo;
Lis óurindello éli tambèn,
        Partèn ensèn.

—Passés pas de-vers l'Americo,
Que poudrias avé de ploumb:
Dóu coustat de la Martinico,
N'en tiron de cop de canoun.
I' a long-tèms que l'an assieja,
      Lou rèi d'Espagno:
Se noun voulès èstre arresta,
      Passas d'eila.

"Welcome, wild nightingale so free,
Now that you've arrived safely
I thought you had come to harm
In Gibraltar's mighty storm.
But from the moment I heard you
      Warbling sweetly,
From the moment I heard you,
      My heart was glad."

"Sir, you have a good memory
To have remembered me so long.
It will always be my wish
To spend summers here with you.
To your love I will respond,
      Warbling sweetly;
Day and night I shall sing
      Here around you."

"I shall give you all the freedom
And enjoyment of my garden.
The gardener has my orders
Not to cause you any grief.
For your nest you'll find a place
      Among the leaves;
For your nestlings you will find
      Enough to eat."

"I can tell, sir, by your look
That you love all little birds.
I shall bring the goldfinch here,
Who will sing new songs to you.

The goldfinch has a pretty song
        When he's alone;
He can sing you charming airs
        In plain song.

"Till the month of September
We'll be your neighbors.
You'll enjoy hearing me
In the night as well as day.
But when it's time to fly away,
        What sadness!
All the trees will be in mourning
        At our flight.

"Goodbye, sir, we're on our way,
For that, you know, is our sad fate.
You may be sure we're sorry
When it's time to leave Provence.
Every year we must go winter
        In the Indies.
The swallows go there too;
        We leave together."

"Don't go near America,
For the air is full of lead.
Over there by Martinique
They are firing cannonades.
For a long time the King of Spain
        Has been besieged:
If you don't want to be stopped,
        Keep far away."

Surely the work of some illiterate living on the banks of the Rhone at the time of the Empire, these naive verses have at least the merit of having preserved the melody that "Magali" made known. As for the theme of love's metamorphoses, launched by the aubade from *Mirèio*, I deliberately took it from a popular song that begins like this:

—Margarido ma mio,   "Margarido, my dear,
Margarido mis amour,   Margarido, my love,

Eiçò soun lis aubado	These are the aubades
Que se jogon pèr vous.	That are played for you."
—M'enchau de tis aubado,	"I don't want your aubades
Emai de ti vióuloun:	Or your violins;
M'envau dins la mar blanco	I am going to the sea
Pèr me rèndre peissoun.	To turn into a fish."

Finally, I heard the name "Magali," which is an abbreviation of Margarido, one day as I was returning from Saint-Rémy. A young shepherdess was watching her flock along the Big Canal. A little boy who was going by on the road called her, "Oh, Magali, aren't you coming?" And that sweet name seemed so pretty to me that I sang on the spot:

O Magali, ma tant amado,	Oh Magali, my much beloved,
Mete la tèsto au fenestroun.	Lean your head out the window.
Escouto un pau aquesto aubado	Listen a bit to this aubade
De tambourin e de vióuloun:	Of violins and little drums:
Es plen d'estello aperamount,	The sky above is full of stars,
L'auro es toumbado . . .	The wind has fallen;
Mai lis estello paliran,	But the stars will grow pale
Quand te veiran.	When they see you.

Some time after that I suffered the grief of losing my old father, the first shadow cast over my unclouded youth. He had grown blind, and we had seen him in a state of sadness that pained us the previous Christmas, for the feast of Christmas had always filled him with joy. In vain the sacred candles shone on the table and on the white tablecloth as usual. In vain I offered him the spiced wine to hear him say, "Good cheer!" Groping his way with his big arms now thin, poor man, he had sat down without saying a word. And in vain my mother offered him the Christmas dishes one after another, the platter of snails, the mullet from Martigues, the almond nougat, and the oil cake. The poor old man had eaten his supper in melancholy silence. A shadow was upon him, a harbinger of death. He had completely lost his sight.

"Last year at Christmas I could still see the candles flickering dimly," he said. "But this year nothing, nothing! Oh, Blessed Virgin, sustain me!"

At the beginning of September of 1855, at the age of eighty-four, he was extinguished in the Lord. When he had received the Lord, as they say, with innocence and faith, the good faith of simple souls, and when the whole household was crying around him, he said to us, "Come now, my children, I am going away. And I give thanks to God for everything I owe Him, my long life and my work, which has been blessed."

Then he called me and asked, "Frederi, what's the weather like?"

"It's raining, Father," I replied.

"Well," he said, "if it's raining, it's good weather for sowing."

And he rendered his soul to God. Oh, what a moment! We put the sheet over his head. Near the bed, that big bed in the white alcove where I was born in broad daylight, a dim taper was lit. The shutters of the room were closed. The plowmen were told to unhitch immediately. In the kitchen the maid turned the cauldrons upside down on the shelf. The hearth fire was extinguished, and we members of the household all sat down in a circle around the ashes without saying anything. My mother, in a corner next to the big fireplace, had put a white kerchief on her head as a sign of bereavement, as is the custom in Provence when women become widows. And all day long neighbors, relatives, and friends came "to observe mourning" with us, one after the other, saying, "May the Lord keep you!" And all lamented long and piteously in honor of "the late master."

The following day all Maillane was present at the funeral. And in praying to God, the poor said, "May as many angels accompany him in heaven as loaves of bread he gave us!" The coffin was carried by hand with napkins on the handles and left uncovered so that people could see the poor body one more time in its white winding sheet with its hands crossed. Behind the coffin Jan Roussière carried the mortuary taper that had kept watch over his master.

As for me, while the passing bells tolled in the distance, I went into the fields by myself to give vent to my grief. For the rooftree of the house had fallen. The Judge's Farm, the farm of my childhood, was now devastated and desolate, as if it had lost its sheltering shade. The eldest of the family, my father, Master Francés, had been the last of the patriarchs of Provence, the faithful guardian of customs and traditions, and the last—at least for me—of that austere, devout, humble, disciplined generation that had stoically borne the famines, afflictions, and death-throes of the Revolution and provided France with the selfless men of her great holocausts and the tireless men of her great armies.

A week later, upon our return from the memorial service, the property was divided. The provisions, the household utensils, the draft animals, the sheep, the poultry, everything was parceled out in lots. The contents of the house, the furniture, our dear old furniture, the big four-poster beds, the kneading trough with iron fittings, the flour-mill, the polished wardrobes, the carved breadbin, the table, the rack for glasses, which I had seen fixed to those walls since my birth; the dozens of plates and the flowered pottery that had never left the shelves of the sideboard; the sheets my mother had spun with her own hand; the farm equipment, the carts, the plows, the harness, the tools, utensils, and various objects of every shape and kind—all that was removed from its place and taken outside, there in the middle of the farmyard, and I had to watch it being divided into three lots on the instructions of an appraiser.

The men of the farm, the hired hands and the part-time help, went away one after another. And finally I had to say goodbye to the farm because it was not in my lot. One afternoon with my mother, the dog, and Jan Roussière, who moved our belongings in the wagon, we left sadly, to live henceforth in the house in Maillane which had fallen to my lot. And now, dear reader, you can understand the nostalgia behind this line from *Mirèio*:

Coume au mas, coume au tèms de moun paire, ai! ai! ai!

Like the farm in my father's day, alas! alas! alas!

XVI
MIRÈIO

he following year (1856), on the feast of Saint Agatha, the patron saint of Maillane, I had the visit of a poet from Paris, whom chance (or rather, the Félibres' lucky star) brought to my mother's house at its chosen time. At fifty, Adolphe Dumas was a fine figure of a man, with an ascetic pallor, fiery black eyes, long white hair, a brown goatee and mustache, always making splendid gestures in the air to accompany his resonant voice. When he walked, he looked like a cypress shaken by the wind, tall and lame, for, unfortunately, he had a crippled leg.

"So you are Monsieur Mistral who writes poetry in Provençal?" he said in a bantering tone when he first shook my hand.

"Yes, I am," I answered, "at your service, sir."

"Yes, indeed, you certainly can help me. The Minister of Public Education, Monsieur Fortoul of Digne, has given me the assignment of collecting the popular songs of Provence, like 'The Ship's Boy from Marseilles,' 'Beautiful Margoutoun,' and 'The Butterfly's Wedding,' and if you know some, I am here to gather them."

And in the course of the conversation, I happened to sing the aubade of "Magali" for him, which I had just adapted for the poem of *Mirèio*.

Adolphe Dumas was astonished and carried away with enthusiasm. "But where did you fish up that pearl?" he exclaimed.

"It's part of a Provençal novel," I said, "or to be exact, a Provençal poem in twelve cantos that I am in the process of revising."

"Oh, these Provençaux! You'll always be the same, stubbornly keeping your rag of a language, like black donkeys going along ditches and browsing some thistle. It's in French, my friend, in the language of Paris, that we must sing our Provence today, if we want to be heard. Here, listen to this:

J'ai revu sur son roc, vieille, nue, appauvrie,
La maison des parents, la première patrie,
L'ombre du vieux mûrier, le banc de pierre étroit,
Le nid que l'hirondelle avait au bord du toit
Et la treille, à présent sur les murs égarée,
Qui regrette son maître et retombe éplorée;
Et dans l'herbe et l'oubli qui poussent sur le seuil
J'ai fait pieusement agenouiller l'orgueil.
J'ai rouvert la fenêtre où me vint la lumière
Et j'ai rempli de chants la couche de ma mère.

I saw again my parents' house, my first home,
Naked and impoverished on its rock,
The shadow of the old mulberry, the narrow stone bench,
The swallow's nest under the eaves,
And the grapevine straying now on the walls,
Missing its master and falling back in tears;
And in the grass growing on the abandoned threshold,
I made pride kneel piously.
I opened the windows where I first saw the light
And filled my mother's bed with songs.

"But come now, recite for me, since you've written a poem, recite some of that Provençal poem for me."

So I read him a passage from *Mirèio*—I no longer remember which.

"Ah, if you speak like that," said Dumas after I had recited, "I take off my hat to you and salute a wellspring of new poetry, of native poetry, that no one had suspected. That tells me—for I left Provence thirty years ago and considered her language dead—that tells me, that proves to me, that underlying the dialect spoken by those who put on airs, the semi-gentlemen and demi-ladies, there is a second language, that of Dante and Petrarch. But follow their method carefully. It did not consist, as some believe, in adopting the dialects of Florence, Bologna, or Milan as they found them, nor in blending them in a casserole. They selected the best to make a language that they perfected as they spread it.

"All that preceded the Latin authors of the great age of Augustus, with the exception of Terence, is Ennius' manure pile. Take only the clean straw from the speech of the common people and any grain it might contain. With your taste and the vigor of your impassioned youth, I am convinced that you were born to do great things. And I foresee the renaissance of a language derived from Latin as pretty and resonant as the best Italian."

The story of Adolphe Dumas was a veritable fairy tale. The child of humble parents who kept a bar at Pierre-Plantade, between Orgon and Cabannes, Dumas had a sister called Lauro, beautiful as the day and innocent, poor thing, as spring water. And it happened that some traveling players came and gave a performance at the little inn one evening. There was one who played the part of a prince, all dressed up in cheap finery that glittered under the stage lamps and made him look like a king's son. As a result poor little Lauro, inexperienced as anything, let herself be seduced by that prince of country fairs, according to the old people of the region. She left with the troupe, landed at Marseille, then quickly recognizing her foolish mistake and no longer daring to go home to her parents, in a panic she took the stagecoach for Paris, and arrived there one morning when the rain was falling in buckets.

And there she was, on the street, alone and in desperate straits. A gentleman happened to be passing by in a carriage, and when he saw that young girl from Provence all in tears, he stopped his carriage and said to her, "What's the matter, my pretty child, why are you crying so?"

In her naive way Lauro told the story of her misadventure. Touched and suddenly smitten, the rich gentleman made her get in with him, took her to a convent, had her well educated at his expense, and then married her. But the beautiful bride had a noble heart and did not forget her relatives. She sent for her brother Adolphe and had him educated at a college in Paris, and that's how Dumas, who was already a poet of a passionate nature, got involved with the Romantic movement of 1830. All kinds of verse poured from his teeming brain, dramas, comedies, and poems in rapid succession: *The City of Men, The Death of Faust and of Don Juan, The Crusaders' Camp, Provence, Mademoiselle de Lavallière, The School for Families, Voluntary Servitude*, etc. But as you know, even though you do your duty in battle, you are not always given a medal, and despite his merits and several good works in the Paris theater, the poet Dumas remained a common soldier, like our drummer boy at Arcole, and that led him to declare later in Provençal:

A quaranto an passa, quand tout lou mounde pesco
Dins la soupo di gus e ié trempo sa lesco,
        Devèn èstre countènt d'avé
L'amo en repaus, lou cornet e la man lavado . . .
—E dequ'a? vous diran.—A la tèsto levado!
—E dequé fai?—Fai soun devé.

In our forties, when everyone fishes
And dips bread in beggars' soup,
        We must be content to have
A soul at peace, a clear heart, and clean hands.
"And what's he got?" they will say. "Self-respect."
"And what does he do?" "He does his duty."

But although he did not become a captain, he won the esteem of his proudest fellow-soldiers. Hugo, Lamartine, Béranger, de Vigny, the elder Dumas, Jules Janin, Mignet, and Barbey d'Aurevilly were his friends.

With his energy, his experience as an old Parisian campaigner, his enthusiasm, and all his boyhood memories of the Durance, Adolphe Dumas happened along at the right moment to bring the Félibrige its ticket to travel from Avignon to Paris.

When my Provençal poem was at last finished but not yet published, our friend Ludòvi Legré, a young man from Marseille who often came to Font-Ségugne, said to me, "I'm going to Paris. Why don't you come with me?"

"All right!" I answered.

Thus on the spur of the moment I went to Paris for the first time and spent a week. Of course I brought my manuscript, and when we had done enough wandering and sightseeing, from Notre-Dame to the Louvre, from the Place Vendôme to the Arc de Triomphe, of course we went to see our friend Dumas.

"Well then, that *Mirèio*," he asked me, "is it finished?"

"It's finished," I said, "and here it is—in manuscript."

"Come then, while we're at it, you must read me a canto."

And when I had read the first canto, Dumas said, "Go on."

And I read the second, then the third, then the fourth.

"That's enough for today," said the good fellow. "Come back tomorrow at the same time, and we'll continue the reading. But I can already assure you that if the work goes on at that rate, you could very well win a finer prize than you think."

The following day I went back and read four more cantos. And the day after that we finished the poem. On the same day (August 26, 1858), Adolphe Dumas addressed the following letter to the editor of the *Gazette de France*:

> The *Gazette du Midi* has already informed the *Gazette de France* of the arrival in Paris of young Mistral, the great poet of Provence. Who is this Mistral? Nothing is known about him. People ask me, and I am afraid to answer with words so unexpected they will not be believed during this period of imitative poetry when poetry and poets seem to be dead.
>
> Ten years from now, after everyone else, the French Academy will bless one more glorious name. The clock of the Institute is often an hour behind the times. But I want to be the first to discover the one who can now be called the Virgil of Provence, the shepherd of Mantua arriving in Rome with songs worthy of Gallus and Scipio.
>
> Our South is doubly Roman, being Latin and Roman Catholic. We have often demanded a poem celebrating that beautiful land, its eternal language, its sacred beliefs, and its unspoiled way of life. I have that poem in my hand. It is written in twelve cantos and signed Frédéric Mistral, of the village of Maillane, and I countersign it with my word of honor, which I have never compromised, and my responsibility, which only aspires to be just.

This preposterous letter produced many jokes. "Come now,"

said the papers, "it seems the mistral is incarnated in a poet. We shall see if it's anything but wind."

But Dumas was pleased with the impression his bomb had created. "Now," he said, shaking my hand, "go back to Avignon and publish your *Mirèio*. We have thrown the mark on the bowling ground in the face of Paris. Let the critics have their say. They will have to bowl their shots one after another."

But before my departure my excellent compatriot was kind enough to introduce me to his friend Lamartine, and this is what the great man later wrote about our visit in the fortieth "Conversation" of his *Informal Course in Literature* (1859):

> At sunset I saw Adolphe Dumas arriving, followed by a handsome and modest young man dressed with quiet elegance, like the lover of Laura when he brushed his black tunic and combed his smooth hair in the streets of Avignon. It was Frédéric Mistral, the young village poet, destined to become, like the Scottish plowman Burns, the Homer of Provence.
>
> His simple, modest, gentle face had none of that tense pride or that startled look that too often marks those men of greater vanity than genius known as popular poets. What nature has given is possessed without pretension or boasting. The young Provençal wore his talent as easily as his clothes; nothing bothered him because he attempted neither to inflate himself nor to raise himself above nature. Perfect decorum governed his behavior, that youthful instinct that gives shepherds the same dignity as kings, the same grace of manner or accent in all circumstances. He had the seemliness of truth; he was pleasing, interesting, moving; in his male beauty one sensed the son of one of those beautiful Arlésiennes, those Greek statues that live and breathe in our South.
>
> Mistral seated himself at my mahogany table in Paris without ceremony, in accordance with the ancient laws of hospitality, as I would have seated myself at his mother's walnut table in her farm-house in Maillane. The dinner was moderate, the interview open-hearted, the evening short and chatty, to the warbling of blackbirds in the cool of the night in my little garden the size of Mireille's handkerchief.
>
> The young man recited some poetry for us in that sweet and sinewy Provençal idiom reminiscent now of Latin, now of Attic grace, now of Tuscan roughness. My familiarity with Latin dialects, which I spoke exclusively in the mountains of my region until the

age of twelve, permitted me to understand this fine idiom. His lyric poetry pleased me but did not intoxicate me. The young man's genius was not in that form; the frame was too narrow for his spirit; he needed his epic poem in order to expand, like Jasmin, that other singer without a language. He was returning to his village to give it the finishing touches there near his mother and beside his flocks. He promised to send me one of the first copies of his poem and left.

Before leaving I went one evening to pay my respects to Lamartine, who lived on the ground floor at 41 rue de la Ville-Lévêque. Overwhelmed by his debts and quite forsaken, the great man was drowsing in an armchair, smoking a cigar, while several visitors conversed quietly around him.

Suddenly a servant came and announced that a Spanish harpist named Herrera asked if he could play a piece from his country to Monsieur de Lamartine.

"Have him come in," said the poet.

The harpist played his piece, and Lamartine asked his niece, Madame de Cessia, in an undertone if there was any money in the drawers of his writing-desk.

"There are two *louis* left," she replied.

"Give them to Herrera," said the generous Lamartine.

Then I returned to Provence to have my poem printed, and when that was done (at the Seguin printing house in Avignon), I sent the first copy to Lamartine, who wrote the following letter to Reboul:

> I have read *Mirèio* . . . Nothing had yet appeared in that inimitable, fertile, native vein of the South. My spirit and my heart were so struck that I wrote a "Conversation" on that poem. Tell Monsieur Mistral. Yes, such a fountain of primitive poetry had not flowed since the Homerides of the Islands. Like you, I exclaimed, "It's Homer!"

Adolphe Dumas wrote to me in turn:

> (March 1859)
>
> Another letter of good news for you, my dear friend. I went to Lamartine's last night. When he saw me coming in, he greeted me with enthusiastic remarks and spoke to me in the same vein as my letter to the *Gazette de France*. He says he has read and understood your poem from beginning to end. He has read and reread it three

times, he has not let go of it, he reads nothing else. His niece, that attractive person whom you met, added that she had not been able to steal it from him for a moment to read it, and he is going to write a whole "Conversation" on you and *Mirèio*. He asked me for biographical notes on you and on Maillane. I am sending them this morning. You were the subject of discussion all evening, and your poem was explained in detail by Lamartine and me from the first word to the last. If his "Conversation" speaks of you thus, your reputation will be made in the whole world. He says you are "a Greek of the Cyclades." He wrote to Reboul, "He's another Homer!" He bids me write you anything I wish and adds that he is so enchanted I cannot overstate it. So be very happy, you and your dear mother, of whom I have such a pleasant recollection.

I want to set down here a very curious case of maternal clairvoyance and intuition. I had given my mother a copy of *Mirèio* but had not spoken of the opinion of Lamartine, which I did not as yet know. At the end of the day, when I thought she had read it, I asked her what she thought of it, and she answered, deeply moved, "An extraordinary thing happened to me when I opened your book. A flash of light that was like a star suddenly dazzled me and made me put off reading until later." People may think what they wish, but I have always believed the good and holy woman's vision was actually a sign from Saint Estelle, that is, of the star that presided, as you know, over the founding of the Félibrige.

The fortieth Conversation of the *Informal Course in Literature* appeared a month later (1859) under the title "Publication of an Epic Poem in Provence." Lamartine devoted eighty pages to the poem of *Mirèio*, and his praise was the crowning point of the innumerable articles that welcomed my rustic epic in the press of Provence, the South, and Paris. And to express my gratitude, here is the quatrain I wrote in Provençal at the front of my second edition:

A Lamartino

Te counsacre Mirèio: es moun cor e moun amo,
Es la flour de mis an;
Es un rasin de Crau qu'emé touto sa ramo
Te porge un païsan.

(*8 de sètembre 1859*)

To Lamartine

To you I dedicate *Mirèio*: it's my heart and soul,
It's the flower of my years,
It's a grapevine of the Crau with all its leaves
That a peasant offers you.

(*8 September 1859*)

And here is the elegy I published after the great man's death:

Sus la mort de Lamartino

Quand l'ouro dóu tremount es vengudo pèr l'astre,
Sus li mourre envahi pèr lou vèspre, li pastre
Alargon sis anouge, e si fedo, e si can;
E dins li baisso palunenco
Lou grouün rangoulejo en bramadisso unenco:
"Aquéu soulèu èro ensucant!"

Di paraulo de Diéu magnanime escampaire,
Ansin, o Lamartino, o moun mèstre, o moun paire,
En cantico, en acioun, en lagremo, en soulas,
Quand aguerias à noste mounde
Escampa de lumiero e d'amour soun abounde,
E que lou mounde fuguè las,

Cadun jitè soun bram dìns la nèblo prefoundo,
Cadun vous bandiguè la pèiro de sa foundo,
Car vosto resplendour nous fasié mau is iue,
Car uno estello que s'amosso,
Car un diéu clavela, toujour agrado en foço,
E li grapaud amon la niue . . .

E'm'acò, l'on veguè de causo espetaclouso!
Éu, aquelo grand font de pouësìo blouso
Qu'avié rejouveni l'amo de l'univers,
Li jóuini pouèto riguèron
De sa malancounié proufetico, e diguèron
Que sabié pas faire li vers.

De l'Autisme Adounai éu sublime grand-prèire
Que dins sis inne sant enaurè nòsti crèire
Sus li courdello d'or de l'arpo de Sioun,
En atestant lis Escrituro
Li devot Farisen cridèron sus l'auturo
Que n'avié gens de religioun.

Éu, lou grand pietadous, que, sus la catastrofo
De nòstis encian rèi, avié tra sis estrofo,
E qu'en maubre poumpous i'avié fa'n mausoulèu,
Dóu Reialisme li badaire
Trouvèron à la fin qu èro un descaladaire,
E tóuti s'aliunchèron lèu.

Éu, lou grand óuratour, la voues apoustoulico,
Que faguè dardaia lou mot de Republico
Sus lou front, dins lou cèu di pople tresanant,
Pèr uno estranjo fernesio
Tóuti li chin gasta de la Demoucracio
Lou mourdeguèron en renant.

Éu, lou grand ciéutadin que dins la goulo en flamo
Avié jita soun viéure e soun cors e soun amo,
Pèr sauva dóu voulcan la patrìo en coumbour,
Quand demandè soun pan, pechaire!
Li bourgés e li gros l'apelèron manjaire,
E s'estremèron dins soun bourg.

Adounc, en se vesènt soulet dins soun auvàri,
Doulènt, emé sa crous escalè soun Calvàri . . .
E quàuqui bònis amo, eiça vers l'embruni,
Entendeguèron un long gème,
E pièi, dins lis espàci, aqueste crid suprème:
Heli! lamma sabacthani!

Mai degun s'avastè vers la cimo deserto . . .
Emé li dous iue clin e li dos man duberto,
Dins un silènci grèu alor éu s'amaguè;
E, siau coume soun li mountagno,
Au mitan de sa glòri e de sa malamagno,
Sènso rèn dire mouriguè.

(21 de mars, 1869)

On the Death of Lamartine

When the hour of setting has come for the sun,
The shepherds on the hills invaded by evening
Release their ewes and yearlings and dogs;
And in the low-lying marshes
The croaking swarms all complain:
"That sun was overwhelming!"

So, Lamartine, my master, my father,
When you poured forth on our world
A surfeit of light and love
From God's magnanimous outpouring of words
In hymns, in actions, in tears, in solace,
And when the world had grown weary,

Everyone gave off his croak in the dense fog,
Everyone hurled the stone from his sling,
For your splendor hurt our eyes,
And a star that's extinguished
Or a god crucified always pleases the mob,
And toads love the night.

Then we saw extraordinary things.
Young poets laughed at him,
They laughed at his prophetic gloom and said
He did not know how to write verse—
That great font of pure poetry,
Who rejuvenated the soul of the universe.

Pious Pharisees cried out on the heights
That he had no religion,
That sublime high priest of God the Highest,
Who exalted our faith in his holy hymns,
Bearing witness to the Scriptures
On the golden strings of Sion's harp.

He had shown great compassion,
Writing his poems on the fall of our old kings,
And building them a mausoleum of stately marble.
But toadying royalists
Pronounced him a revolutionary at the end,
And all withdrew quickly from him.

He was the great orator, the apostolic voice,
Who made the word Republic flash forth
In the sky of exultant peoples.
Yet in a strange frenzy
All the mad dogs of Democracy
Growled and bit him.

He was the great citizen who threw
Life and soul and body into the flaming maw

To save his country from the volcano.
Yet when the poor man asked for bread,
The bourgeois and the bigwigs called him a wastrel
And shut themselves up in their town.

So, seeing himself alone in his misfortune,
He climbed his Calvary with his cross,
And there toward nightfall some good souls
Heard a long groan
And then this supreme cry:
"Eli! Eli! lamma sabacthani!"

But no one ventured toward the deserted summit.
So he wrapped himself in heavy silence,
With both eyes closed and both hands open,
And calm as the mountains,
In the midst of his glory and woe,
Without saying a word, he died.

(21 March 1869)

I have now come to the end of the "elucidation" (as the troubadours would have said) or explanation of my beginnings. This is the culmination of my youth. From now on, my story is that of my works and belongs like so many others to publicity.

I shall finish these Memoirs with several episodes about the free and easy existence led by the leaders of the muses or chorus of our Renaissance in Avignon to demonstrate how we led the troubadour life on the banks of the Rhone.

XVII

AROUND
MOUNT
VENTOUX

ne fine day in September, in the company of Aubanel, who was a menace when it came to organizing excursions, and our friend Pèire Grivolas (senior), the painter from Avignon who took part in all our festivities, we climbed Mount Ventoux.

We left about midnight from the village of Bédoin at the foot of the mountain and reached the summit a little before sunrise. I won't tell you about the ascent, which we made easily on muleback, conducted by guides through the rocks, cliffs, and hills of the Combe-Fillole.

We saw the sun rising like a splendid king of glory among the dazzling snowy peaks of the Alps and the wide shadow of Ventoux extending its great triangular point down over the whole width of the Comtat Venaissin and across the Rhone as far as Languedoc off in the distance.

At the same time, big white scudding clouds rolled in under us, clouding the valleys, and beautiful though the weather was, it was not warm. After having a bite to eat, we began our descent about nine o'clock, but on foot this time, with steel-tipped walking sticks and knapsacks on our backs.

However, we went down the other side this time, that is, by the "shady" slope, as they call the north side of all mountains and Ventoux in particular.

Now that other side of Mount Ventoux is so rough and so steep that Father Laval tells the following story:

In his day (in the eighteenth century), the mountain folk who went on pilgrimage to the chapel on the summit on September 14 came back down by the north slope simply by sliding, sitting on their heels on a double plank three spans square, and when they went too fast or came close to a precipice, they stopped suddenly by thrusting their sticks into the ground in front of them.

In that way they went down in a half-hour—and you must realize that Ventoux has an altitude of one thousand nine hundred and sixty meters above sea level. We had the idea of taking shortcuts like that, but we went astray—that's what happens when you don't know your way!—in a steep ravine called The Wolf Den of Ventoux, so rocky and so dangerous that we spent the whole day getting down.

The Ravine of the Wolf Den, as its name indicates, is frequented only by wolves, and it drops abruptly from the summit to the foot of the mountain between slopes so steep that once you're inside it, getting out is the very devil.

Anyhow, there we were, climbing down and down, in the stony rubble and debris of rockslides, over trunks of pines, beeches, and larches that had been uprooted and swept away by fierce storms and impeded our way at every step, when suddenly the bottom of the ravine dropped off in front of us and left us gaping at a sheer precipice that fell about a hundred fathoms.

What to do? Go back up? That was very difficult, especially when we saw big black clouds above our heads that would have drowned us in floods of water if they had burst. Willy-nilly, we had to go down by the gorge, that frightful gorge where we had gone astray.

So we threw our coats and knapsacks down into the abyss, and commending our lives to God, creeping, crawling, and mostly slipping, we let ourselves slide down that almost vertical cliff, where only a few roots of boxwood or lavender, which we grabbed with our hands, kept us from falling headfirst.

We thought we were safe when we reached the bottom of the precipice, and after gathering our baggage, we had cheerfully resumed our descent down the ravine, when an even steeper and more abrupt cataract blocked our way again. And at the risk of our lives, we had to slide down again, and still a third time after the first two.

Finally at dusk we arrived at Saint-Léger, a miserable little village at the foot of Ventoux inhabited by charcoal-burners and strewn with lavender, where we could not find a place to stay.

Though it was night and we were dog-tired, we had to push on for a couple of hours more to Brantes, another little village perched on cliffs facing Ventoux, where we were very happy to have an omelet with salt pork and then to sleep in a hay-loft.

The nicest part of it was that our host had locked us in for fear we might carry off his sheets—for it appears that we looked no better than we should. And on the following day, having just about recovered from our ordeal of the day before and having learned that it was the saint's day of the nearby village of Montbrun, we cheerfully left that village "that rocks without wind" (as its neighbors call Brantes) and walked around the north side of Ventoux through Savoillans and Reilhanette.

But as we stood on the banks of the babbling Toulourenc, marveling at the height of the frightening cliffs and brooding crags that touched the clouds, two gendarmes—to whom the innkeeper at Brantes had probably given our description—came up the road after us and accosted us, "Your papers!"

You know, we had escaped wolves, storms, and precipices, but look, whoever you are, if ever you are forced to escape from the Jesus-grabbers, always avoid the roads.

"Your papers! Where have you come from? Where are you going? Come on!"

I took some old scribbling in Provençal out of my pocket, and while one of the constables was straining his eyes and twisting his mustache trying to figure out what it meant, Aubanel was saying, "We are Félibres on a walking tour around Ventoux."

"And artists," Grivolas added, "studying the beauty of the landscape."

"Oh sure, that's a good one! You would have us believe that you come to the Ventoux to study its charms," replied the gendarme who was trying in vain to read my Provençal. "Tomorrow, you jokers, you'll go tell that to His Honor the Imperial Prosecutor at Nyons. Now follow us."

Recalling the saying of General Philopoemen that "one must suffer the consequences for one's bad looks" and realizing that we were in fact got up like brigands, with our arrogantly cocked felt hats, our steel-tipped sticks, and our knapsacks—and besides, I must admit that it amused us—we followed the oppressors of the poor.

As we were going along, a prosperous farmer, carrying his jacket on his shoulder, came up and said, "God give you a good day! Are these gentlemen going to the festival at Montbrun?"

"Oh, yes, a fine festival!" we answered. "We were coming down Ventoux, from the summit of Mount Ventoux, to see if it's true as they say that the sun hops three times when it rises, and these gendarmes, who took us for robbers because we have no papers, are taking us to Nyons."

"Really? But can't you see from their way of speaking," the good man said to the gendarmes, "that these gentlemen are not from far away? that they speak Provençal? that they come from good families? Well, I have no hesitation about answering for them and inviting them to my house for a drink when they are in Montbrun, and you government gentlemen too, if you would do me the honor."

"In that case, gentlemen," said the cops from Dauphiné, after they had conferred with one another, "you may go. But see here, is it true, as you were saying a moment ago, that the sun hops three times when it rises up there on the summit of Mount Ventoux?"

"That," we replied, "must be seen to be believed. But seriously, it's as true as you are good men."

And leaving them on that note as we arrived in Montbrun, we went straight to the inn to take a little refreshment with that peasant who had decently spoken up for us.

There is nothing so pleasant, when you are traveling and when you are tired, as a country inn on a saint's day. Now just imagine our feelings as we entered the inn at Montbrun and saw chickens, turkeys, rabbits, hares, and partridges—oh, what a blessing!—heaped on the floor in abundance that did not suggest hardship. People were plucking them here and bleeding them there. In front of the fire a pair of long spits loaded with game and larded with bacon turned and dripped very slowly into the dripping pans, filling the air with the aroma of roasting game. The host and hostess briskly set the tables with bottles, knives, and forks. And all that for the first guests who asked for dinner, that is, for us. Oh, what good luck! what bliss! And on top of that—at no extra cost, mind you—the hostess' daughters had such pleasing ways that we stayed there as long as the festival lasted, merely for the pleasure of being served by them.

"At Montbrun," they used to say in Dauphiné, "if you arrive at two o'clock, you'll be hanged at three." Which goes to show that proverbs are not always true. But I believe that one must refer to the reputation of the terrible Montbrun, the Huguenot captain who was lord of the village. Charles du Puy, called "the brave Montbrun," is the one who opposed the king of France, arguing that "arms and games make men equal." He's the one who besieged Mornas, which was a Catholic town, and when he had taken the castle, hurled its garrison down the precipice at the point of his soldiers' halberds (1562). Whence the people of Mornas have kept the nickname of "rampart-jumpers" to this day.

One of those poor devils, they say, when his turn came to take a dive, backed up to get a running start, and when he was near the horrible precipice, took fright and suddenly stopped. He went back and ran again and—reasonably enough—stopped again.

"You coward," cried the fierce Montbrun, "you've taken two running starts, can't you make one jump?"

"My lord," replied the poor Catholic, "if you want to try, I'll let you have it for three."

And for that retort they say that Montbrun granted him a reprieve.

We visited the baron's castle, which Francis II had destroyed.

Some frescoes attributed to Andrea del Sarto remain. And they showed us the spot on the terrace where the Huguenot lord entertained himself with his crossbow by knocking down the monks who were reading their breviaries in the garden of the monastery down below.

Finally we resumed our journey, going along the Touroulenc, a river that separates Provence from Dauphiné, passing at the foot of the Ventouret, and following the gorge of the Oule, which opens out in the smiling valley of Sault.

"Shall we have a siesta?" we asked one another, and all three of us stretched out on the edge of a meadow next to the road to wait for the heat of the day to pass.

"Goodbye, Ventoux!" Aubanel exclaimed, "you certainly made us pant and sweat enough, you villain."

Grivolas gazed at the play of light and shadow among the oaks and walnut trees. And I looked at the sun to see what time it was, then sucked a little brandy from the flask.

At that moment we saw an old man coming down the white road in the burning sunshine. He wore a blouse, big hobnailed boots, a big black cape and carried a grape switch in his hand. Something special and imposing about his open sunburned face attracted our attention as he passed, and we said hello to him.

"Good day to all the company," he said to us in a pleasant voice. "Are you having a little rest?"

"As you see, good man. Don't you want to do the same?"

"Well, I don't mind. I've come from the town of Sault, where I had a little business, and I'm beginning to get tired. That, my friends, is not how I was at your age. Then Bertha spun; now Martha unwinds."

And as he said that, he sat down near us on the grass.

"If I am not being too inquisitive," he said, "are you herbalists? Ah, if we knew the properties of the herbs we trample underfoot, we would never need apothecaries or doctors."

"No," we replied, "we have come from Mount Ventoux."

"Wise is he who does not go back, and mad is he who does," said the old man sententiously. "Ah, now I see, I see, you are probably snake oil salesmen from Venice."

"Snake oil? What's that?"

"Surely you know, gentlemen, that there is a sovereign remedy called 'snake oil,' which is made, they say, from the fat of vipers. And in our mountains, on Ventoux, on Ventouret, even in this valley, there are plenty of vipers, if that's what you're looking for."

"Not us, we don't want anything to do with them!" we exclaimed.

"Excuse me if I have offended you," the good fellow replied, "but there are no foolish occupations.

E, coume dis lou reinard,   And, as the fox says,
Cadun jogo de soun art.   Each plays according to his skill.

"You see, the good Lord (whom I hail) has spread a little of His light on everyone. By himself, man knows nothing; all together, we know everything. I, for example, am a dowser."

"Oh, wonder in the name of thunder!"

"Yes, such as I am, I can discover underground springs through the power of that stick I am holding in my hands."

"Really! And look, if we are not being too inquisitive ourselves, how do you manage to find springs that are in the ground?"

"How do I do it? To tell you," replied the dowser, "might be a bit difficult. It's all a matter of faith. Look, when the sun is blazing, I can sometimes see the waters steaming and evaporating seven leagues away. I can see them (my God, I thank you), I can see them when the sun draws them up and colors them. Then the stick twists and turns by itself in my hands and does the rest. But I tell you, you have to feel it to understand: that's the question of faith. You can ask about me, if you wish, at Sault, at Villes, at Verdolier, in all the villages around here. I'm from Aurel, which you can see over there. They call me Fourtunat Aubert. Ask if I am lying to you. They will show you the springs that I have set flowing everywhere."

"Grandfather Fourtunat," we said, joking, "could you find the Golden Goat with your stick?"

"And why not? If God willed, it would be no more difficult than sitting here, you see, on this bank. But the One above has more sense than all of us. Isn't a fountain of water better when you're thirsty than a fountain of gold? And this meadow, don't you think the slightest dew does more good to its grass than a royal coach loaded with gold and silver? To help our neighbor when we can, as we are bid, that, my friends, that is how the good Lord comes to our assistance. And as proof, listen to the story I am going to tell you now.

"Last year the servant of our parish priest at Aurel (who would vouch for it) summoned me to the rectory. 'Master Fourtunat,' she said to me, 'I am very worried. Here Monsieur le Curé went this morning to the assizes in Carpentras, where they are judging a young relative of his accused of arson. He promised to return early, but it's already nightfall, and I see no one coming. I don't know what to think. If you could use your skill to tell me what is going on down there, oh, how you would please me!'

"'We shall try,' I answered. 'Give me some of those wafers they make into communion hosts.'

"And then I placed the wafers on the table to represent Him Who is invisible, Supreme Love, the good Lord.

"Next to the wafers I placed a glass of unadulterated wine to represent Justice.

"In front of Love and Justice I placed a glass of water. That represented the accused.

"And behind the accused I placed a glass of wine adulterated with water. That represented the lawyer.

"Then taking my stick with faith, I humbly asked God, the Supreme Love, if they had condemned the accused.

"My friends, the stick moved no more than these stones.

"Good! Then I asked if they had acquitted him. The stick turned joyfully between my fingers, as if dancing.

"'Mademoiselle,' I said to the servant, 'you can sleep peacefully. The accused has been acquitted.'

"'While we're at it, Fourtunat,' Mademoiselle said to me, 'ask a little about the witnesses.'

"I took up the stick again and asked the unadulterated wine, or, if you prefer, Justice, if the witnesses were going home and if they were on their way.

"The stick remained silent.

"Humbly I asked if they were being prosecuted. The answer was that they were being prosecuted, severely prosecuted.

"Well, would you believe, gentlemen, that the parish priest of Aurel arrived the next morning and confirmed everything we had seen the night before! At Carpentras they had acquitted the accused and detained the witnesses.

"But come, you must think I'm a great windbag," said the old man rising from the bank. "God be with you, and take care not to catch a chill there in the shade."

The dowser went off up the hill with his stick in the direction of that section of Aurel called Saint-Trinit, later sung by Fèlis Gras in his great and lively poem entitled *The Charcoal-Burners.*

And we went by a steep path and found a lodging in Sault, the town of the "sow-stranglers."

In the castle ruins we paid our respects to the coat of arms and the glory of its old lords, the barons of Agoult (which in German is "wolf"), and the historic name of the Countess of Sault, who controlled Provence at the time of the League. Then we went on to Monieux, whose parish priest appears as a character in a series of merry popular tales.

That priest had a cow. And behold, a poor man, who had a heap of children, stole and killed the cow, fed it to his children, and after the feast, he made them say the following little prayer as a kind of "grace":

> Rendèn gràci, moun Diéu,
> Au curat de Mouniéu,
> Que, s'avèn bèn soupa, Diéu-merci à sa vaco!

> My God, we give thanks
> To the priest of Monieux,
> For if we have eaten well, thank God for his cow!

But children tell everything. The priest caught wind of it and questioned one of the little eaters, saying, "Is it true, sweetheart, that your father has taught you such a pretty prayer as your grace after meals? Let's see, how does it go?"

And the boy recited:

> Rendèn gràci, moun Diéu,
> Au bon priéu de Mouniéu
> Que, s'avèn bèn soupa, Diéu-merci à sa vaco!

> My God, we give thanks
> To the good priest of Monieux
> For if we have eaten well, thank God for his cow!

"Oh, what a nice prayer!" said the priest. "Well now, you know what we must do, sweetheart? Tomorrow is Sunday, and you must come and find me at the first Mass. You will climb into the pulpit with me, won't you, sweetheart? Then you will recite the little prayer your father taught you in front of everyone, so that they will all learn it."

"All right, Father."

And the boy lost no time in going to tell his father the priest's proposal. And the father, who was a sly fox, said to the boy then, "Well, if you speak of a cow in the pulpit, you'll make everyone laugh. I am going to teach you another prayer of thanksgiving, my son, which is even finer:

> Vous rènde gràci, o moun Diéu,
> Que noste curat de Mouniéu
> A fa de sa parròqui tóuti lis ome couquiéu,
> A la reservo de moun paire
> Que noun a pas pouscu lou faire!

> Oh my God, I give you thanks
> That our priest of Monieux
> Has cuckolded all the men in his parish,
> With the exception of my father,
> Who wouldn't let him do it!

"Will you remember that tomorrow?"

"Yes, I'll remember, Father."

The following day at Mass, then, the priest climbed into the pulpit with the boy next to him and began his sermon: "My brothers, you must know that our cow has been stolen. But I don't want to speak to you of that. However, it's always good to know the truth, and the truth always comes from the mouths of the innocent. Come now, sweetheart, say what you know."

And the boy recited:

> Vous rènde gràci, o moun Diéu,
> Que noste curat de Mouniéu
> A fa, de sa parròqui, tóuti lis ome couquiéu,

> A la reservo de moun paire
> Que noun a pas pouscu lou faire.

> Oh my God, I give you thanks
> That our priest of Monieux
> Has cuckolded all the men of his parish,
> With the exception of my father,
> Who wouldn't let him do it!

You can imagine how they laughed!

From Monieux we followed the gorge of the Nesque, a wild little river that rushes, as Gras says,

> Entre dous baus taia, clafi de bouissounas,
> Ounte li pastre pènjon l'esco
> Pèr aganta li merle.

> Between two sheer cliffs covered with thickets,
> Where shepherds hang bait
> To catch blackbirds.

And we blundered among the rocks there in the hope of reaching Vénasque the same day if we could. But he who counts without the innkeeper, they say, counts twice. At sunset we were still wandering at the foot of a horrible cliff called Candle Rock, which I later used as a setting for an episode in *Calendau* when he discovers the beehives:

> La Nesco, peravau, afrouso
> Durbié sa gorgo tenebrouso. . . .

> Down below the frightful Nesque
> Cuts through its gloomy gorge. . . .

And as the shadow of night gradually overtook us in a place called the Pas de l'Ascle, which was a regular labyrinth, we could no longer see well enough to go on and were in danger at every step of slipping and falling down below, God knows where.

"My friends," I said, "it would be foolish to leave our bones down some precipice here before we have accomplished our work as Félibres. I'd suggest we turn back."

"What!" said Grivolas, "let's go on. In a while we shall see the 'moonlight effects' on the gorge of the Nesque."

"My friend Pèire," Aubanel said to him, "if you want to fall off a cliff, feel free. But I have no desire to be eaten by wolves."

And thereupon we climbed back up, groping our way here and there to get away from the cliffs. We were exhausted, weak with hunger, and drenched as ducklings, when fortunately we saw a little light shining in the dark some distance away.

We went there, and it was an isolated farmhouse called Les Bessons. We knocked, they opened the door, and those good people (a family of goatherds) provided for us as well as they could. And they told us, "You certainly did well to turn back. One winter night several years ago we heard cries but didn't know what was happening. In the morning when we went to see, we found a poor priest in the Nesque who had fallen down the cliffs and had been battered to death over there by the Pas de l'Ascle."

"So you see, you fool," said Aubanel to Grivolas, "if we had followed you. . . ."

"Pooh!" the painter replied, "you are soldiers of the Pope."

Meanwhile the farmer's wife had put the pot on the fire. With garlic, sage, and a handful of salt, all well seasoned with olive oil, she quickly made us a fragrant garlic soup, so good that Aubanel, small as he was, emptied eleven platefuls. And the great Félibre kept such a good memory of that tasty soup and of the sound sleep we had at the farm of Les Bessons that he described it in his *Book of Love* as follows:

> La femo, vivamen, emé lou taio-lesco
> Chaplo lou bèu pan brun; vai querre d'aigo fresco
> Emé soun bro de couire; e pièi, sus lou lindau,
> Sort, e sono si gènt que rintron dins l'oustau.
> E la soupo es vujado e, d'enterin que trempo,
> L'oste amistous vous fai béure un cop de sa trempo;
> Pièi, chascun à soun tour, rèire, ome, femo, enfant,
> Tiron uno sietado e se lèvon la fam;
> E manjas de la soupo, e sias de la famiho.
> Mai, lou repas fini, deja cadun soumiho:
> L'oustesso, em'un calèu; vous vai querre un linçòu,
> Un bèu linçòu rousset qu'es tout rufe e tout nòu.
> Lou lassige dóu cors es de baume pèr l'amo . . .
> Ah! que fai bon dourmi dins li jas, sus la ramo,

Dourmi sènso pantai, au mitan di troupèu,
D'èstre pièi reviha que pèr li cascavèu
Di cabro, lou matin, e d'ana 'mé li pastre
Se coucha tout lou jour e sèntre lou mentastre!

Quickly the wife cuts the good brown bread
With the slicer, fetches fresh water
In her copper jug, then on the doorsill
Rings for her family to come in the house.
And the soup is poured, and while it steeps,
The friendly host gives you a taste of his wine;
Then each in turn, grandfather, husband, wife, and children,
Take a plateful and allay their hunger;
And you eat the soup and become part of the family.
But when the meal is over, they are all drowsy.
The hostess goes with a lamp to get you a sheet
Of fine unbleached linen, new and rough.
The body's weariness is balm for the soul;
How good it feels to sleep on green boughs in the pens,
A dreamless sleep amid the flocks,
Then to be awakened in the morning
To the ringing of goat bells and to join the shepherds,
Lying down all day and smelling the wild mint.

The next day we again followed the gorge of the Nesque, all abuzz with swarms of bees sipping honey from the flowers, and arrived at the village of Méthamis in a heat that made the lizards gape. We asked for the inn. But we called in vain. We found the door closed. The host and hostess had gone harvesting.

We went into the café to see if they would fix us some dinner.

"That I am forbidden to do," the café owner told us, "just as I am forbidden to kill a man!"

"And how come?"

"Because the inn, which belongs to the town, is leased on condition that no one else have the right to serve food."

"So we must starve to death?"

"Go find the mayor. I couldn't serve you anything but drinks."

We had a drink to refresh ourselves. Then, all covered with dust, we went to find the mayor of Méthamis.

The mayor, a big boor with a face as dark and pock-marked as a chestnut roasting pan, thought he was dealing with tramps and spoke to us rudely, like someone you have disturbed, "What do you want?"

"Your Honor," I said, "since your inn happens to be closed, we would like you to authorize the café owner to serve us food."

"Do you have any papers?"

"What the devil! we're only from Avignon. If you can't take a step or eat an omelet in the region without having papers. . . ."

"Now don't give me any arguments! You will go and explain yourselves to the district police chief, with my two constables as an escort."

"Good heavens, are you joking? You can see that we're worn out."

"Oh, I'll have you taken in my cart. I have a good mule."

By thunder, we were beginning to find this not so funny any more, especially on empty stomachs.

"Your Honor," said Aubanel, "if you would conduct us to the house of the parish priest, I am sure he will recognize us."

"Let's go, then, let's go," said the mayor peevishly.

And when we were in the rectory in the presence of the priest, he said, "Look, Father, see if you know these fellows."

First the parish priest of Méthamis invited us to sit down in his little parlor. And then, walking around us and examining our faces, he said, "No, Your Honor, I don't know these gentlemen."

"But, Father," said Aubanel, "take a good look at me. Don't you remember having seen me in my bookstore in Avignon?"

"Oh, Monsieur Aubanel?"

"Exactly."

"Monsieur Aubanel!" exclaimed the parish priest of Méthamis, "bookseller and printer to our Holy Father the Pope! Jacoumouno, Jacoumouno, quick! bring the little glasses so that we can drink a drop of ratafia from Goult to the health of *The Provençal Almanac* and the Félibres!"

And as we turned around to see the look on the mayor's face, he was fumbling for the door, which he could no longer find, and muttering, "I won't have a drink, Father, I won't have a drink. I have work to do."

All right. Some time later, when we came out, the innkeeper on his doorstep and the café owner in front of his café called us, "Gentlemen! you may come, gentlemen. His Honor has just said that if you should want a bite to eat. . . ."

But we were offended and disdainful as the apostles when they had not been recognized, and tightening our belts, we shook the dust from our shoes on Méthamis and went hobbling on our way again down the Nesque.

"Well now, my valiant Pèire," said Aubanel, "you see that the soldiers of the Pope are still good for something."

"I won't argue," said Grivolas, licking his beard hungrily. "But if we should come upon a heap of rabbits, chickens, hares, and turkeys at Vénasque like those at the festival in Montbrun, I suspect we would soon put a dent in it, my friends."

Day follows day, but alas, not in the same way. The innkeeper at Vénasque, who was a wheelwright by trade—the blockhead!—made us a supper we couldn't choke down, a thick stew of potatoes, browned in a casserole with dregs of olive oil.

As if that weren't enough, the sadist made us lie down on a pile of holm-oak with a bundle of straw as a mattress, which leaked out so much during the night that the sharp, rough logs stuck in our backs and we couldn't sleep a wink.

To conclude: Sunburned, shabby, and down at heels, but happy and savoring the taste of Provence, we finally came back across a ridge of bare mountains named La Barbarenque, by way of Vaucluse, the Abbey of Sénanque, Gordes, and Le Calavon—not without further adventures, which would take too long to relate in full—and returned to the flatlands of Avignon.

XVIII
THE SPREE AT TRINQUETAILLE

1

lphonse Daudet has written fluently about several of his escapades with the first Félibres in Maillane, on Barthelasse, at Les Baux, and at Châteauneuf in his reminiscences of youth (*Letters from My Windmill* and *Thirty Years in Paris*)—with the first crop of Félibres, I say, who at that time were constantly gadding about Provence for the pleasure of gadding and bustling, and above all to soak the new art of the troubadours back into the old well of the people. But he didn't tell everything by any means, and I must tell you about a jolly spree we went on together a good forty years ago.

At that time Daudet was the secretary of the Duc de Morny, who presided over the Senate—the honorary secretary, you may be sure, for the young man went at most once a month to see if his patron was in good health and spirits. And his choice vine, which has since yielded so many fine vintages, was only in its first leaf. But he had written, among other elegant little works, a pretty love poem entitled "The Plums," which all Paris knew by heart. And when Monsieur de Morny heard it in a salon, he asked to be introduced to the author, who pleased him and whom he took into his favor.

To say nothing of his wit—which was a gem, as they say of precious stones—Daudet was a good-looking lad, with a pallid complexion, black eyes and long, fluttering eyelashes, a budding beard, and a thick head of dark hair, which covered the

241

nape of his neck so luxuriantly that every time the author of "Plums" came to the Senate to see him, the Duke touched his hair with a condescending finger and said to him, "Well, poet, when are we going to lop off that wig?"

"This coming week, my lord," the poet would reply, bowing.

And so every month the great Duc de Morny made the same remark to young Daudet, and invariably the poet gave him the same reply. But the Duke fell before Daudet's mane.

At that age the future chronicler of the prodigious adventures of Tartarin de Tarascon was already a merry bird who watched which way the wind blew: avid to know everything, boldly unconventional, and free in his speech, launching into the swim of everything that was life, light, noise, and pleasure, and only too eager for scrapes. He had quicksilver in his veins.

I remember one evening when we were having supper at the Chêne-Vert, a pleasant cabaret outside Avignon. Daudet, hearing the sound of nearby music from a dance that was being held below the terrace where we were, suddenly leaped from a height of eight or nine feet, I would say, and fell through the vines of a grape arbor into the very midst of the dancers—who took him for a devil.

Another time, on the road that goes along the base of the Pont du Gard, he dove into the Gardon to see how deep the water was, without knowing how to swim. And but for a fisherman who hauled him out with his gaff, my poor Alphonse would most certainly have had his last drink.

Another time, on the bridge between Avignon and the island of La Barthelasse, he climbed on the narrow parapet and ran along it at the risk of plunging into the Rhone below—that fiend!—shouting to scandalize several bourgeois who could hear him, "From here, by God's thunder, we threw the body of Brune into the Rhone, yes, of Marshal Brune! Let that be a warning to the French and the Allobroges who would come back to plague us!"

2

Well, one September day in Maillane, I received a little letter from my friend Daudet, one of those letters small as a parsley leaf, well known to his friends, in which he said to me:

My dear Frederi, tomorrow, Wednesday, I shall leave Fontvieille to come and meet you at Saint-Gabriel. Mathieu and Grivolas will join us there via the road from Tarascon. Our meeting place is the bar, where we shall expect you about nine o'clock or nine thirty. And there, at the bar of Sarrasino, the beautiful hostess of that spot, we shall have a drink together and leave on foot for Arles. Don't fail us.

Your
RED RIDING HOOD

And between eight and nine on the appointed day, we were all at Saint-Gabriel, at the foot of the little church that watches over the mountain. At Sarrasino's we savored a cherry in brandy. And off we went, down the white road.

"Do we have far to go?" we asked a road-mender, "to get to Arles?"

"When you reach the Tomb of Roland," he answered, "you'll still have two hours to go."

"Where is that tomb?"

"Off there, where you see a clump of cypress trees on the banks of the Vigueirat."

"And who was that Roland?"

"From what I hear tell, he was a famous captain at the time of the Saracens. He's sure been dead a long time."

Hail, Roland! We never expected to find the legend and glory of Charlemagne's companion alive amid the stubble and ploughed fields of Trébon as we got under way. But on we went, talking away, and arrived in Arles, where the Man of Bronze was striking noon as we entered by the Cavalry Gate, all white with dust. And since we had empty stomachs, I can assure you, we went straight to dinner at the Pinus Hotel.

3

We were not too badly treated. And you know, when you are young, among close friends, and happy to be alive, there's nothing like a good dinner to release laughter and playfulness.

There was something that annoyed us, however. A waiter dressed in black, with his head covered with pomade and two sideburns bristling like a whiskbroom, constantly hovered around us, with his napkin over his arm, keeping his eye on us, and on the pretext of changing our plates, obviously listening to all the crazy things we said.

"Do you want to make that bootlicker leave?" said Daudet, who had lost his patience.

"Waiter!"

"If you please, sir!"

"Quick, go get us a silver platter."

"What for?" the waiter asked him, baffled.

"To put an ass on it!" Daudet replied in a thundering voice.

The plate-changer immediately disappeared and from that moment left us alone.

"What is ridiculous in these hotels," said good old Mathieu, "is that ever since traveling salesmen introduced northern tastes to the fixed menu, they now serve you the same dishes everywhere, whether in Avignon, in Angoulême, in Draguignan, or in Brive-la-Gaillarde: carrot soup, veal with sorrel, half-cooked roast beef, cauliflower cooked in butter, and other foods that have neither flavor nor savor. So if you want to find regional cooking again in Provence, our old cooking that's so tasty, you have to go to a cabaret where the common people eat."

"Shall we go to one this evening?" asked the painter Grivolas.

"Let's go!" we all cried.

4

And having decided that, we paid, lit our cigars, and went to a little café for a cup of coffee. Then we strolled slowly until nightfall through the narrow streets lined with old, freshly whitewashed houses, looking at those Arlésienne queens in their doorways or behind their transparent curtains—who were a good part of our reason for coming to Arles.

We saw the Roman amphitheater with its wide open portals, the Roman theater with its pair of majestic columns, Saint-Trophime and its cloister, the Head that has lost its nose, the palaces of the Lion, of the Porcellets, of Constantine, and of the Great Prior.

Sometimes on the streets we ran into the donkey of some "barreler" selling water from the Rhone. Sometimes we met the tanned "campers" coming back to town with their bundles of gleanings neatly piled on their heads and the "snailers" crying, "Ladies, who wants harvest snails?"

Then in going by La Roquette, there by the fish market, as the sun was setting, we asked a woman who was knitting a stocking, "Could you tell us of some little inn, or even a tavern, where you can eat properly in the good old apostolic tradition?"

Thinking that we were joking, the old woman shouted to the other women of the neighborhood, who at the sound of her laughter had come out on their doorsteps, their heads coquettishly covered with white scarves with a knot of red ribbons on top. "Hey!" she cried, "these gentlemen are looking for a tavern for supper. Do you know of any?"

"Send them," one replied, "to Yokel Street."

"Or to the Big Old Cat's," said another.

"Or to the Widow Come-Hither."

"Or to the River Gate."

"No, no," I said, "we aren't joking, dear ladies. We want a modest cabaret that everyone can afford, where plain folks go."

5

"Well, then," said a fat man with a face red as a beggar's gourd, who was sitting on a cornerstone smoking his pipe, "why don't you go to the Comber's? Come on, gentlemen, I'll take you there," he said, rising and shaking out his pipe, "I have to go that way. It's in the suburb of Trinquetaille on the other side of the Rhone. It's not a first-class inn, to be sure, but the river folk, the rafters, and the boatmen from Condrieu take their meals there, and they aren't too dissatisfied."

"And how come," said Grivolas, "they call him the Comber?"

"Because he's from Combs, a village near Beaucaire that produces sailors. I myself am a skipper and have done my share of sailing."

"Have you gone far?"

"Oh no, I've only done coastwise sailing as far as Le Havre. But,

Noun es de marinié	There's no sailor
Que noun s'atrove en dangié.	Who doesn't know danger.

"And indeed if the great Saint Marys had not always watched over us, my friends, we would have sunk long ago."

"And what's your name?"

"Skipper Gafet, entirely at your service if you'd like to go down to Le Sambuc some time or to the sandbars at the mouth of the river to see the ships that have run aground there."

6

And as we chatted away, we arrived at the bridge of Trinquetaille, which at that time was still a bridge of boats. When you walked on that moving floor placed on flat-bottomed boats fastened side by side, you felt the river breathing beneath you, powerful and alive, and as its breast rose in waves, you rose, and as it fell, you fell.

After crossing the Rhone, we turned to the left of the riverbank, and under an old arbor we saw—how shall I describe her?—a slatternly woman and blind in one eye to boot bending over the trough of a well and skinning some wriggling eels. At her feet two or three cats growled as they gnawed the heads she threw them.

"It's the Comber's wife," Master Gafet announced to our surprise.

For poets who had been dreaming since morning of beautiful and noble Arlésiennes, this was somewhat disconcerting. But there we were.

"Comberess, these gentlemen would like to have supper here."

"Oh now, you're not serious, are you, Master Gafet? What the devil are you bringing us? We don't have anything for people like that."

"Come now, don't be stupid, haven't you got a fine dish of eels there?"

"Well, if an eel stew will make them happy. . . . But look, we have nothing else."

"Oh!" exclaimed Daudet, "there's nothing we like better than eel stew. Let's go in, let's go in, and you, Master Gafet, we invite you to sit down with us."

"Thank you very much, you're very kind."

In short, the fat skipper was prevailed upon, and all five of us entered the cabaret of Trinquetaille.

7

In a low room with a floor of rough mortar but with very white walls, fifteen or twenty "rivermen" were sitting at a long table, having kid for supper, and the Comber was eating with them.

From smoke-blackened rafters hung "fly-catchers," bunches of tamarisk where the flies settled and were then caught in a bag. And we sat down on the benches around another table across from those men, who fell into a deep silence when they saw us coming in.

Then while the eel stew was cooking on the hearth, the Comber's wife brought us as appetizers two big Bellegarde onions, a plate of pickled peppers, some sharp cheese spread, pickled olives, fish roe from Martigues, and several slices of braised cod.

"And you just told us you had nothing, you bitch," said Skipper Gafet to the Comber's wife as he sliced bread with his hooked knife, "why, this is a feast!"

"Well," replied the one-eyed woman, "if you'd given us advance notice, we could have prepared a lamb *blanquette* or some juicy omelet for you. But when people happen in on you at supper time like hairs in a soup, you must understand, gentlemen, that you give them what you can."

All right. Daudet, who had never seen such a feast of the Camargue in all his life, took an onion, one of those beautiful flat onions gilded like Christmas bread, and set to work with teeth and mouth, tearing and swallowing it leaf by leaf, sometimes with the cheese, sometimes with the cod. But it's only fair to add that we all did our best to keep up with him.

Skipper Gafet, raising the pitcher from time to time, full of excellent wine of Crau such as you never find any more, said, "Come on, lads, shall we drink a bit? Onions make you thirsty and keep you thirsty."

In less than half an hour you could have lit a match on our cheeks. Then came the eel stew, salty as the sea and peppery as the devil, in which a shepherd's crook would have stood upright.

"Salting and peppering," observed fat Gafet, "make the wine taste good. Come on, clink glasses, here's to your health."

8

Meanwhile, the rivermen, having eaten their kid, ended their meal in the fashion of the boatmen of Condrieu, with a dish of greasy soup. And after mixing a big glass of wine in their soup, they all drank together from their plates, which they held in both hands and emptied with gusto at one gulp, smacking their lips.

Then a raftsman who wore a neck beard sang a song which, as I recall, ended like this:

Quand notre flotte arrive	When our fleet arrives
En rade de Toulon,	In the harbor of Toulon,
Nous saluons la ville	We salute the town
A grands coups de canon.	With a loud cannonade.

"Thunder in the name of joy!" Daudet said to us. "Aren't we going to show them our teeth too?"

And he started off this song from the time of the war against the Protestants of the Lubéron:

Chivau-lóugié moun bon ami,	Light-horseman, my love,
A Lourmarin s'espanson!	They're gutting each other in Lourmarin!
Chivau-lóugié moun bon ami,	Light-horseman, my love,
Moun cor es esvani.	My heart faints for you.

Then the riverfolk, not wanting to be left behind, sang in chorus:

Li fiho de Valènço	The girls of Valence
Sabon pas fai l'amour:	Don't know how to make love,
Aquéli de Prouvènço	While those of Provence
La fan, la niue, lou jour.	Make it night and day.

"Our turn, friends!" we shouted to the singers. And all singing at once and snapping our fingers like castanets, we gave them this splendid reply:

Li fiho d'Avignoun	The girls of Avignon
Soun coume li meloun:	Are just like melons:
Sus cènt-cinquanto	Of a hundred and fifty
N'i a pas un de madur;	There's not one that's ripe;
La plus galanto. . . .	The prettiest. . . .

"Quiet!" said the one-eyed woman, "if the police came by, they'd give us a ticket for making a racket at night."

"The police?" we cried, "we don't give a good damn about the police!"

"Here," said Daudet, "go get us the register where you write down the names of those who stay at the inn."

The Comber's wife brought the book, and the gentleman-secretary of Monsieur de Morny immediately wrote down in his finest handwriting:

A. Daudet, secretary to the president of the Senate;
F. Mistral, chevalier of the Legion of Honor;
A. Mathieu, the Félibre of Châteauneuf-du-Pape;
P. Grivolas, master painter of the School of Avignon.

"And if anyone," he said, "ever comes to pick a quarrel with you, whether it's a police chief, a gendarme, or a sub-prefect, you need only put these fly tracks under his mustache, see? and if they give you any trouble, write to us in Paris, and I promise to make them dance."

9

We paid and went out, like princes who have just revealed their identity, leaving the public awestruck. And as we reached the landing of the bridge of Trinquetaille, the charming and indefatigable author of "The Pope's Mule" said, "Let's dance a round of the farandole on the bridge. The bridges of Provence are made for that."

And away we went, dancing on the bridge by the light of the September moon reflected in the water, and singing:

La farandoulo de Trenco-taio,	The farandole of Trinquetaille,
Li gènt soun tóuti de canaio!	Where all the people are canaille!
La farandoulo de Sant-Roumié,	The farandole of Saint-Rémy,
Tóuti li gènt pisson au lié!	Where all the people piss in bed!

Suddenly, as we reached the middle of the Rhone, what did we see coming toward us in the shadowy darkness but a procession of lovely Arlésiennes, each with her escort, walking slowly, all chattering and laughing. The rustling of their dresses, the swishing of silks, the murmur of couples conversing softly in the peaceful night against the shudder of the Rhone as it glided between the boats, was something exquisite.

"A wedding," said fat Skipper Gafet, who was still with us.

"A wedding?" asked Daudet, who was short-sighted and not fully aware of all that was going on, "an Arlesian wedding! a wedding by moonlight! a wedding in the middle of the Rhone!"

And seized by a mad impulse, our mischief-maker sprang forward and threw his arms around the bride's neck with no end of kisses.

Oh my God, what a broil! If ever in our lives we were in a jam, it was then. Twenty young fellows crowded around us with their fists raised, saying, "Into the Rhone with the bums!"

"What's this? what's this?" cried Skipper Gafet, pushing the crowd back, "can't you see that we have just been drinking to the health of your bride in Trinquetaille and that it would do us harm to drink any more?"

"Long live the newlyweds!" we all cried. And thanks to the fist and the presence of mind of that worthy Gafet, whom everybody knew, the matter went no further.

10

Where shall we go now? The Bronze Man had just struck eleven o'clock.

"We must go," we said, "on a tour of the Alyscamps."

Proceeding down the Promenade and around the ramparts, we ended up walking by moonlight down the lane of poplars leading to the old Roman cemetery of Arles. And in wandering amid the moonlit tombs and rows of sarcophagi, we found ourselves solemnly reciting the splendid ballad of Camihe Reybaud to each other:

> Li piboulo dóu cementèri
> Saludon-ti li trepassa?

S'avès pòu di pious mistèri,
Passas pu liuen dóu cementèri!

IÉU.

Di blanc toumbèu dóu cementèri
Lou curbecèu s'es revessa.

TOUTI.

S'avès pòu di pious mistèri,
Passas pu liuen dóu cementèri.

IÉU.

Sus lou gazoun dóu cementèri
Tóuti li mort se soun dreissa.

TOUTI.

S'avès pòu di pious mistèri,
Passas pu liuen dóu cementèri.

IÉU.

Tóuti li mort dóu cementèri,
Fraire mut, se soun embrassa.

TOUTI.

S'avès pòu di pious mistèri,
Passas pu liuen dóu cementèri.

IÉU.

Es la fèsto dóu cementèri,
Li mort se meton à dansa.

TOUTI.

S'avès pòu di pious mistèri,
Passas pu liuen dóu cementèri.

IÉU.

La luno es claro: au cementèri
Li vierge cercon si fiança.

TOUTI.

S'avès pòu di pious mistèri,
Passas pu liuen dóu cementèri.

IÉU.

Atrovon plus au cementèri
Si calignaire tant pressa.

TOUTI.
S'avès pòu di pious mistèri,
Passas pu liuen dóu cementèri.

IÉU.
Oh! durbès-me lou cementèri:
Lis ame, li vau caressa . . .

Do the poplars of the cemetery
Salute the dead?
If you're afraid of holy mysteries,
Don't go near the cemetery.

I.
The cover has been removed
From the white sarcophagi.

ALL.
If you're afraid of holy mysteries,
Don't go near the cemetery.

I.
All the dead are standing
On the cemetery lawn.

ALL.
If you're afraid of holy mysteries,
Don't go near the cemetery.

I.
All the dead in the cemetery
Are silent brothers who embrace.

ALL.
If you're afraid of holy mysteries,
Don't go near the cemetery.

I.
It's the feast day of the cemetery,
All the dead begin to dance.

ALL
If you're afraid of holy mysteries,
Don't go near the cemetery.

I.

The moon is bright; in the cemetery
Virgins seek their fiancés.

ALL.

If you're afraid of holy mysteries,
Don't go near the cemetery.

I.

They find their lovers no longer
So eager in the cemetery.

ALL.

If you're afraid of holy mysteries,
Don't go near the cemetery.

I.

Oh, open the cemetery for me,
I want to caress the spirits. . . .

11

Oh, my dear friends in God! from a gaping tomb three steps
away—would you believe it?—a deep, doleful, sepulchral voice
spoke to us:

Leissas dourmi aquéli que dormon!   Let sleepers rest in peace!

We stood there, petrified. And all around us in the moonlight
all was silent again.

"Did you hear that?" Mathieu whispered to Grivolas.

"Yes," answered the painter, "it's there, in that sarcophagus."

"That?" Skipper Gafet burst out laughing, "that's one of
those vagrants who 'sleep in their clothes,' as we say in Arles,
who come and sleep in these empty sarcophagi at night."

And Daudet said, "What a pity, though, that wasn't a real
ghost, some beautiful Vestal Virgin who had awakened at the
sound of the poet's voice and had come to kiss you, Grivolas!"

Then he sang in a resounding voice, and we joined in:

—Se dóu couvènt passes li porto,   "If you go by the convent gate,
Tóuti li mounjo trouvaras   You'll discover all the nuns
Qu'à moun entour saran pèr orto,   Hovering around me,
Car en susàri me veiras.   For I'll be in my winding sheet."

—O Magali, se tu te fas	"Oh Magali, if you turn into
La pauro morto,	A poor corpse,
Adounc la terro me farai:	Then I'll turn into earth
Aqui t'aurai!	And there I'll have you."

And with that we all shook hands with Skipper Gafet and hurried to the railway station to catch the train for Avignon.

Seven years later, in the year of the debacle, alas, I received this letter:

> Paris, December 31st, 1870.
> Dear Chief, I am sending you a big load of kisses by the hot-air balloon, and I am happy I can send it in Provençal. That way I can be sure the Barbarians won't be able to read my writing and publish my letter in the *Swabian Gazette*, if the balloon should fall into their hands.
>
> It's cold, it's dark, we eat horse, cat, camel, hippopotamus. (Oh, if only we had the good onions, the eel stew, and the spiced cheese of the Spree at Trinquetaille!) The guns burn your fingers. Wood is becoming scarce. The armies of the Loire have not come. But it doesn't matter. The cockroaches of Berlin will be bored a while longer before the walls of Paris. And then, if Paris is lost, I know several good patriots who will show Monsieur Bismarck the way in the little streets of our poor capital.
>
> Farewell, dear Chief, and three big kisses, one for me, another for my wife, the last for my boy. And with that a happy New Year and many happy returns from today till a year from now.
>
> Your Félibre,
> Alphonse Daudet.

And yet they tell me that Daudet was not a good Provençal! Because he joked and ridiculed the Tartarins, the Roumestans, the Tante Portals, and all the idiots of Provence who want to affect French speech—is that why Tarascon holds a grudge against him?

No! the lioness does not resent and will never resent the lion cub, though in playing it sometimes scratches.

ANNOTATED INDEX

Parenthetical notes are intended to explain literary and historical allusions in the text. Although first names of Provençal writers may be given in their Provençal form in the text, here they appear only in their French form. Only geographic names that figure prominently in the Memoirs are listed.

Informal Course in Literature (Lamartine), 219–20, 221
Invalides, 66

Jacobins (powerful political club during the Revolution, revived in 1848), 66,
    136
Janin, Jules (1804–74, literary critic), 217
Jano (Joanna I, 1326–82, Queen of Naples and Countess of Provence; Mistral
    wrote a tragedy based on her life), 4, 127
"Jarjaio in Heaven," 168–71
Jasmin (nom de plume of Jacques Boé, 1798–1864, self-educated precursor of
    the Félibres, a celebrity for his poems in *langue d'oc*), 74, 79, 128, 140, 220
Jesèto, "the little Maillanais," 2, 61, 146
Jirome, Uncle, 97, 99–100
John, Saint (feast day, June 24), 5, 89, 111, 112, 136
Joseph, King (eldest brother of Napoleon, successively King of Naples and
    Spain), 99
Jourdan the Headsman ("*Jourdan Coupe-Tête*," nickname of Mathieu Jouve, blood-
    thirsty commander of the Revolutionary forces in Avignon in 1793), 66
Judge's Farm, xiv, 3, 11–16, 18–19, 95, 110–13, 131, 133, 213

Klopstock, Friedrich Gottlieb (1724–1803, German poet), 128

Lacordaire, Jean Baptiste Henri (1802–61, famous preacher and liberal deputy),
    110
Lacroix, Mathieu (1819–64, a mason by trade), 142, 143
Lafare-Alais, Marquis de (1791–1846, like Jasmin, a precursor of the Félibres),
    79, 128
Laidet, Hippolyte, 142
Lamartine, Alphonse de (1790–1869, great Romantic poet, orator, and states-
    man, head of the provisional government during the revolution of 1848),
    105, 109, 110, 219–20, 221–25
Lambert, Louis Siméon (1815–68), 142
Lamennais, Felicité Robert de (1782–1854, Christian democrat and Catholic
    apologist until denounced by the Pope), 110
Lamouroux, 185–92, 196
langue d'oc (the group of dialects spoken throughout southern France), xii, xiii, 81
Languedoc (the region of southwestern France across the Rhone from Pro-
    vence), 128, 197, 226
Laura (the woman who inspired Petrarch's love poems), 67
Laurens, Bonaventure (1801–79, artist specializing in paintings and drawings of
    Arlésiennes), 140, 162
Laval, Father, 227
Lawyer Pathelin (a medieval farce rendered into Provençal in 1684), 65
League (see Catholic League)
Legré, Ludovic (1838–1904, historian and botanist, close friend and biographer
    of Théodore Aubanel), 217
Lejourdan, Jules, 142
Letters from My Windmill (*Lettres de mon moulin*, 1868, Daudet's collection of Proven-
    çal sketches, including a visit to Mistral on a feast day in Maillane), 241